"BULLET" BILL DUDLEY

THE NATIONAL FOOTBALL LEAGUE
UNIFORM PLAYER'S CONTRACT

The........Pittsburgh Steelers Foot Ball Club Inc.................herein is called the Club,
and........William M. Dudley........, of........Blue Field Virginia.
herein is called the Player.

The Club is a member of **The National Football League**. As such, and jointly with the other members of the League, it is obligated to insure to the public wholesome and high-class professional football by defining the relations between Club and Player, and between Club and Club.

In view of the facts above recited the parties agree as follows:

1. The Club will pay the Player a salary for his skilled services during the playing season of 19.42., at the rate of........$ 500.00........dollars for each regularly scheduled League game played, provided he has not been released by the Club prior to the playing of the first League game. For all other games the Player shall be paid such salary as shall be agreed upon between the Player and the Club. As to games scheduled but not played, the Player shall receive no compensation from the Club other than actual expenses.

Clauses numbers 15 and 16 attached here to are fully a part of this Contract as much so, as if they appeared over the signatures of the parties here to.

2. The salary above provided for shall be paid by the Club as follows:
Seventy-five per cent, (75%), after each game and the remaining twenty-five per cent, (25%), at the close of the season or upon release of the Player by the Club.

3. The Player agrees that during said season he will faithfully serve the Club, and pledges himself to the American public to conform to high standards of fair play and good sportsmanship.

4. The Player will not play football during 19.42. otherwise than for the Club, or in games contracted for by the League, except in case the Club shall have released said Player, and said release has been approved by the officials of **The National Football League**.

5. The Player will not participate in an exhibition game after the completion of the schedule of the Club and prior to August 1 of the following season, without the permission of the Commissioner of the League.

6. The player accepts as part of this contract such reasonable regulations as the Club may announce from time to time.

7. This contract may be terminated at any time by the club giving notice in writing to the player within forty-eight, (48), hours after the day of the last game in which he has participated with his club.

8. The Player submits himself to the discipline of **The National Football League** and agrees to accept its decisions pursuant to its Constitution and By-Laws.

9. Any time prior to August 1st, 19.43, by written notice to the Player, the Club may renew this contract for the term of that year, except that the salary rate shall be such as the parties may then agree upon, or in default of agreement, such as the Club may fix.

10. The Player may be fined or suspended for violation of this contract, but in all cases the Player shall have the right of appeal to the Commissioner of **The National Football League**.

11. In default of agreement, the Player will accept the salary rate thus fixed or else will not play during said year otherwise than for the Club, unless the Club shall release the Player.

12. The reservation of the Club of the valuable right to fix the salary rate for the succeeding year, and the promise of the Player not to play during said year otherwise than with the Club, have been taken into consideration in determining the salary specified herein and the undertaking by the Club to pay said salary is the consideration for both the reservation and the promise.

13. In case of dispute between the Player and the Club the same shall be referred to the Commissioner of **The National Football League**, and his decision shall be accepted by all parties as final.

14. Verbal contracts between Club and Player will not be considered by this League, in the event of a dispute.

Signed this........27........day of........August........A. D. 19...42

Witnesses:

Pittsburgh Steelers Football club inc
(Club)

By _Bert Bell Pres_

William M. Dudley
(Player)

Duplicate copy to be held by Player

Bill's first contract with the Steelers—all one page of it—signed by Bert Bell and witnessed by Bill's father.

"BULLET" BILL DUDLEY

THE GREATEST 60-MINUTE MAN IN FOOTBALL

Steve Stinson

LYONS
PRESS

Essex, Connecticut

An imprint of Globe Pequot, the trade division of
The Rowman & Littlefield Publishing Group, Inc.
4501 Forbes Blvd., Ste. 200
Lanham, MD 20706
www.rowman.com

Distributed by NATIONAL BOOK NETWORK

British Library Cataloguing-in-Publication Information available

Library of Congress Cataloging-in-Publication Data

Names: Stinson, Steve, 1952- author.
Title: Bullet Bill Dudley : the greatest 60-minute man in football / Steve Stinson.
Description: Lanham : Taylor Trade Publishing, [2016] | "Distributed by NATIONAL BOOK
    NETWORK"—T.p. verso.
Identifiers: LCCN 2016018047 (print) | LCCN 2016032489 (ebook) | ISBN 9781493018154
    (hardcover : alk. paper) | ISBN 9781493018161 (e-book) | ISBN 9781493068661 (paperback)
Subjects: LCSH: Dudley, Bill, 1921-2010. | Football players—United States—Biography. |
    Veterans—United States—Biography. | Politicians—Virginia—Biography.
Classification: LCC GV939.D82 S75 2016 (print) | LCC GV939.D82 (ebook) | DDC
    796.33092 [B] —dc23
LC record available at https://lccn.loc.gov/2016018047

♾️™ The paper used in this publication meets the minimum requirements of American National
Standard for Information Sciences—Permanence of Paper for Printed Library Materials, ANSI/
NISO Z39.48-1992.

I believe Dudley was as good as any football player who ever played in the National Football League. Coaches told their passers, "Don't throw in Dudley's territory." He had intuition. He wasn't fast, but nobody caught him. He couldn't pass, but he completed passes. He was one of the top kickers in the game. The best all-around ballplayer I've ever seen.

Our coaches used to say to me, "Well, he don't hit the hole." I'd tell them, "I don't want him to hit the holes. If he started hitting the holes, he'll turn the game into such a one-sided farce that nobody will come out to see us play."

He's always been a classy guy.

—ART ROONEY

FOREWORD

"Bullet" Bill Dudley had an outstanding NFL career, which was spread out over three teams. When I was growing up, he was "The Man" that could do it all! With his exceptional versatility, Bill was a fierce tackler, an elusive runner, and a reliable punter and placekicker.

Getting to know Bill after his illustrious career was a real big deal for me. He was a hero to me as I was growing up, trying to do some of the things that Bill did on the field. I played both ways at LSU and kicked field goals. Bill got to play a lot more like this in the pros, as I would have liked to do, but being ten to fifteen years after him, things had changed.

He really set the standards for me, not just as a great ball carrier, but as an even better person. Serving our country, being a great husband, father, and friend to many. He was called upon time after time to give back and he never let you down.

Bill was inducted into the Pro Football Hall of Fame in 1966 and I went in 1976. After that, we got to spend a lot of time together at golf outings, dinners, sporting events, and other galas raising money for various charities. I feel truly blessed to have known him and his lovely bride, Libba. Bill was such a positive influence and touched my life and many others'!

—Jim Taylor

CHAPTER ONE
Eight Players in One Uniform

THANKSGIVING DAY, 1941: BILL DUDLEY SAT ON THE BENCH AND watched the last two minutes tick away. He had been on the football field for 113 plays before being carried off on the shoulders of his teammates. Every spectator—24,000 of them—at North Carolina's Kenan Stadium had risen in salute. They were still standing, still applauding.

He was silent, exhausted. He could no longer feel the weight of the moment. The crowd noise was a blur, like it came from elsewhere. Somebody tossed a blanket around his shoulders. Another handed him a cup of water. Already, he could feel the sweat salt caking on his shoulders. Aches and bruises whispered. They would shout tomorrow. The water was welcome. The clock labored on, disconnected, erasing its own domain of time.

In the pressbox above, it was near bedlam. Men in fedoras typed out what the radio boys had already told a national audience and what the standing spectators were telling each other—they had just witnessed the greatest individual performance in college football, ever.

The pressbox boomed. Cigar smoke blew, fingers smacked keys, writers barked into phones, and announcers searched for words as autumn lowered behind the pines around Kenan.

It was Bill Dudley's final game in a University of Virginia uniform. Behind him lay childhood and struggle and sudden stardom. Ahead were triumph and heartache and a fairy tale love story.

In seventeen days, the world would be at war.

It is a rare and wonderful thing to be the best at what you do—to be The Most Valuable. Bill Dudley got there by being better at many things.

An NFL team today suits up eight men to play the positions Bill played by himself on offense, defense, and special teams in a single season. He called plays and signals, he passed the ball, he ran the ball, he caught the ball, he intercepted the ball. If you had the ball, he took you down hard. He kicked off and punted. He was the most feared kick and punt returner in the NFL. He was one of the first free-roaming safeties.

Coaches designed offenses around him. Opposing coaches changed theirs.

He played in the NFL for nine years—losing three playing years to World War II—and led every team he played for in scoring.

He holds records that will never be broken. In 1946 he won the only Quadruple Crown in pro football, leading the league in rushing, punt returns, interceptions, and lateral passes.

He is the only player elected Most Valuable Player in college, the pros, and the military. He was a Hall of Fame inductee, college and pro.

There are eleven ways to score in a football game. Bill scored using ten of them. Hint: He never downed the ball for a touchback. He once crawled for a touchdown.

In a modern NFL combine—a day of physical tests where NFL coaches appraise aspiring players—Bill would have none of the measurables—speed, strength, and size. Bill's measure of himself was candid, "I was small, but I was slow." His hands could barely grip a ball. He threw sidearmed and ran like he was about to fall over. Nobody copied his kicking style. Nobody wanted to. And yet . . .

You can't separate football from the man. The game gave him everything and Bill said as much. But you can separate the man from football. As a husband, father, businessman, and citizen, he put far more into this world than he took out. Three years before Bill died, he asked me to write his story. Here it is.

The Virginia Cavalier team with coach Frank Murray, 1941.

Bill: "*The Good Book says there's only one winner. If I really want to do something, I think I can do it. I know no one would try any harder. It's not a question of being the best—it's a question of trying. The harder I tried, the more I wanted to learn to do better.*"

CHAPTER TWO

The Ruthless Meritocracy of Little Boys

HARVEY MANSFIELD, HARVARD PROFESSOR AND LIFELONG STUDENT OF all things American, once described Americans like this: "We are a can-do people. We like to take shortcuts. We don't like to 'stand on ceremony.' We say what we mean, and we like to speak bluntly, without flourishes and without diplomatic niceties. We like efficiency and don't like to waste time. We get impatient easily."

He might as well have been describing William McGarvey Dudley, who was born on Christmas Eve, 1921. His birth was unremarkable in every aspect but one—his mother, grandmother, and great-grandmother were also born on Christmas Eve.

The third of four children, he was delivered at the family home three streets off and overlooking the brick facades of downtown Graham, a small town in the coal country hills of southwest Virginia. It was a pleasant home and a no-nonsense household.

His father, Shelby—Sheb to his friends—was a traveling meat salesman. He worked the company stores and grocers along a coal country circuit from Monday to Thursday. He started out as a railroad man, learned the meat trade during seventeen years with Wilson Packing, and formed his own meat distribution firm, the Dudley Provision Company, the year Bill was born. The company was successful and became a major distributor for the Swift and High Grade brands. Sheb was a local boy with a fourth-grade education. His grandparents had been pioneer settlers in the county.

His mother, Jewell Jarrett, was from Charleston, West Virginia. She had completed high school. She kept a warm, clean household. There was always a spread—the unassuming, but not artless, fare we call country cooking—on the table. When she read, she read the Bible. She never called Bill anything but William.

Oldest brother Jim would play an important role in Bill's later life. Older sister Margaret was a free spirit who followed her own path. Younger brother Tom was the quiet one in a windy family. He followed Bill into college football at Virginia. The brothers were close despite their age differences—close and uncommonly competitive. In the manner of the day, sister Margaret was little involved in boyish things.

Both parents dealt discipline in full measure. Their authority was absolute. There was no foolishness. Today, we might say they weren't good listeners. The wrong retort got you a mouthful of lye soap. The wrong move got you the strap. Shelby issued hot and swift punishment for transgressions. Jewell, too, exercised the strap.

Sheb could be volatile. On one hot day in downtown Bluefield, pass-ersby watched as Sheb Dudley pulled his car over, pulled Margaret, age twelve, and Jim, age ten, out of the car, dropped their pants, and whaled them right there in the street. If the witnesses had an opinion about this, they kept it to themselves. They knew Sheb kept to his own advice. He was the mayor.

The center of the Dudleys' lives was Memorial Baptist Church, which was visible from the Dudley front door. Services were Wednesday nights and Sunday mornings. Both parents taught Sunday school. They were Baptists who fused Old School Baptist tenets with elements of Calvinism—Little Bill took his middle name from a circuit-riding preacher. There was also a hint of modernity. You could deal a hand of Rook on Sundays, but first, close the blinds.

The Dudley home was open. People felt comfortable dropping in, often toting a guitar or banjo or fiddle. The home was filled with music. Margaret played piano. It had a hoedown feel. Everyone in the family sang. The reviews were good. Here's one from the *Bluefield Daily Tele-graph* "Social Notes":

Billy Dudley, 3, lays claim to the youngest platform entertainer. This young man, the son of Mr. and Mrs. Sheb Dudley, performed in the high school building Friday morning during an entertainment and sang several songs without a bobble. Among his selections were "Let Me Call You Sweetheart" and others. Billy is just three years of age, but is one of the best known citizens of East Street, his home.

Sentimentality ran in the family. Sheb wrote long, tender poems and composed his own Christmas cards. Jewell could be a wit and a prankster and was known throughout Bluefield for her Halloween witch act.

The family business, so to speak, was being busy. Jewell shouldered her civic duties at the church. Sheb was active in civic organizations locally and nationally. He formed Bluefield's first Business Men's Club. He was active in the Boy Scouts and was the first regional chairman of the organization. When Graham changed its name to Bluefield, population 4,500 (they advertised 5,000) in 1924 and was chartered as a Virginia city, Sheb Dudley was elected the first mayor. He introduced the first city manager form of government in the region. The *Bluefield Daily Telegraph*: "The Dudley family seems to have more energy than anybody else in town. They just excel in everything they do."

When Sheb was on the road, older brother Jim would assume his role. Here's Jim on what it was like to be Billy Dudley's big brother:

The only thing I heard for the first four years of his life was, "Would you go find William?" I could find him at Bill Holbrook's store. Bill Holbrook's store was a place with a barrel of crackers, a barrel of pickles and great big wheel of cheese and some overalls for sale hanging there and a checkerboard and a bunch of people standing around a pot-bellied stove watching a two-year-old doing a soft shoe shuffle and singing "It Ain't Gonna Rain No More." People were throwing nickels and dimes at him. The two-year-old was William.

We had a boy we called Vapors. We called him that because whenever there was trouble Vapors would disappear. One day mother says, "Go find William." I go down to the play lot and here comes Vapors running down the street. Bill is chasing him. I say, "Where

*you going?" Bill says, "I'm going to beat the hell out of him. He called
mom an S.O.B."
I went after them. Vapors hits his back door and tries to lock it.
Bill hits it right behind him and follows him into the kitchen. Bill is
pounding on Vapors and Vapors' mother is standing there screaming.
She picks up the party line and calls Maude. Maude runs the
party line. Maude announces all over the party line that Bill is over
at Vapors' house beating the hell out of Vapors.*

In his later years Bill would sometimes get the same treatment from
his older brother. Bill would recall being pinned to the floor, straddled,
and getting cheek slapped by Jim. The message to the bull-headed little
boy: "You aren't the only one who lives here."

They were an emotional, mercurial family. Extraordinary outbursts of
temper were considered normal. Equally strong demonstrations of affection
were commonplace. The parents preached and practiced a hard-wearing
ethic—work, perseverance, and plenty of it. Their moral convictions were
anchored and changeless. Above all things, the family name should be pro-
tected. It was constantly reiterated: In the end, your name is all you have.

The Dudleys expected and rewarded personal responsibility and
punished its absence. They prized independence and were willing to
sacrifice for it. They argued. The tone was blunt and confrontational and
full-throated. This would work for and against Bill Dudley all his life.

The boys thrived. Sheb spent time with them. Margaret didn't thrive.
As a female, she was burdened with restrictions and she wasn't the kind
for restraints. But she wasn't restricted from the strap. She would struggle
with this imbalance until she left the home as an adult.

Post–World War I America was a nation in transition. The industrial
might of the nation shifted to domestic production. Prosperity followed.
The word *consumerism* made its way into the language. Cars, appliances,
radios, telephones, ready-to-wear clothing—anything that could be
mass-produced and advertised—were available to a vibrant and increasingly affluent culture.

Installment buying and buying on credit allowed large purchases—especially cars—to be an option. The Sears, Roebuck catalog was in every home. Large department stores were built.

Somebody had to make the products and build the stores and man the service stations and the roadside diners. There was plenty of work and people had money to spend.

A huge cultural shift was under way. By the end of the 1920s, more Americans would live in towns and cities than on farms. Mass culture followed. Radio stations appeared in 1920. In ten years there were radios in more than twelve million homes. In a little Virginia hill town, you knew what they were singing and dancing to in California and New York. In 1923 Graham McNamee invented what we now call play-by-play sportscasting and brought the drama of sports into the living room, from the Gene Tunney vs. Jack Dempsey long count to Babe Ruth's called shot home run.

The Dudley family dipped a cautious toe into this rising tide. Modernity and Calvinism didn't play well together. The radio that brought in Gershwin's new "Rhapsody in Blue" also blared coverage of the Scopes Monkey Trial. In movie houses there were the first Disney cartoons, but there was also a silent Garbo in *Flesh and the Devil*. Another horror: Cigarette production doubled in the 1920s and the advertising was aimed directly at women. Prohibition was fine with the Dudleys. There was never alcohol in the home. But they were also aware, like everyone else in the country, that the real outcome of Prohibition was increased drinking.

It was easy enough for the Dudleys to pick and choose their way through the 20s—vacuum cleaner, yes, cigarettes for women, no. Jewell Dudley remained singularly frugal even as Sheb's meat business grew—a practice that served the family well in the next decade. When she sent a child to the grocery store, she knew the exact price of every item on the list. She would pick through her palm-sized coin purse, hand over what she had, and tell the delivery child how much change she expected upon return.

Unlike so many Americans unleashed by their new cars, the Dudleys didn't travel. The family took two trips in the 20s—one to Virginia Beach and one to a nearby hot spring.

Like so many Americans, the Dudleys discovered the picnic. They often made the five-mile trip to Falls Mills—a man-made lake for the railroad, which also had a swim and fishing club—for the day. Sheb's prowess at the grill—he was, after all, a meat salesman—was envied. Restaurant outings, though, were restricted to Christmas Eve birthday celebrations in Bluefield, West Virginia, the sister city across the state border, where a bug-eyed little Billy ate his first raw oyster.

There are few places better than small-town America to be a little boy, then and now. Given the freedom to explore, he can feel that he owns the place. For Billy Dudley, it was a matter of getting past the chores.

From the front the Dudley home had a typical small-town look—a two-story frame house with wide porches overlooking a front yard split by a sidewalk. Behind it, though, was a five-acre spread that climbed into the hills and the woods. There was a barn and enough space to till a garden, keep chickens, and graze a cow or two and a goat.

At age ten, Bill inherited the daily chores from brother Jim, who was off to Washington & Lee College. Milk the cow. Gather the eggs. Do whatever else Jewell put on the list. That same year, Bill got a paper route with the *Bluefield Daily Telegraph*. The routine was set and unchanging. Up at 6:15 to deliver the papers—118 of them. Home in an hour to milk the cow, then off to school. On Saturdays, it was off to the Tower Ground.

Every small town in America had its version of the Tower Ground—a patch of dirt and grass big enough and flat enough for football and baseball. The Tower Ground bordered the railroad tracks in Bluefield. Trains would slow there to leave or take up delivery bags posted at a tower that reached engineer level, hence the name.

The Tower Ground, as in every other small town, was owned and operated by boys, or at least they thought so. Games were self-organized and structured according to attendance. Yes, you can play baseball with three on a team. They were governed by a ruthless, but fair, meritocracy. You may get picked last, but you get picked. There were no parents or leagues or coaches. The boys made and enforced the rules. This is where boys tested themselves and each other. They found their limits and their potential. Some boys discovered what leadership feels like. Other boys discovered what leadership looks like. If Waterloo was won on the playing fields of Eton, a world war was won on countless cousins of the Tower Ground.

As soon as little Billy was shown the Tower Ground, he decided it was his. He stood there, leaning slightly forward, ready to be what he dreamed of being—a baseball player. "I wanted to play professional baseball," Bill said. "I could hit and get on base. I played a lot of baseball growing up." He was four years old and he already knew he could hit and field the ball. He was a Lou Gehrig fan, and quick to add that he wasn't a Yankees fan. Baseball was the most popular sport in the region. Sheb played the game.

Bill would later say he couldn't recall his first football. He guessed it was a Christmas gift. However it happened, the moment benched baseball. The Tower Ground became witness to a new force of nature.

"When he was the age of eight, we were into sandlot football," said Jim Dudley. "He wants to play. At fifty pounds he can't play much, we didn't think. So we put him all the way back as far as we can so he wouldn't get hurt. He was going to be the safety man.

"The first guy got through the line, this fifty pounds of whatever hit him and he left with a sprained ankle. A few minutes later another one left with a bruised rib. A few minutes later a guy left with a bruised thigh. We had to call off the game."

It wasn't long before little Billy became the organizing force at the Tower Ground. The boy who had wanted to become a baseball player now embraced football and he wasn't letting go. He was seldom without one. He asked for, and received, a football every Christmas and also received a swift and painful instruction about gratitude one year when he complained about the quality of the ball. He played it in his front yard and the nearby church yard with his brothers and his neighbors, but the Tower Ground was the real thing. It is hard to wear out a football. Billy Dudley put one in tatters every year.

It was difficult to organize the other boys. Baseball was the town sport. Boys like sports and they like dirt, but tackle football played on dirt demands a certain kind of boy. You needed a shirt nobody cared about or no shirt at all. When it was cold you played in two pairs of pants. It was a contact sport, and you could find yourself lined up against a boy twice your age and you could expect no quarter. On the other hand, if you showed up, you played. The only boys sent home were the cheats and the dirty players.

Over time the organizing paid off. Teams showed up, usually defined by neighborhoods. The game of the year was the Onion Bowl. The East End would meet the West End. It began as a fall game and became a fixture. The event grew and was moved to New Year's Day and grew again. Spectators started showing up. Sometimes the boys could recruit an adult referee. The game even got a mention in the *Bluefield Daily Telegraph*.

Schooling in 1920s America was varied. Small towns had their own ways of doing things. In Bluefield, children went to kindergarten in private homes until they were sent to elementary school at age seven. From there, procedures were undefined.

Billy Dudley was placed in the third grade after Christmas at age seven. Because of the mid-year entry and his late-year birthday, he was still seven when he started the fourth grade. You could say it was the opposite of redshirting. So, it was a transition from kindergarten to fourth grade. He got through it, although he was known for crawling into his teacher's lap for a nap. He was an indifferent student with no favorite subject.

When the town of Graham became the city of Bluefield in 1924, the high school kept the old name. Graham High School had about 200 students in 1933. Freshman Billy Dudley was one of them, age eleven. He tried out for the football team. He weighed 105 pounds. He didn't think that mattered. The year before, University of Michigan quarterback Little Harry Newman ran, passed, and kicked his way onto the All-America team. He was a hero. He was five feet eight inches tall. If he could do it, why couldn't little Billy?

Graham coach Ted Fix declined. He told the boy the team didn't have a suit that small. This was true, but he told Sheb it was the boy who was too small.

The Graham team practiced on the Tower Ground. For Billy Dudley this was a gritty thing to swallow. He thought he owned it. Now, he was a spectator. While the other boys practiced, he jerked sodas at the down-town drugstore. At least he had sandlot ball on Saturdays and Sundays, plus the Onion Bowl.

He turned his paper route into a workout. He ran it, heaving the papers and not looking back. It proved costly. He paid eight cents for each paper. The customers paid him sixteen cents. The difference was his pay. After he ran a route, the phone would inevitably ring with a call from a customer: "Bill, where's my paper?" Usually, it was on the roof. Each rooftop toss cost him eight more cents.

He also fashioned another workout. People who happened by the railroad tracks would notice a little bowlegged kid standing by the tracks, breathing in the industrial incense of creosote. He would be leaning forward, looking into the distance. Suddenly, he would sprint down the tracks, headlong for a telephone pole. At the last second, he would cut and sidestep the pole and sprint to the next pole and the next and the next and the next. Then he would walk back, stopping at each pole to examine his footprints and measure the distance between his print and the base of the pole. He used the skill he honed by the tracks for the rest of his career.

Bill: "I caught a punt once at Washington. I caught the ball and couldn't run—I stood there and dodged three men and never moved a step forward. They all had a shot at me. They all missed."

He showed up for the football team again his sophomore year. He was 110 pounds. The coach said no. He showed up his junior year. He was 120 pounds. Coach Fix let him suit up, but he was never more than practice fodder. Even then, Bill could hear the coach yelling "Don't hit him" when plays came his way. Bill never got into a game.

He did make the basketball team that year. In the jargon of the day, he was a "floor man"—a ball handler and passer. He played guard and was a starter. Games were low-scoring affairs—40 points could usually win it. At his height, Billy didn't get many shot opportunities. If he got free, he could sink a corner shot.

He could also sink a corner shot on a pool table. He never mentioned what they thought of that at Memorial Baptist.

The Dudley children would be educated. This was an article of faith in the home. Sheb Dudley preached it again and again: Responsibility and independence—education gives you both. If you are educated, nobody can tell you where and when to work or how much you can earn. When you can think and act for yourself, you have nobody to blame but yourself. If you threw some modern jargon at him about empowering people, Sheb would have rejected it as a bunch of hooey. People empower themselves.

Nobody knew this better than Sheb. A fourth grade education is something you have to overcome. Sheb used every ounce of talent and determination within himself to build his business and become a consequential member of the community.

He had worked the company stores for years, and he had seen what happens to men with no options—men whose lives were negotiated by unions and managed by coal companies. This was not to be the fate of his own children. It would be college for them.

By 1935 two of his children were in two of the best, and most expensive, colleges in Virginia. Jim Dudley was at Washington & Lee and Margaret was at William & Mary.

Also in that year Sheb Dudley had a nervous breakdown at age forty-nine. Today, we might say he suffered from depression. This may have been the case, but probably not in the clinical way we use the term now. That year there was plenty to be depressed about. Coal anchored the local economy. Bluefield, West Virginia, was the regional headquarters of the Norfolk & Western Railway. From the docking yards there, coal cars made their way across the state and down to the shipping yards in Norfolk, Virginia, on the Chesapeake Bay.

The Depression was in its fifth year. Nationally, unemployment had been above 20 percent for the previous three years. In coal country it was much higher. Mines were failing and, with them, the company stores. For stranded miners and their families, it was either try your luck on a mountain farm or move away. Many chose to move. Towns were failing and, with them, the grocers. Nobody had any money. Business was bad.

The economy of Bluefield, Virginia, came to a standstill. It would be twenty years before the city expanded again. Dudley Provisions Company was shuttered. Little Bill found himself with customers who couldn't pay for a paper. Grown men pleaded with him to carry them just one more month. He did. For a few, the debt piled up for years.

Downtown businesses began to fail. The empty buildings became venues for cheap, pass-through entertainments. When an auto dealership went bust, promoters put the building on the professional wrestling circuit. A kid could sneak through a window and watch Strangler Lewis get done in by Cowboy Luttrell. The show came to town often enough that even a kid could figure out that the good guy/bad guy drama was phony, especially when the wrestlers switched sides.

Sheb wasn't productive for a year. Then, he put himself back together and entered the life insurance business and built a new and successful career. But the financial damage was done. Jim was called home from Washington & Lee and followed his father into the life insurance business. Margaret had to leave William & Mary. For young Bill Dudley, with another year of high school ahead, tuition was out of the question. The promise of college had vanished.

In the spring of 1937, Bill faced a choice. He was about to graduate from high school at age fifteen and enter an unwelcoming working world. He didn't have much of a resume. He jerked sodas, tossed papers, and pumped gas. A summer stint on a local construction crew was the closest he had come to an adult job.

At age fifteen, Bill made a life-altering decision. He would stay in school one more year. He had made the football team the previous fall. Maybe if he stuck around, he would actually play in the upcoming fall and earn a college scholarship.

Looking backward through the telescope, the choice seems obvious—a Hall of Fame football player sees his future and controls it. But viewed from the ground at that moment, the audacity of his choice is even now difficult to grasp. He still weighed less than 130 pounds. He had yet to enter a single high school football play. Nobody thought he ever would. Nobody except him. In his fifth year at Graham High School, he took one course—Home Economics.

CHAPTER THREE

A Triple Threat Gets a Nickname

MARSHALL SHEARER WAS A THIRTY-FIVE-YEAR-OLD FORMER NAVAL commander when he took over the Graham High School football program from Coach Fix. He had played football with Bo McMillin and Matty Bell at Centre College in Kentucky, and he was determined, along with his assistant Mark Gillespie, to establish what the locals called a "Big Time" program at a small school.

Coach Shearer soon discovered the same problem little Billy Dudley had experienced at the Tower Ground pickup games—finding enough coal country boys who wanted to play football and who knew the game. His first encounter with Bill was at Memorial Baptist Church.

The boy wanted to play ball and Shearer needed warm bodies. In a town that size, a coach hoped for eleven players and a second string that he never needed. He already knew there was more to the Dudley boy than met the eye. He'd seen the 1935 roster and made inquiries. One more factor cinched it. Bill had a talent rare among high schoolers. He could kick. Shearer went to Sheb Dudley. There would be a light bench that fall. If Bill made the team, he would play. Shearer was unsure. Did Sheb think Bill was too young and too light? "If he makes the team, let him play," Sheb told Shearer.

So, it looked like a shot at the varsity for Billy Dudley. He had been playing sandlot football for twelve years. A bond quickly formed between Bill and Coach Shearer. The two loved to talk football. They began regular Thursday night meetings at a booth at the corner drugstore downtown—milkshakes and football for a couple of hours. When the season arrived, the meetings became strategy sessions.

Right away, Shearer altered Bill's kicking style. He stopped by the Tower Ground one afternoon while Bill was practicing dropkicks. That, he told the boy, wouldn't work anymore. They were changing the shape of the ball. The footballs of the day were heavy and shaped more like rounded rugby balls. What we know as the modern football shape—longer, narrower, and more pointed—would be used in the upcoming season. The new, pointed ball would deliver a less predictable rebound from a drop. Teams were switching to placeholders for field goals.

It all probably started something like this: Two Stone Age guys are walking somewhere. Stone Age Man One sees something in the path ahead. He kicks it. The thing travels a bit, but lands again in the path. When the two guys get to it, Stone Age Man Two kicks it. His kick goes farther than Stone Age Man One's kick. They look at each other. A skill is born. It doesn't have much utility, but it's fun.

Bill Dudley found kicking plenty useful. It got him into football when he was young and it kept him in the game when he got older. To him, it was art and science. He approached kicking much as a golfer approaches a shot—keep it low in a headwind, high in a tailwind. Adjust for conditions of the field or a wet ball, which is heavier. After he made the team at Virginia, Bill designed a shoe for kicking and running. It was a standard football shoe, but the sole on the right foot was extended in front and cut square. To Bill, kicking was a little bit art and a little bit science and a lot of practice:

> *Sam Baugh was the best holder I ever had. And the holder is important. He's got to set the damn ball down there right for you. I wanted the ball straight up and down. A good holder, 90 percent of the time, he's gonna have that ball down there for you with the laces facing where you want them.*
>
> *My laces are always gonna be straight up and down with the ball. Doesn't make a difference where I am on the field, when he sets the ball down, we're aligned toward the goal post.*

Your good holders are gonna do that. Now, if the holder can catch that ball with the laces near the front, he can get that ball down a lot quicker. If the ball comes back with the laces at the wrong angle, then he has a little bit more trouble setting the ball down. In fact, you can work it out with the center. You can practice it so the ball revolves from the snap so that it arrives in the holder's hands right. It's gonna make the same number of revolutions every time.

Your coaches don't tell you that. It's something you have to work out to make yourself better. It's worked out between the holder and the kicker and the center. It makes a big difference in the success of the kicker.

Handling a football requires a peculiar set of skills. This is designed into the game. Most players in a game never touch the ball. You can do four things with a football—carry it, kick it, throw it, and catch it. Carrying a football is simple. The other three aren't. Watch two kids tossing a baseball in the front yard and you'll see the ball go back and forth in a steady rhythm. Switch them to a football and you'll see a scramble as the ball goes short, wide, or over the mark. When it does hit the mark, there's half a chance it will be bobbled.

Kicking a football head on with accuracy and distance is the most difficult of the four. All kicks were head on in that era. From that day Bill stopped practicing dropkicks, it would be another twenty-four years before Pete Gogolak swung a leg sideways at a football and introduced the soccer-style kick. Field goals and extra points were not routine plays. When Bill was 31 for 31 in extra point kicking with the 1950 Redskins, the perfect season was considered remarkable.

At Centre College, Coach Shearer had played with a back named Red Roberts who employed an odd, standing pendulum swing on placekicks. He did not take an approach step. He stood at the point of the hold. After the snap, he swung his leg back from a standing position and kicked it head on. He was accurate, and the absence of an approach step shaved time off the play. It was harder to block.

Bill soon perfected the pendulum technique and used it through college and in the pros. He didn't use an approach step until the kick was about 35 yards. In the pros, his longest standing field goal was 34 yards. His longest approach step field goal was 48 yards.

Roberts had also used the "rocker" step when he punted. Instead of taking a stride and a half before kicking, the punter rocks his weight back—stepping backward on his kicking foot—when he receives the snap. When the kicker shifts forward on his other foot, it gives enough momentum so that the ball can be punted from the point where it was caught. Again, no approach step. Again, harder to block.

There were no permanent goalposts on the Tower Ground. Bill placed canvas bags as markers for the two posts and estimated the crossbar height in order to practice kicks. By fall, he was the best punter and kicker on the squad.

Shearer noted Bill's running speed. The kid wasn't fast overall, but he had a sprinter's start and he could cut. He had an awkward, sidearmed throwing motion that, astonishingly, worked. The boy had an instinct for the game. Shearer was beginning to see the kind of triple-threat back who made a single wing offense work.

By fall, he had two dozen boys signed up for the team. After a few scrimmages, Shearer began to design his offense around Bill. The kid who'd never played a varsity game knew how to use his blockers. He knew more about the game than any other boy on the squad. What he didn't know, he wanted to learn.

The week before the opening game, Stubby Currence, columnist for the *Telegraph*, had Bill picked to lead the team. "Bill Dudley looks like a sure shot for the quarterbacking job and he is a good one. Bill has lots of football sense, is fast and has the moxie to put in across in winning fashion."

Nobody talked much about his size anymore. He started the first game and never left the field after that. He wore number 7.

The Graham team was equipped like most high schools of the day. The uniforms were loose-fitting jerseys and pants of coarse, heavy cotton, almost like canvas. The helmets were leather. Shoulder pads and hip pads were either cardboard or leather. Knee pads were sewn into the pants. The shoes were leather high-tops, with flat cleats made of layered leather on a copper base. The players wore whatever the team had available. There were no custom fittings.

The team played the coal towns in Virginia and West Virginia. Sometimes they traveled in a bus. Sometimes it was a caravan of cars.

Bill at quarterback called the plays from the field, using an odd system of hand signals. The G-Men—as the Graham team was known—huddled two yards off the ball within easy hearing distance of the defense. They used three formations, designated by palm up, palm down, or a fist. Plays and counts and holes were called with the fingers and the back of the hand. A pinky meant a pass play.

This wasn't Coach Shearer's system. The boys came up with it. Other teams thought they were crazy. From the huddle, the center would get the count, turn, and be on the ball. Using audibles of "hep," "hike," and "shift," Bill could shorten or prolong the count. They used a precise count—rehearsed endlessly during the first three days of practice to be exactly one second apart—along with audibles and long counts to draw defenses offsides. A hike seven—a very long count with seven audibles of "hike," each called with different intensity—worked more than half the time.

Until 1935, Graham games were played on the Tower Ground. Temporary goalposts were erected and fans stood on the sidelines. In 1935, a 10,000-seat stadium was built in Bluefield, West Virginia. Mitchell Stadium was a Works Progress Administration project—a federally funded New Deal program designed to boost employment. Graham played their home games at Mitchell after '35, likely making them the only high school in the country that played home games in another state. They played day or night games, depending on the schedule of the Bluefield team.

Shearer and Bill were quickly adjusting to each other in game situations. Shearer kept Bill at safety when he realized the boy was adept at reading formations and anticipating plays. It also helped that he was a punishing tackler. Offensively, Bill was learning real game tactics.

I called all the plays. I made one mistake from which I learned plenty. We were playing Tazewell—they were always a tough opponent. And we ran the ball from our own 30 yard line right all the way down to their 5. First down and I threw four passes and all of them were incomplete. Coach didn't get mad, he just said, "Bill, why in the world did you start throwing the football when we made all that ground running?" I said, "Coach, I felt I could complete at least one out of four." He shook his head and said, "Well, we won't do that anymore, will we?" I said, "No, sir."

In another situation, it was Shearer who did the learning. He and Bill were walking the field in the pregame against North Fork. Like many level places in that part of the world, the North Fork field was carved out of a mountainside. A spring dripped and puddled on the mountain side of the field at the 5 yard line. Bill and Shearer agreed it would be a great place to land a punt, which is exactly what Bill did later in the game. When the refs ruled the ball dead, Dudley—acting as captain—allowed the ball to be moved. It was centered on the field, out of the water, giving North Fork a usable field position.

Shearer was hot. It wasn't what they discussed. Assistant coach Mark Gillespie could hear Shearer muttering about what he was going to say when he got his hands on Dudley. Later in the half, Graham recovered a North Fork fumble in the same puddle. The refs again moved the ball to the center of the field, this time setting up an easy score for Graham. "Now," Gillespie was reported to ask, "What are you going to say to Dudley?"

The G-Men had a good season. They were 4-2-1 for the regular season. Graham had a loyal following, but the wins and the new stadium grew the crowd. The Graham High School janitor, Flapper Pancake, lived up to his name. He ran the chain crew and exhorted the boys and the fans. It was a show and one that Depression era Bluefield needed.

They defeated Gary, North Fork, and Bristol handily. They beat Elkhorn on a 35-yard breakaway Dudley run in the fourth quarter. The *Telegraph*'s Wally Longworth covered the game and supplied Bill with his first of many nicknames—Paperweight Dudley.

They tied a heavily favored Tazewell squad. The G-Men had four boys out with injuries. The Graham boys were cocky against underdog

Richlands and paid for it with a 0–0 tie. The only loss was an away game against Salem.

So it was three wins against West Virginia teams and one win, two ties, and a loss against Virginia teams. This set up the "Mythical Two Virginias Championship."

A homemade playing card—a hand-tinted cutout photo mounted on cardboard— probably made by Bill's mother during his final year of high school football.

CHAPTER FOUR

A Lifetime in One Kick

GRAHAM HIGH SCHOOL HAD NEVER PLAYED THE TEAM FROM PRINCE-ton, West Virginia. Most of the G-Men, including Bill, had never been there. The Two Virginias game was added late in the season. It was the border state area championship—contrived and unauthorized, but consequential in the Virginia/West Virginia coal country. It was a bragging rights game. In a grand misuse of both words, sportswriters called the game a "mythical championship." Princeton was favored.

Princeton was a much bigger town. The Tigers were rated in the top three in West Virginia. They had beaten the Bluefield, West Virginia, Beavers, a AAA team. Graham was AA. The Graham team was down to seventeen players from twenty-four at the start of the season. In the barbershops, the sages foretold—the question was whether Graham would lose as bad as the Beavers did, or worse.

Princeton supplied bulletin board material the week before the game. Graham had suffered several costly fumbles in the regular season, and the Tigers labeled them the "Fumbling Herd"—a play on the "Thundering Herd," the name of the Marshall University team in Huntington, West Virginia—in the local press.

The G-Men didn't need motivation, though. The championship game gave four Graham seniors one more shot in a G-Man uniform. They weren't going out losers.

Bill: "Good, better or indifferent, if I participate, I want to win, period. I can't do it for just fun. Now, I may not win. Half the time

I didn't. I've never been told there's anything wrong with that. I've been a good sport, even when I lose, but I don't like it."

Coach Shearer always played the pessimist with the press before games. For this game, he clammed up. Two weeks before the game, he moved practice off the Tower Ground. The team scrimmaged on a farm three miles out of town, veiled from the eyes of likely Princeton scouts. There, Shearer and his boys rehearsed new defensive schemes.

The schemes worked. Little Graham held the Princeton offense. It was a low-scoring game on a rain- and snow-soaked field. Princeton led at halftime 7–0. Graham lost two touchdowns to penalties, but came back and tied the score in the fourth quarter. The game stayed knotted until the G-Men found themselves fourth down on the Princeton 23 yard line with a minute to play.

On its previous possession, Princeton tried to pin the G-Men deep in their territory with a quick kick. The quick kick was a useful offensive weapon in the era of the single-wing offense. It's a low-scoring offense and coaches were willing to trade loss of possession for field position. A good kicker could catch a defense off guard on third down and pin the opponent deep in their territory. They called it "flipping the field." The Redskins' Sammy Baugh was peerless at it. Bill always said he could sense a quick kick coming. He would get a little smile and say, "Sam Baugh never got a quick kick over my head."

When the Princeton eleven lined up, Bill, playing safety, saw a quick kick coming and lulled the offense by playing close to the line. At the snap, Bill hotfooted it back, made an over-the-shoulder catch on his 35 yard line, and returned it to the Princeton 35. Three plays later, the G-Men were on their 27 and out of downs and out of time.

Dudley huddled the boys and called a play. When Shearer saw the formation, he called a timeout. He met his young charge at the sideline.

"What are you gonna do?" asked Shearer.

"I'm gonna kick a field goal," Bill replied.

Bill would later recall that Shearer didn't bat an eye. To Bill, it was simple: He'd either make it or miss it.

The setback position of the goalpost and the position of the holder made this a 37-yard field goal. It was unheard of in high schools at the time. Nobody in the stands had ever seen one. In 1937, a kick of this distance was scarce even in college games. The G-Men on the field, though, were unfazed by the call. They'd seen too many Billy Dudley moments like this on the Tower Ground. They were poised for the play.

At the snap, Bill kicked using an approach step. When the ball cleared the crossbar, it was game over.

Here is how they reported it the next day in the *Bluefield Daily Telegraph*, Saturday, November 20, 1937:

GRAHAM FLOGS PRINCETON 10-7
Gives G-Men Grid Title Of Area;
Bill Dudley In Hero Role As Kick Wins
That's the final chapter of the story of how Marshall Shearer and his G-Men drove through to the mythical championship of Southern West Virginia and Southwest Virginia. Playing on a water-logged field, and under the most deplorable weather conditions imaginable yesterday afternoon at the Princeton field, the G-Men turned in one of the biggest surprises of the 1937 pigskin semester.

The victory was one well earned. The G-Men outplayed Princeton and might have won by a much larger margin had not penalties nullified two other Graham touchdowns. It was the parting shot of the campaign which goes down in history as the finest one ever experienced by Graham high school.

The unerring accuracy of the good right toe of little Billy Dudley, brainy little quarterback of the Virginia Siders, provided the margin of victory. With the two teams knotted in a 7-7 deadlock, Dudley dropped back to the 27 yard line and booted the ball squarely between the uprights. It traveled a total of 37 yards to clear the bar.

Dudley's kick was a fitting climax for the ball game as it was the little G-Man field chieftain who dominated the play most of the afternoon. He intercepted the Princeton pass deep in county seat territory that paved the way for the Graham touchdown.

When the clock ran out, the boy was swarmed by players and spectators. He didn't know it, but Paperweight Dudley had just kicked his way into the University of Virginia.

Jack "Doc" Whitten was an old bachelor and farmer who cussed like a sailor. He was a friend of Sheb Dudley, and he was the state legislator representing Tazewell County. Mostly, he was the benefactor of lost boys in southwest Virginia. He took them off the streets, gave them work on his farm, and made sure they were educated.

One of the many things that Whitten cussed about was the absence of University of Virginia athletic recruits from his district. He had boys who could play. Where were the coaches?

In January 1938, Whitten was on the state finance committee when the university came calling for funds. He vowed they wouldn't get a dime until somebody came to southwest Virginia with scholarships ready. The school—and the new football coach Frank Murray—heeded.

To the extent that Dudley thought he would go to college at all, Virginia wasn't on his list. Virginia Tech, North Carolina, and Tennessee were in easier traveling distance. Those were the teams he followed as a young fan.

Coach Shearer knew coaches at North Carolina, Southern Methodist (SMU), Kentucky, and other schools, but it was tough to peddle a 130-pound back with one season of varsity ball from a distant border town in Virginia.

Tennessee was Bill's first choice. They declined. UNC said no. Matty Bell at SMU was interested, but the moment passed. Virginia Tech said no. Washington & Lee, no. Virginia Military Institute (VMI), no. Kentucky never called.

By June, Bill was ready to make other plans. He was working as a crate handler on a Nehi soda delivery truck. It was a job, but it wasn't job enough. Autumn would be upon him. He needed to support himself.

One day a car pulled the Nehi truck over. It was Coach Shearer. "Drop what you're doing. We're going to Tazewell." Dudley shrugged at his dumbfounded Nehi driver and got in the car. Shearer took him home. Bill changed clothes and they were in Tazewell forty minutes later.

Doc Whitten had gotten wind that Coach Murray was making a southwest Virginia swing. He arranged for Shearer and other coaches to bring prospects to his house. When Bill arrived, he was the fifth and final prospect.

Murray's Virginia Cavaliers had gone 2-7 in his first year as head coach. The kicking game was bad all season and cost them a win against rival Maryland. Shearer had already made sure Murray knew about Bill's performance in the Princeton game.

Bill would later recall they just talked. Murray asked about the Princeton game and kicking in general, but it seemed like he was simply sizing up the boy.

Five weeks later, a representative from UVA arrived at the Dudley home with an offer—$500 for room, board, books, and tuition. Bill didn't have to make the team. The scholarship, funded by a group of Richmond businessmen, was good as long as he stayed academically eligible.

All that was required of the Dudleys was to say yes or no. It was done on a handshake. There was no letter of intent, no contract, and no money changed hands.

Bill later learned that the better prospects received $800 scholarships, but he didn't care. A year of Home-Ec had paid off. He would play college football.

CHAPTER FIVE

A World Apart in a $23 Suit

EVERY STATE HAS A SENSE OF ITSELF, SOME MORE THAN OTHERS. IN THE state of Virginia, it's more.

There's the natural and architectural beauty—the Chesapeake Bay on one end and the Shenandoah Valley and Blue Ridge Mountains on the other. Between are the horse-fenced colonial spreads that are somehow majestic and understated at the same time.

There's the shared destiny with the nation. The Jamestown Colony. Williamsburg. Revolutionary War battles. Yorktown. The founding of the Republic. The "Mother of Presidents"—Washington, Jefferson, Madison, Monroe, Harrison, Tyler, Taylor, and Wilson. The Civil War—Manassas, Chancellorsville, Petersburg, Appomattox, and more than a hundred other battles. Stonewall Jackson and Robert E. Lee.

And there was the mystique of the Cavaliers, swashbucklers who fled Britain's Roundheads for America and Virginia in the mid-1600s and brought their extravagant customs with them—hard drink, hard work, and hard play mixed with exalted honor and rectitude and gallantry.

Nowhere in Virginia is this sense of self more evident than in Charlottesville, home to the University of Virginia. The place is marinated in it. The aura of Thomas Jefferson spreads outward from the grounds and buildings he designed and is as inescapable as the scent of English boxwood. The Cavalier was a model for manhood. Manhood meant something, and in 1938, the University of Virginia was all male. To them, the mystique was unique. Within the state today, University of Virginia students and alumni still refer to the school as "The University."

A fellow who just moseyed into town might wonder what all the fuss is about. In Charlottesville, the answer is: It's special here. We are a world apart. You either get it, or you don't.

Bill Dudley got it. He felt it the moment he stepped out of his brother's car and took in the school.

It's hard to put into words my feelings about UVA. I was so young when I went there. There was an air about Charlottesville, the University, Jefferson and the way athletics have been taken along with an education. There's nothing wrong with being the best in medicine, the best in law, and having the best football and basketball teams. There's something about playing at the University of Virginia that's not like playing at any other school.

Brother Jim had insisted on making the five-hour drive, knowing his father would linger for the day in Charlottesville and get in the way. On the drive up, Jim and Bill stopped in Lexington and lunched at Jim's former frat house at Washington & Lee. Jim had played end on the W&L team. When Jim informed the Sigma Chi boys that he and his brother weren't staying, that Bill would play for rival Virginia, every piece of silverware hit the floor. The Dudleys made it out alive.

Jim had dressed his kid brother for school. Back in Bluefield he explained that Virginia students wore coat and tie to class. Bond's Clothing store on the West Virginia side was having a sale. Two-pants suits were priced at $19.99, $21.99, and $22.99. Buy one and get another free. The boys went all out. Twenty-three dollars later, Bill had two jackets and four pairs of pants. In those days, the store threw in the tie. Jim's only remaining task was to explain what garters were and how they worked.

Jim did not linger in Charlottesville. He dropped Bill at Alumni Hall and drove away. Bill made his way to Mrs. Van Leer's boarding house. It was across the street from the entrance to the grounds (Virginia eschews the term "campus"). Everything was as they said it would be. His name was on the register. The rent—thirty-eight dollars per month—was paid.

The grounds were at the edge of town. The view from Scott Stadium opened up to a few houses, hills, and farmland. The place was a world of its own.

Bill followed the other students from other boarding houses—UVA had few dorms then—and frat houses to sign up for classes. He took English, chemistry, Latin, economics, and math. At the bookstore, he charged his books to his scholarship. And, like that, he was one of 2,934 Virginia students.

He didn't know a single person there. The school was a mystery to him. Charlottesville was a long, twisty, mountain-quelling drive from Bluefield. To him, Charlottesville was just a remote place where the state's annual high school essay and debate contests were held in spring. He was sixteen.

He felt lucky to be there. Virginia was, after all, the only school that wanted him.

It was a defining year for UVA—1938 was the fiftieth anniversary of the football program at the school. Two years earlier, the school had begun extending athletic scholarships. It had to. Virginia was already late to the college athletics party.

Football began at UVA in 1888. For the next twenty-eight seasons, they posted winning seasons. From 1916 on they went from average to bad to awful.

Virginia fielded teams with walk-ons. There were good athletes. There just weren't enough to field good teams. The school was forbidden scholarships under Southern Conference rules. The UVA Honor Code nixed under-the-table deals. A student found accepting payment would have violated the code and would be expelled.

Nothing much had changed over the first fifty years of Virginia football. By the mid-1930s, the UVA football coach, Gus Tebell, was also the basketball coach. He drove players to away games in his own car. He kept to the Honor Code. Meanwhile, other college coaches around the country and in the conference weren't bound by a code. They could recruit and keep players with jobs, clothes, meals, and cash—which came in handy during the Depression. The disadvantage was visible every fall weekend. To many students and faculty in Charlottesville, this was just fine. The school would regard and treat an athlete as any other student. If you wanted to be special at UVA, you did it in the classroom. You might say the school and student body were cold to the idea of Bigtime Sports, as they called it. Such a thing would sully Mr. Jefferson's academic grounds.

An abundant sense of self hollows out fast when everybody else thinks you're a loser and can prove it. In 1933, Ohio State sullied Mr. Jefferson's grounds 75–0. In the final game of 1935, Virginia's biggest rival, North Carolina, beat them 61–0. Soul searching was followed by a search for a coach. How could UVA get in the game and keep its character? Who could answer the dual demands and keep athletics and academics on equal footing?

If you went to central casting and told them to send over a Hall of Fame football coach, the last person you'd expect to see returning would be Frank Murray. He was small and quiet and bespectacled. He had a master's degree in English and a doctorate in philosophy from Harvard. He taught political science. He had never played a down of football.

But he had a first-rate football mind and a perceptive, elegant way with young athletes. He had coached Marquette to a winning record over fifteen seasons and took the team to the first Cotton Bowl his final year there. He was the man Virginia wanted, and the school hired him in 1937. UVA then left the Southern Conference. Football scholarships followed.

Tebell stayed on as an assistant football coach and head coach of the basketball team. He remains the third most successful basketball coach in school history.

Murray had a complex system and a thick playbook. He liked fakes and reverses. He liked to think. He was Bill's kind of football man, "Murray was a brilliant offensive mind. He would spend hours looking at film, diagramming plays on a board, moving men around."

Murray had done a stint as a journalist and it was said he penned a column or two for Chauncey Durden, the dean of Virginia sportswriters at the *Richmond Times-Dispatch*. Murray didn't like profanity. He considered himself a teacher, which he was until he landed the Marquette coaching job. He was willing to listen and experiment, and this made him the perfect coach for young Bill Dudley. Murray knew how to discover the strengths in a young athlete. As Bill said, "A young man would go into his office. Coach Murray would close the door. The boy would come out forty-five minutes later just beaming."

Sheb Dudley and his son agreed it would be classes and football only. The boy wouldn't take a job his first year. He would just have to get by. He also wouldn't play other sports, although Bill was itching to play baseball.

Bill arrived at the first day of practice listed as the seventh most promising recruit for the backfield, a diplomatic way of saying he was the least promising recruit. Freshmen weren't allowed in varsity games. The first-year boys would play four games against other freshman teams. These games had the feel of exhibition games. Player development was as important as winning and losing. Playing time was intermittent. However, the freshmen scrimmaged with the varsity. So, once again, the boy was fodder, but this time it was different.

> Bill: *"I loved to return punts. They used freshman backs for that. We had a couple of kids who didn't want to run back punts against the varsity. I looked forward to it. I broke one loose now and then. I got to know the varsity players that way."*

It was different in another way. Everybody was bigger and older. Everybody. He told them he weighed 150 pounds, but telling it doesn't make it so. He was one of three battling for the tailback spot. Did he think he could make the team? "I never thought I was. I never thought I wasn't. I never thought about size. Everybody was bigger than me."

In Murray's first year, 1937, his Virginia team was 2-7. The 1938 season, though, was his first with experienced scholarship athletes, including star junior Jimmy Gillette, the first Cavalier to be drafted into the NFL, where he became an All-Pro. The team went 4-4-1 in 1938. More importantly, they defeated or tied every in-state rival. They won over Washington & Lee, William & Mary, and Virginia Tech. They tied VMI.

Even in the lean years, the other schools in Virginia despised UVA teams. A little too much Cavalier swagger will do that for you. The state schools had a "Big Six"—Virginia Tech, VMI, W&L, W&M, Richmond, and UVA. Sportswriters could pen articles about yet another mythical championship. One school could claim the Big Six championship. Nobody, and that means nobody, wanted UVA to win it.

The 1937 Virginia Tech game was the Hokie homecoming in Blacksburg. When the UVA team arrived at the stadium, they were met by a Cavalier hung in effigy with a sign pinned onto it:

Here lies the bier of the Cavalier.
He died in a wreck At Va. Tech.

UVA won 14–7 that day—with Gillette scoring off a double reverse—and it was the first win over Tech in eleven years. Now, a hint of genuine swagger returned to Charlottesville, but the debate was on. There were two very conflicting schools of thought about Murray: He was too flashy. He was too conservative.

There was one more big difference at Virginia. Some of Dudley's Graham classes had been listed as college prep. You could say they gave him a false confidence. There was no denying it—the boy was below average in the classroom. It was not for lack of trying. Students in those days studied in the Rotunda—Jefferson's signature Palladian dome structure that anchors the grounds—or the new library. Dudley was in one or the other every night. He just couldn't get the gist of it.

In his first semester he passed English, but that was about it. He flunked Latin cold, even though the prof was one of the few at UVA who favored jocks. "I spent a lot of time on the subjects," Bill said. "I thought I knocked a test cold and then I'd get a 60."

His scholarship was based on academic performance. When the grades came in, the academic committee made Sheb Dudley an offer. If he would pay $175, his son could stay in school and earn his scholarship back. Sheb borrowed $200—no easy thing for a man rebuilding his career during the Depression—and it was back to Charlottesville. Young Dudley was on probation at Virginia and he was on a more severe probation back home in Bluefield, and he knew it.

His classroom performance improved in the next semester. A sense of purpose was developing. He would get a degree in education and he would teach and coach.

With his first season behind him, Bill was freed of afternoon practices. His social life improved quickly. His social circle widened beyond football players. He got to know the boys at the SAE fraternity house. The manager of the football team befriended him. He learned to dance. He went out on dates. Everybody was older. It didn't matter.

He also became friends with some boys from Lynchburg, Virginia, just down the road. He became close with one—Bobby Watts would remain a lifelong friend and play an important role in Bill's life.

He discovered that Coach Murray and his assistant, Art Guepe, liked to talk football. It was like being with Marshall Shearer, without the drugstore booth. Bill came to think of Murray as the finest coach he had, college or pro. He was a finesse coach more than a power man.

Whether or not you played that fall was decided in spring practice. There were five tailbacks on the varsity roster. After spring practice, Dudley was fifth, but he was still there. He knew he was on the squad.

He passed all his courses that semester except one—Latin again. The scholarship was renewed, although he had to make up the lost Latin credits in summer school. He arranged with Mrs. Van Leer to wait tables at her boarding house in exchange for summer lodging and he earned pocket money as a cashier in a restaurant.

He never mastered a foreign language class in all his years at Virginia, and if you ever asked him to read a menu at an Italian restaurant, you'd know why. The man was wired for English.

CHAPTER SIX

1939: A Coin Flip and a Star Is Born

GREAT ATHLETES WILL TELL YOU THEY MAKE THEIR OWN LUCK. WHEN the break happens, you must be prepared for it. In Bill Dudley's case, the break was the flip of a coin.

Things felt different in the fall of 1939. In Bluefield, the mines were reopening. People were returning to work. In Charlottesville returning students whispered about a winning season. It was Gillette's senior year. Could it be?

Bill was already in town. The first game was three weeks away. He shared an apartment with lineman Jack Murden. He was rushed by the SAE boys, but he couldn't afford to join.

Usually there was no football practice in the offseason. Staying in playing shape was a matter of road work and pushups. Athletes and students normally arrived at school on the same day. This year, Murray had the team in early training at the naval base in Norfolk. Bill showed up ready to scrimmage. He knew Murray's thick playbook. He said he weighed 158 pounds. This time it was true.

College football teams were beginning to number players by offensive position. It was said the idea was suggested by radio announcers. It wasn't a rigid system. Backs were numbered 1 through 40. On the line, centers were in the 50s, guards in the 60s, tackles in the 70s, and ends in the 80s. Bill was given number 35. It wasn't a solemn moment. It was just another number. Nobody present had a clue that it would someday be retired.

The Cavaliers opened against Hampden-Sydney. They won 26–0, but it was a bad outing. Virginia's top two tailbacks were injured. Bill got in the game, but fumbled on the goal line.

"I was distressed. Guepe patted me on the shoulder and sent me to the bench. I thought that might have finished me, but it didn't."

The next game was against Navy, a team that played in football's big league. They had a good first team and a strong bench. The Middies would be tough even if the Virginia squad was at full strength. They weren't. Virginia's third-string tailback was injured in practice. There were only two left. In pregame press coverage, Murray made little of the injuries. He'd scouted Navy's Middies and said they could be beaten. He had a good word for his new starter, sophomore Bill Dudley. "He's young and he's light—he weighs only 158 pounds, you know—but he's got confidence."

What Murray didn't tell the press boys was that Dudley got the starting spot through a coin flip. Murray had two healthy tailbacks remaining and the coaches had no preference between the fourth- and fifth-stringers. Dudley won the toss. The players weren't told about the flip. A star was about to be born. Navy won 14–12. Rarely has a loss generated so much enthusiasm. The next day's headlines were all Dudley. The *Richmond News-Leader*: "Dudley Stars as Cavaliers are Beaten." The *Richmond Times-Dispatch*: "Dudley Stars as Cavaliers Are Beaten." The *Washington Post*: "Rise of Dudley, Cavalier Soph, Is Brilliant."

Virginia outplayed the Middies for fifty-seven minutes on a hot, muscle-sapping afternoon in Annapolis. Two failed extra points and two fluke plays cost Virginia the game. The postgame excitement was caused by the kind of football that would become a Bill Dudley signature—breakaway, broken-field runs and punt returns.

In the second quarter, it was Dudley around end on a Murray double reverse. He took the ball through heavy traffic 45 yards for a touchdown. The fans had to check the scoreboard to see who wore number 35. The extra point failed.

The Cavaliers led 6–0 at the half. In the third quarter, Navy made it 7–6 after a fluke play. Navy was in punting formation, fourth down and 5 deep in their own territory. The snap was high and the punter couldn't get the kick away, but the Virginia end had dropped back to block for the return. Suddenly, the punter found himself with a wide open field to his right. He took the ball downfield for 50 yards. Two plays later, Navy scored and the extra point was good.

Bill soon answered when he broke loose on a punt return and ran 43 yards to the Navy 5, but the Cavaliers failed to get in from there.

A Gillette lapse set up Navy's second touchdown in the third quarter. Bill was playing safety. The Middies had just gained 10 yards on a reverse and the play was over. A Navy linemen continued to rough up Bill after the whistle. Gillette went over and let the Navy boy have it. As it works so often, the refs didn't see the first offense, but they did see the second. Gillette was flagged. The penalty put the Middies on the 1 yard line. Navy scored and the extra point was good. Navy 14, Virginia 6. UVA then made it 14–12 with a touchdown followed by a blocked extra point.

Navy coach Swede Larson used his deep bench against the heat. Faced with fresh opponents, and down two points in the fourth quarter, the Cavaliers went to the air. Again and again, it was Dudley to Gillette or Gillette to Dudley, but Navy controlled the ball and time ran out.

Bill had 124 yards rushing for the day. It was the first time Gillette's yardage was exceeded by a teammate. Not that Gillette didn't have a good day. The Middie defense keyed on him. Even so, Gillette broke loose for a long run that set up the second UVA score. He had a great game defensively, including two interceptions, one for a 90-yard return. The Cavs failed to convert that one, too.

The press often sees the way refs do. They dwelt on Gillette's costly loss of temper. Little was made of the fact that it was a Dudley-fumbled lateral that put Navy in scoring position in the first place.

There was some revisionism in the postgame coverage. Murray recalled that he had picked Dudley as the class of the freshman crop in 1938 and that nobody agreed with him at the time. The coaching staff said his sudden arrival was startling, but they'd seen more promise from him than any other sophomore. Nobody mentioned the coin flip.

They were surprised. Very surprised. Early in the game, two big Navy linemen laid out Bill with the kind of double-team tackle that puts players out of a game. The kid shook it off. Murray's offense was complex. It should have been out of reach for the young tailback. Bill knew the book in and out. The boy was a weapon. The Navy defense marked Gillette, but the Virginia coaches saw how Middie coaches and players reacted when Dudley touched the ball. He scared them.

When the Navy coaches reviewed game film on Monday, they counted eight midshipmen who had shots at Bill on his touchdown run. None touched him. They said it was like trying to catch a ghost. Perhaps it was more like dodging telephone poles.

What happened? For Bill, football was a mental game. When he watched two teams on a football field he didn't see the same thing that spectators, or even other players, observed. He saw patterns of play. He saw situational play calling. What would he call? He saw player tendencies. He saw linemen who couldn't move left or receivers who telegraphed patterns or passers who couldn't switch to the secondary receiver. He didn't spend all those hours with Marshall Shearer and Coach Murray for nothing. He knew the game. He read it all and stored information in a data bank in his head as the game progressed.

The Good Lord gave me a brain and I was able to use it. I tried to use my faculties I wasn't big enough to run over anybody.

I always felt that football was played as much with your mind as your body. I was always trying to think one step ahead of the defense if I was on offense, and one step ahead of offense if I was on defense. If I got the idea they were gonna try to do something, I would move out of position to give them the impression that what they wanted to do was gonna be wide open. I'd move over to the right spot at the last minute and counteract their play.

I can remember several times when I knew exactly what the other team was going to do. When I was with Detroit, we were playing Pittsburgh. The Steelers had a play where they fake an end run to the right and throw left. And if called at the right time, it invariably worked. Pittsburgh had a tendency to call it at certain times. I remember talking with Coach Grey on the sidelines, "They're gonna call that play, let me go in." He said, "Oh, Bill, don't worry about it." I didn't go in, and sure enough, this kid goes out there, goes down the

field and catches a pass for about a 30–40 yard gain. I wanted to be in
there so bad, and knew it was gonna be coming up and I could have
intercepted it. But that just came with knowing the personnel they
had and knowing what was going to happen.

In order to absorb these tendencies and exploit weaknesses, Bill
needed to be in the flow of the game. The exhibition-style freshman
games negated that. His lucky sophomore flip put him where his talents,
all of them, could come together. The coaches learned more about Bill in
one game than they had in the entire previous season.

The coaches learned even more about their new star on the ride home.
Bill smoldered over the loss. They should have won. The Cavaliers had
missed two extra points and failed to score twice on possessions inside
the Navy 10 yard line. One Navy TD was set up by a blown Cavalier
punt defense. The other TD was set up by his own fumble. When another
player asked him what the problem was, Bill told him what he was thinking. The player replied, "You had a good game. I had a good game. What's
the problem?" Bill detonated. If there had been a strap on the bus, the boy
would have gotten the Sheb Dudley treatment. Bill would never name the
player later, but everybody within hearing distance knew.

Bill kicked off for Virginia that day, but he didn't kick extra points.
For the rest of the season, and the rest of his Virginia career, he kicked
extra points, too.

Newspaper sportswriting in pre-television years was colorful and for-
mulaic. Nimble running backs were swivel-hipped. Burly linemen were
stout. Passers lobbed aerials or aerialists lobbed passes. Receivers were
sure-handed or light-footed or both. The end zone was The Promised
Land. There was a breathless quality to it. Here is the description of the
new Cavalier star from the *Richmond Times-Dispatch*:

Stars were numerous on both teams, but standing out was Dudley,
the smooth-as-silk sophomore who bids fair to become one of Virginia's
immortals. After turning in that 45-yard touchdown jaunt in the
second quarter, the little fellow kept Navy supporters on tenter-hooks
all the while he was in the game. In the third quarter, he took a Navy

punt out of the air, danced in and out of harm's way for a couple of moments and ran 43 yards to the Tars' five-yard line. But the Virginia strategy went awry and the ball went over.

And players had nicknames. The rush was on to pin a name on the new Cavalier star. Prior to the Navy game, he was Little Bill Dudley. After the Navy game he was Little Billy, Bounding Bill, Bouncing Bill, Beacon Bill, or the Bluefield Beacon. None of them stuck until he was eventually labeled The Bluefield Bullet the next season, which was reduced to "Bullet" Bill his senior year.

The Cavaliers had forced a powerhouse team to rally for a win. In Charlottesville and in the press, anticipation was high. There was, as they say today, a narrative. Gillette would play big brother. Dudley would be the able aid.

The *Virginia News-Leader* predicted this: "The slender 158-pound sophomore from Bluefield, who stepped up from a substitute role last week to put on an amazing offensive display against Navy, is assured of more time in the Cavalier backfield and probably will remain the starting lineup against Maryland Saturday."

Bill didn't start against Maryland. Murray didn't want to bring the boy along too fast. He was so young. Most boys his age were working up through high school ball. What if he got cocky? Bill played in every game for the rest of the season, but he only started four. When he went in the game, though, he stayed. Bill would later credit Murray for this. "I think he cared about winning, but I think he felt it would be better for me and better for him if he brought me along slow. Evidently, he saw something that a lot of other people didn't see."

Dudley and Gillette did play well together. Murray liked to spread the end to the left side, then he'd put a flanker away, which opened up the field for both players. Bill always said the best college play he was in was a Gillette to Dudley touchdown pass over VMI star Pounding Paul Shu. From the *Roanoke Times*:

With the ball on the VMI 23 with the fourth period about six minutes gone, Billy leaped up behind Shu over the goal line to take a beautiful pass from Gillette for the second Virginia score. So marvelous was his catch, so difficult the position he caught it in, he fell hard to the ground just inside the end zone but he held the ball.

The whispers of a winning season became boasts. The Cavaliers went 5-4, the first winning season in seven years. They lost, though, to their three biggest rivals—VMI, Virginia Tech, and North Carolina.

In spring, the SAE house offered Bill a scholarship. Spring intramurals were approaching. There were the usual sports—softball and basketball—and there was boxing. Bill took the scholarship.

It wasn't unusual for an American household to have boxing gloves at the ready in those years. The Dudley home did and the boys laced them up often. At the University of Virginia, boxing was the premier intramural sport. The boys of that era grew up with Jack Dempsey. The Manassa Mauler was one of the most popular sports figures of the era and a cultural icon. You don't have to be an art lover to know the George Bellows painting of Dempsey knocking Angel Firpo out of the ring. In 1937, Joe Louis became heavyweight champion and he whipped Max Schmeling in 1938. He, too, was a cultural icon.

For the intramural matches, the UVA boys fought three two-minute rounds in gloves and no headgear. When Bill entered the ring for his final match, he found himself facing a much bigger opponent—a med student who had boxed in the Navy. Round one went to the Navy boy. It was pugilistic style vs. brute strength. Style lost: "I tried to box. Bingo. I'm on the floor."

It didn't get better from there. At the end of the second round, Bill's cornerman had some advice—start slugging or get carried out the door. Bill took the advice. Over the course of his sports career, Bill clipped and sent home only one article, from *College Topics* (today the *Cavalier Daily*):

Friday night saw the most thrilling fight of the year staged between Bill Dudley of SAE and Campbell of Phi Beta Pi. Haymakers and knockdowns were as frequent as Russian bombs. At the sound of the first bell, the taller Campbell rushed out and dug into his man with a succession of heavy blows. He continued to spear Dudley with a bruising right, and had the latter in troubled water in a neutral corner. Bill weathered the storm however, and surged back with a murderous assault of his own. Campbell was holding on at the bell.

The boys increased their pace in a blistering second round. Once again the taller lad had the upper hand. A flurry of blows drove Dudley to the ropes, another right chop dropped him. He was up shortly and immediately caught his opponent with the same blow. It was Campbell who held on this time. Dudley followed with a savage succession of rights and his man went down. He was up at nine and managed to last the round.

The crowd expected a knockout in the last canto, but nothing of the sort happened. It was all Dudley however as he subjected his man to a nasty beating. Campbell was out on his feet, his hands helplessly at his sides as the fight ended. Dudley's decision drew a great cheer.

At spring practice there was no debate about whose name would occupy the number one tailback slot. There was debate, though, about the fall schedule.

There was an open week. Murray decided to let the players vote on the opponent. The list of available opponents included beatable schools like in-state Hampden-Sydney, as well as heavier opponents, like the University of Tennessee. The Tennessee Volunteers were 10-1 the previous season and were the Southeastern Conference champions. They were a national powerhouse. Bill talked his teammates into choosing Tennessee. Murray called him aside after the vote.

Murray: "Bill, we can't play Tennessee."
Bill: "What do you mean, Coach?"
Murray: "They're just too good for us."
Bill: "They're the best. I want to play the best."

Murray shook his head. The game was on. Bill knew Murray was right. The Cavs had no business playing in Knoxville. Tennessee was, indeed, the best. He also knew they had refused him a scholarship.

Bill's grades were acceptable, although he did have to make up one class that summer. This time it was French. There was time, though, for a return to Bluefield. It was a family reunion, of sorts. Brother Jim was home, working with Sheb for Home Life Insurance. Brother Tom was a rising high school senior. Sister Margaret was home and unhappily so.

She had returned to college, this time to Longwood, a day's drive from Bluefield in Farmville, Virginia. Unfortunately for her, Sheb got wind that she was singing in nightclubs—with a band, no less. Now, there was music and there was *music*. Sheb took a train to Longwood, packed her trunk, and took her home.

Bill filled out his summer working at a coal mine. He never referred to himself as a miner, then or later. He was a laborer outside the tunnel. He was a welcome addition to the miners' baseball team, but he found himself unwelcome in another way.

After a few weeks at the mine, Bill was approached by a miner. There was a union meeting Monday night. He made it clear Bill needed to be there. Bill—with Sheb's admonitions echoing—declined. Sheb's low opinion of unions was thoroughly fixed in his son. The next week, another miner approached Bill. There was, he said, another meeting Monday. This time the invitation was less cordial. Again, Bill declined. He, too, was less cordial. The first encounter was a cool standoff. This one had the potential to heat up. The third week, a foreman approached. He wanted to know how many shifts Bill had remaining for the summer. Bill told him.

"Work every shift until Monday," the foreman said. "That will get you all your guaranteed hours. Don't be here Monday."

CHAPTER SEVEN

1940: Third Team All America

THE 1940 SEASON BEGAN WELL. IN CHARLOTTESVILLE, OPTIMISM WAS high. In the previous season, the Murray-recruited freshman squad went undefeated. Now they could play for the varsity. Murray had a headliner. Bill would take over the running, passing, and kicking. Preseason publicity focused on the new triple threat. Bill was a fan favorite. The crowds would be big. Most important for Murray: His star hadn't gotten cocky.

The Cavs beat Lehigh in the home opener 32–0 with Dudley touchdown runs of 31 and 37 yards. He also threw a 56-yard touchdown pass and returned an interception for 37 yards.

The next week they upset Yale 19–14 on the road before 25,000 spectators. Although Bill was young and untraveled, he rarely played the role of the wide-eyed boy from Bluefield. At Yale, it was different. Yale was a good team. Just playing in the Yale Bowl had him slack-jawed. It was also meaningful to him in ways he didn't know. Yale, Harvard, and Princeton were the Big Three. They drew students from the New York Social Register. Ivy League games were covered by the New York, Boston, and Philadelphia sportswriters—men who had plenty to say about who was and wasn't an All-Star. They listened to what the Yale men had to say. Yale chief of staff Spike Nelson called Dudley "the most dangerous back I have ever seen in the Yale Bowl."

The next week, Virginia beat Maryland on the road, 19–6 with two Dudley passes and one run for touchdowns. The Cavs were 3-0. The fans cheered. The writers raved. Then things went south.

The Cavs lost two close games to in-state teams. VMI beat them 7–0 at home. William & Mary beat them 13–6 away.

The Cavs started November facing rival Virginia Tech on neutral ground—Foreman Field in Norfolk. The Hokies didn't take the field for pregame warmups. This was a sign, Murray warned his team—this meant the Tech boys were ready when they got there. It was a low-scoring match, but Tech was, indeed, ready. Tech scored a TD on a 40-yard pass in the second quarter and missed the point after. It was a defensive game from there. Tech won, 6–0.

Virginia returned to form the following week, defeating Washington & Lee 20–6 on Dudley touchdown runs of 30 and 39 yards. The Cavs had gone from 3-0 to 3-3, losing to in-state schools. A winning season would mean defeating either Tennessee or North Carolina. It didn't look likely.

The Tennessee Volunteers were that good. Coach Bob Neyland took them to the Orange Bowl in 1938 and the Rose Bowl in 1939. The AP chose them number 2 in the nation both years. They had not lost a game so far in 1940, outscoring opponents 225–12. Alabama scored all 12.

The Virginia boys took the train to Knoxville, riding in sleeper cars. They were greeted at the stadium by a sellout crowd. For three quarters, the Cavaliers gave them a game. Going into the fourth quarter it was 21–14, Tennessee. The Virginia highlight was a Dudley touchdown kick-off return for 87 yards in the second quarter. That had never been done to a Neyland team at home. But, the Volunteers were bigger and faster and stronger. They scored three times in the fourth quarter. Final score, 41–14, Tennessee.

If there was such a thing as an acceptable loss to Bill, this was it. The Cavs were overmatched and responded with a good game. The Tennessee game generated the first national publicity for Bill.

Wilton Hazzard of *Illustrated Football Annual* wrote "Dudley is one of the most hair-raising halfbacks in America."

The *Knoxville News-Sentinel* wrote:

The young athlete did everything but consume the hog's hide, and he probably would have done that if an injury hadn't forced him to the sidelines in the closing minutes of the game. When Dudley limped reluctantly from the battlefield near dusk, the crowd scrambled to its frozen puppies and paid the Cavalier a tribute such as is seldom heard at Shield-Watkins Stadium. For several minutes the customers remained standing, clapping, yelling, and whistling their appreciation.

North Carolina, Virginia's biggest rival, was 5-4 going into the final game. The Tarheels were coming off three straight winning seasons. It was another close loss for the Cavs. They scored on a Dudley pass and extra point, but UNC stayed ahead by a field goal when a Dudley Hail Mary was intercepted in the end zone on the last play of the game. UNC won 10–7.

It should have been a better year. Even so, something was changing in Charlottesville. The University of Virginia was becoming a sports school. The indifference was gone and the new outlook had a great deal to do with Bill.

College Topics: *"His outstanding spirit and heart have won for him the admiration and respect of thousands, and realizing that he has another year, we expect greater things of him still."*

For the year, Bill led the team in rushing, passing, and scoring. He ranked eighth in the country in rushing and fourth in passing. He averaged 37 yards per punt. He gained 509 yards on punt and kickoff returns. He was named Third Team All-American.

Bill had a good year academically. He stayed in the fraternity both semesters. It was a good time to be in a frat house. Glenn Miller's "In the Mood" was number 1 on the charts in fall. In spring it was Duke Ellington's "Take the A Train." On the dance floor, girls told Bill he was a good leader. He discovered champagne. He faced fifteen-time world champion

Willie Mosconi in a straight pool exhibition match. "I ran the table twice. Then I missed one. Willie took over and never looked back." It was beginning to dawn on Bill that he'd never return to Bluefield to stay.

The world had a bad year. The Olympics were canceled; Nazi armies invaded Holland, Belgium, and Luxembourg; Nazi bombs fell on England; and Paris was about to fall, but that was all an ocean away.

Bill was elected team captain at spring practice. He stayed in Charlottesville that summer to make up classroom hours: French again. He worked odd jobs in restaurants and at the UVA tennis courts. He also got his first taste of the movie business.

Actor Sterling Hayden was filming a movie in Charlottesville. He needed stagehands. Bill's job was to man a firehose. Before the director called "roll 'em," he signaled Bill, who would blast nearby trees with the hose. It kept the katydids from chirping.

Two weeks after the North Carolina loss, Coach Murray took the train up to Griffith Stadium to watch the Washington Redskins vs. the Chicago Bears in the NFL championship game. It looked to be a good game. The Redskins had beaten Chicago 7–3 only three weeks earlier.

The Bears beat Sammy Baugh and the Redskins 73–0. It was the most lopsided win in NFL history. In Murray's mind, though, the Bears didn't defeat the Redskins. The T-formation did.

CHAPTER EIGHT

1941: One Man for the Bastard T

It's CONFUSING. FOOTBALL'S OLDEST OFFENSIVE FORMATION IS THE T-formation. With the advent of the forward pass, it was replaced by the single-wing formation. The single wing was then replaced by the T, only it wasn't the same T, and the new T was better for passers.

There are so many options in the single wing—a talented backfield could feature four players who could run, throw, and kick the ball. On paper, the single wing appears to be the better offense. This may explain why the single wing lived another decade after its obituary was written.

The variations on the two formations will make your head swim. Here are the basic—very basic—differences between the single wing and the T-formation.

The basic T-formation is symmetrical. There are an equal number of linemen on opposite sides of the center. The quarterback is behind center. Halfbacks are to his left and right. The fullback is in the rear.

The basic single wing is asymmetrical. The line is unbalanced. There are more linemen on one side of the center than on the other. The backs are arranged in various formations. Nobody is under center.

In the T-formation, the quarterback takes the snap from center. In the single-wing formation, any back can take the snap from center.

In the T-formation, the snap can be hand to hand or a 3- to 5-yard shotgun. In the single wing, the snaps are about a 2-yard toss.

In the T-formation, the quarterback is the key player and takes the snap from center. In the single wing, the tailback often calls the plays and often takes the snap, but the key player is the center. He doesn't snap the ball to the quarterback. He passes the ball to any of the back positions, sometimes to a player in motion. He must have the same command of the backfield playbook as the T-formation quarterback. The center also must have his eyes on the backfield and both hands on the ball before snapping. This inhibits his takeoff as a blocker, or, in the lingo of the day, it made it harder for him to "fire out."

In the T-formation, the running backs are farther off the line. They can hit the hole at full speed after taking a handoff at running start. In the single wing, the running backs are closer to the line and take the ball directly from center.

In the T-formation, the man-on-man blocking may create multiple holes for a runner. In the single wing, double-team blocking is designed to create a single hole.

In the T-formation, a quarterback can fake a handoff and pass or lateral the ball.

In the single wing, the back who gets the snap usually keeps it or throws it or kicks it. Handoffs are for misdirection plays, like reverses.

In the T-formation, the primary pass receivers are ends. In the single wing, a back might catch as many passes as he throws.

It is these final two differences that make the triple-threat player vital to the single wing. A back who can do a lot of things with the ball once he gets it can make a defense hesitate. This back was usually the tailback.

In 1906, Bradbury Robinson of Saint Louis University was the first player tagged as a triple threat. He was a great passer, runner, and kicker. He is also credited with throwing the first legal forward pass.

In 1940, Bill Dudley was Frank Murray's triple threat. But, Murray wanted to use the T-formation. He wanted to spread the offense and thereby spread the defense. He had used a wide end and flanker for years. This was right up his alley. But, what to do with Dudley?

Murray designed what he called "My Virginia T." The press called it the Dudley Bastard T, at least amongst each other. Dudley would do all the passing, like a modern quarterback, but Murray didn't want Dudley under center. He'd lose the running advantage. Dudley played left halfback like a tailback, and he called plays like a quarterback.

A big advantage of the T-formation is that it spread the defense. Murray wanted it wide open. He used a balanced line and spread the distance between his offensive linemen. He spread the ends and used backs in motion to open up the secondary. With the quarterback under center, Dudley called the signals.

If it was a pass play, the quarterback shifted at the last moment and Dudley got a shotgun snap. If it was a rollout pass, the quarterback took the snap and lateraled to Dudley. It was their most effective pass play. The same formation and movement on a running play could work more or less like an option play.

The quarterback could take the snap under center and hand off like a modern quarterback. Any back could go in motion and get a direct snap.

Murray had more than a new offense. He had filled out his coaching staff. Art Guepe, his star quarterback at Marquette, was already in Charlottesville as the backfield coach. Murray brought on Art Corcoran, a colorful football sage who had played with Jim Thorpe and the Canton Bulldogs. Former Michigan All-American Ralph Heikkinen was the line coach.

Guepe was an able assistant. He would follow Murray as UVA's head football coach, and he became the second-winningest coach in school history. His role in 1941, at least during games, was to hold the reins on his boss during games. The professorial coach could get aroused on the sidelines. Guepe was the calming agent.

Murray also had nine returning seniors and some standout underclassmen. Junior Eddie "Flash" Bryant was a good halfback, running and blocking. Murray also had junior Ed Suhling at center.

Murray's modified T needed a single-wing center. In the single wing, the center was a key player. He needed to keep his head in the game. Literally. He had to play head down at the line of scrimmage and snap the ball cleanly to the correct back. In the T-formation, the ball has only one place to go—the quarterback—and a T-formation center plays head up, even in the shotgun.

Playing head down might not seem like much, unless you're the center and you consider the guy across the line who wants to cream you when the ball is hiked. Suhling was a tough and athletic player.

Six of Murray's linemen were converted backs. This would be one very fast team. The Virginia linemen knew their star runner followed their blocking. They knew he was a threat to break one loose on any play. Murray already understood what Riley Smith, the head coach at W&L, said after the 1940 season—that Virginia's blockers were more inspired and determined when Dudley had the ball. Bill saw it another way. "I had to use my blockers. I couldn't outrun them."

To Murray, his new formation was a "desperate gamble" that hinged on one player.

When practice started, Murray reminded his seniors they had never beaten VMI, Virginia Tech, or North Carolina.

Bill had roomed at the SAE house his junior year. This year he was a dorm counselor. The job paid for his room and board—$185 per semester. He started the year as vice president of the senior class. He knew the Bastard T playbook before practice started.

Murray's worries were misplaced. The new Murray offense worked. It wasn't a gamble, desperate or otherwise. The Cavaliers opened at home with a 41–0 thumping of Hampden-Sydney. Everybody got in the game, but the real test would be the next week.

Virginia faced heavily favored Lafayette the following week. In the previous season, the Leopards were undefeated and were third in the nation in scoring. Star running back and scoring machine Walt Zirinsky returned in 1941. Zirinsky, who would score 55 points against Lehigh that season, was smothered by the Cavalier defense. Virginia upset the Leopards 25–0 in a game that saw a 90-yard Dudley punt return for a score. Surely the wind was at Virginia's back going into the upcoming Yale game.

Virginia played at Yale, the second away game there in two seasons. This time, the Bulldogs were prepared. They let the grass on the field grow seven inches long and wet the field before the game, the better to slow the quick-breaking Cavaliers. They scouted Murray's T.

It was an abnormally hot October day in New Haven. Virginia came out fast. In the first half they scored twice on a 16-yard Dudley pass and a short Dudley run. A Dudley pass set up a third TD, but Virginia failed to convert on two extra points. Murray had trained another player as an extra point kicker. He wanted Bill to focus on his punting motion. This proved to be unwise.

At halftime, it was Virginia 19–0. In the second half, Yale staged one of its greatest comebacks. They won, 21–19. For its part, the Cavalier team stumbled with the Murray offense for the first time and they lost possessions to fumbles. For the rest of his life, Bill swore that the Yale Elis cooled off by taking showers at halftime. Why, he would ask, didn't we think of that? It was the only game Yale won that season. It was the only game Virginia lost.

Extra point kicking duties were returned to Bill for the rest of the season. For the year, two of his attempts were blocked. The rest were good. In today's college game, the extra point attempt is almost automatic. It's a yawner of a play. In Bill's college era and until his final pro season in 1953, the extra point was anything but automatic. Too many things could go wrong with a straight-ahead kick. The advent of the soccer-style kick took the drama out of the play.

The next week was a Virginia Big Six game against Richmond. The Cavaliers reset their winning pattern and won 44–0 with three Dudley touchdown passes, a Dudley rushing score, and a Dudley field goal.

The upcoming VMI game was billed as "The Battle of the Backs." VMI had two backs who would go on to NFL careers—sophomore fullback, linebacker, punter, and placekicker Joe Muha and junior halfback Bosh Pritchard. It was these two vs. "Bullet" Bill Dudley.

VMI fielded powerhouse teams in that era. VMI was playing at home, and leaked they had installed an "anti-Dudley" defense. Virginia already had its own anti-Pritchard defense. In the previous season's game, Murray reminded his boys, Dudley stopped Pritchard when he ran right—into Dudley defensive territory. The lone VMI score in 1940 came when Pritchard ran left.

Murray also reminded his boys once again—this squad had been together for four years and had never beaten VMI. The Cavaliers won 27-7. Bill passed for a touchdown. He stopped Muha and Pritchard, whether they ran left or right.

Bosh Pritchard: "He ran funny. He kicked funny. He threw funny. But, he'd find different ways to beat you."

Next up, Virginia Tech, number two on Murray's list of unbeaten rivals. The Hokies were 4-2 going into the game. They had upset nationally ranked Georgetown. The game was played on a windy day on a neutral field in Norfolk. How windy was it? One Hokie punt that went high landed behind the punter. The Cavaliers routed the Hokies 34–0 on two Dudley rushing touchdowns and two Dudley passing touchdowns. He gained a total of 241 yards—109 passing and 132 rushing. The game received national attention. The *New York Times* wrote: "Dudley's performance was a masterpiece of football versatility."

Meanwhile, the Virginia student paper *College Topics* rubbed it in: "There were many mutterings to the effect that the only gentlemanly thing to do was to let Tech threaten once."

Another Virginia Big Six game followed. The Cavaliers defeated W&L 27–7 on three Dudley touchdowns—two rushing and one passing. Bill left the game early because of an injury.

The next game against Lehigh was, as the press observed, "over early." Bill was fully recovered. The Cavs scored early on a 33-yard Dudley pass. The next time Virginia got the ball they scored after a 59-yard drive on four plays—a Dudley pass and three Dudley rushes. Final score: Virginia 34–0. Bill rushed for 167 yards and passed for 81. He returned five punts for 78 yards.

The Cavaliers were 7-1. The Murray offense had rolled up 251 points. The defense had allowed 35. They had knocked off VMI and Virginia Tech. Now, Murray instructed his boys, it was time for the big one.

CHAPTER NINE
A Game for the Ages

THE VIRGINIA VS. NORTH CAROLINA RIVALRY IS ONE OF THE OLDEST IN college football. The teams faced each other twice in 1892. With the exception of four seasons in the early 1900s, the schools have played every year since.

In 1941 the game was billed as The South's Oldest Rivalry. It was a natural rivalry—the schools are just down the road from each other and are cousins, academically and socially—and it was a genuine rivalry.

At the beginning of the 1941 season, the series was tied 21-21-3. But UNC had not been kind during Virginia's drought years. The last Virginia win was in 1932. UNC had outscored UVA 248–27 since, including five shutouts. Bill Dudley was ten years old the last time Virginia defeated North Carolina.

Things were different in 1941. UVA was favored. Going into the final game, the team had its best record in twenty-six years. They led the nation in offense. And it was lean times for the UNC Tarheels. They were 3-6 and were coming off a bruising loss against Duke and their star halfback Steve Lach.

There was plenty of drama—a season-ending rivalry game on Thanksgiving Day that augured something Virginia had never seen, an All-American. There had never been a First Team All-American football player from the state, much less the school. Three backs at southern schools contended for the honor that season: Frank Sinkwich of Georgia, Lach of Duke, and Bill Dudley.

There are All-America teams and there are All-America teams. In 1941 there were nine, but the team that mattered was the *Collier's* magazine eleven, chosen by Grantland Rice, the absolute monarch of sportswriters.

Lach had played a great game against UNC the week prior. His Duke Blue Devils were unbeaten and untied. Sinkwich was headed for the NCAA rushing title.

There was more drama. Dudley was poised to break the NCAA rushing and passing total yards record for a nine-game season. He could also break the record for average yards per game.

There was more. Virginia started nine seniors. Ross Craig, Johnny Neff, Howard Goodwin, and Dudley filled the backfield. Bill Preston and Jim White played end. Jack Sauerback, George Palmer, and Bill Mirman were down linemen. They had never beaten North Carolina, and it was their last chance.

There was more. Would Cavalier halfback Eddie "Flash" Bryant play? Bryant averaged 7 yards a carry and was a fierce blocker. He was out with a pulled leg muscle. Coach Murray wasn't conceding anything to the Tarheels. They were bruised and beaten, but they were still among the best Virginia would meet that year and they'd be up for the game. He needed Bryant.

There was more. The game would be broadcast by radio to a national audience.

The team bussed to Chapel Hill and roomed at the Carolina Inn adjacent to the UNC campus. The game was at 2:00 the next day. When Bill awoke, he noticed a note card had been slipped under the door. There, handwritten in capital letters, it said, "NINE LONG YEARS." Everybody on the team got one. Nobody ever found out who wrote them.

In later years, Dudley would often claim he never got overly excited about a game—that he showed up for all of them ready to play. It was serious business. "My mind was totally on the game. It could have been a hundred people or a hundred thousand or ten people at the Onion Bowl. It didn't affect me."

This wasn't exactly true.

A typical Virginia game in the '41 season began with a Dudley running play, but Murray saw in the pregame warmups that his boy was manic. He told quarterback Neff to keep the ball clear of Dudley until he settled down. Dudley returned the opening kickoff to the Virginia 33. After a few non-Dudley plays from scrimmage, Bill had a clear enough head to ask why he wasn't getting the ball. After that, he got it, and with a heavily taped-up Bryant alongside him in the backfield, the show was on.

In the first series the Cavaliers moved upfield easily and scored on a Dudley to Preston pass from the UNC 22. Extra point, Dudley. Two minutes later, Dudley returned a punt from his 20 to the Virginia 33. On the next play from scrimmage he sprinted around end, cutting in and out of traffic behind what he described as "gorgeous interference" to score on a 67-yard sweep. He later credited his team. "The blocking was fantastic. I trotted in the last 15 or 20 yards."

Extra point, Dudley. While the team returned to kickoff formation, Bill passed near the chain gang on the sidelines. There, grinning ear to ear, was Flapper Pancake, manning a stick. Bill never found out how Flapper got the gig. It didn't matter. It was a sign, even for a man who didn't believe in signs.

The first quarter ended with the score 14–7, Virginia. The Cavalier fans were going nuts, locking arms and reveling in the "Good Old Song" with every score, which is an especially nettlesome way to rub it in. The second quarter was scoreless, with a Dudley field goal attempt blocked at the UNC 5. Halftime.

John Derr of the Greensboro Daily News: *"He did all the kicking, all the passing, most of the running and quite a bit of the tackling . . . It was as much like a one-man show as anything revealed around here in years."*

The third quarter was scoreless until, with three minutes remaining, the Cavaliers were fourth down and 11 from their own 21. They went into deep punt formation. Dudley took the snap. It was a fake. He sprinted right. Sprung by a Bryant block, Dudley ran to the sideline, sidestepped two Tarheels, broke to the center, and was untouched for the last 50 yards. Third quarter score: 21–7, Virginia.

On the sidelines, Hugh Morton was positioned to frame the kind of shot that sports photographers dream about. Cameras of the day that were suitable for journalistic work were bellows cameras. The bellows—a pleated extension that folded like an accordion—connected the lens with the body of the camera. To focus, the photographer moved the lens toward or away from the body. Focusing was an elaborate and slow process. It was exactly the wrong camera for sports photography, but it was about the only camera.

Sports photographers often shot from a distance, perhaps a tower. Sideline photographers pre-focused on a spot on the field and waited for a play to come to the spot. Bill Dudley swept right into Hugh Morton's focus.

Morton caught Bill steaming around end with a string of hapless Tarheels in the background. It became Morton's most famous sports shot. It is the most reproduced shot of Bill.

The Tarheels in the photo look like they've given up. The play took the fight out of them. Extra point, Dudley.

The fake punt play delighted Bill for the rest of his life. He designed it with Marshall Shearer at one of those drugstore sessions in Bluefield. Bill cajoled Coach Murray all season to put it in, but Murray balked. Just prior to the UNC game, he put in a series of plays, including the fake punt.

The final, fourth quarter scoring drive covered 82 yards. It closed with a Dudley to Preston pass for 48 yards to the UNC 7. Herb Munhall took it to the 3. Bill took it over. Extra point, Dudley.

Murray pulled Bill with two minutes left in the game. His teammates carried him to the sideline on their shoulders while the 24,000 spectators at Kenan Stadium—both Virginia and Carolina fans—gave him a standing ovation. The press described the moment as "a remarkable and gracious tribute."

Final score: 28–7, Virginia. For the day, Bill was on the field for 113 plays. Of the 54 Cavalier offensive plays, Bill carried, passed, or kicked the ball on 38 of them. Take out the 4 plays he was denied the ball at the beginning of the game and the two minutes he sat at the end, and you have what amounts to a one-man offense. He had a hand or a foot in every score. He had 215 yards rushing for a 15.6 yard average. He was 6 of 11 passing for 118 yards. He kicked four extra points. He punted eight times for a 40-yard average. He kicked off for a 50.5-yard average. He returned all punts and kicks for a total of 158 yards. He had key tackles and an interception.

The game put him over the top for three NCAA titles for the year. Total yardage, 2,460. Total scoring, 134. Per-game yardage average, 273, an intercollegiate record. For the season, Bill played 500 of a possible 540 minutes. Burke Davis of the *Charlotte News* reported:

> *He did it all today. The kid captain of the Virginias made himself into a sight of All-American selections. Writers and coaches won't have to talk, boost or argue . . . The stories will call him Dixie's offensive genius of the generation . . . a real kid leader who's going to be an even greater ballplayer if some money club can spare the cash. What he did in his last college game, before he rode out on orange shoulders to rocking applause, is going to start some arguments. But it won't do any good.*

The performance gave Chauncey Durden of the *Richmond Times-Dispatch* his most quoted sentence: "He came. They saw. He conquered."

"Everything went right that day from the opening gun," Bill said. "There was a good feeling on the ball club."

After the game, it was a very pleasant ride back home to Bluefield and Thanksgiving. On the way, the boy who would later claim he never got too excited about a game realized he had forgotten his football shoes. It was later reported they were seen, briefly, in the UNC trophy case.

That night two carloads of youngsters wheeled up before the Dudley home in Bluefield. The mood was boisterous. Send out the hero. It was time to party. Bill watched from the window as his father sent them away. His boy, Sheb explained to the crowd, was only nineteen.

"There are two things a boy your age needs—milk and sleep," Sheb told his son.

Bill had played his final college game at the same age that Ace Parker, Duke star and future NFL Hall of Famer, played his final high school game.

For the year, the Cavaliers outscored opponents 257–35. Yale got 19 of those. The Yale game was Virginia's only loss and Yale's only win. Virginia's attendance for the year topped 121,000. It was a 10,000 increase over 1940 and a record. It was time to celebrate.

The week after the Carolina game, UVA threw a Virginia Victory Ball that capped a Bill Dudley Day. The walls and balconies of Jefferson's famed Rotunda were draped with pennants and lit red with spotlights. Students, faculty, fans, and dignitaries danced to swing music. Bill was presented with a statuette and the crowd sang the university's "Good Old Song."

Virginia threw a ball because they couldn't have a bowl. Postseason bowl games were a Depression era innovation. Until 1935, the Rose Bowl, which started in 1902, was the only game in town. In 1935 the Orange Bowl, Sugar Bowl, and Sun Bowl were introduced. The Cotton Bowl started in 1937. They were hugely popular from the get-go—a bowl appearance could cement a team's legacy. And who doesn't want one more game from two top teams?

Charlottesville stirred with expectation. There was also talk of a postseason match with William & Mary for the mythical Big Six title. It would be played at a neutral site. The gate—and it would be a big one—would go to charity.

Virginia athletic director Norton Pritchett snuffed it all. Virginia wouldn't even consider any feelers. The school had an exam schedule and it would not change. Big Time Football be damned.

Meanwhile, the school publicity department hustled. They wanted their first All-American and they wanted Bill Dudley in the College All-Star Game. At the time, most All-Star players had been selected from the Big Ten and the Southwest. Very few had come from the South.

Bill's stats were out there. The publicity boys burnished them with copy celebrating the unimpeachable boy who made good against the odds. Articles with titles like "Just Bow-Legged Enough" churned out tales of the exemplary plugger who read his Bible and who was never cocky, even before cheers of adulation. They noted that the nineteen-year-old had already been invited to speak at fifteen banquets. Coach Murray was Bill's biggest cheerleader:

About all you can get out of him when you are coaching him is "no sir" and "yes sir." If we told him to jump out the window, he'd more than likely jump. I've never had a player who worked as hard as Bill. He sops up instruction and never thinks of questioning a coach's orders. He's just 19, but he's a shrewd football player.

At the *Richmond Times-Dispatch*, the Dudley story was more than a sports story. It was about character:

Both on and off the field, his conduct is exemplary. In the game he plays hard, but always cleanly. Some have expressed amazement that he should, for example, go out of his way to help a member of the opposing team off the ground, especially if that opposing player apparently was trying to put him out of the game a minute before by some questionably rough work.

At the *Roanoke Times* the story was about fame: "Rare is the day that passes that a state journal does not carry his likeness."

The *Virginia News-Leader* picked up the Golden Boy theme: "He has straight, blonde hair, thick shoulders and a naivete to match his youth."

At the *Knoxville News-Sentinel*, they were cheeky about his popularity: "If this Bill Dudley was to run against Roosevelt tomorrow in the Commonwealth of Virginia, Roosevelt would look like Alf Landon."

The publicity department got what they wanted when, echoing sportswriters across the country, Bill Corum of the *New York Journal-American* wrote, "I don't know how many All American teams Bill Dudley will make, but I have the feeling that few better backs will be on All Americas from this coast to the Pacific."

Virginia got its wish. Bill was named First Team All-American by Grantland Rice, AP, UPI, and Newsweek. He was named Player of the Year and given the Walter Camp Trophy by the Touchdown Club of Washington, DC. He was awarded the Maxwell Memorial Award for best college player of the year from the Maxwell Football Club in Philadelphia. He placed fifth in the Heisman ballot, which went to Bruce Smith of Minnesota.

Bill was chosen to play in the East-West Shrine Game in January. He would also play with the College All-Stars against the Chicago Bears the next fall. Two years later, he was picked the number 1 halfback in the South for the 1933–43 period by *Illustrated Football Annual*, the top football magazine of the era.

Back home in Bluefield, the family didn't get too excited about it. Sheb rarely saw even a high school game. Jewell never went to one. Their son's football career was something that was just out there living a parallel life.

> *Bill: "I was honored to make the All American Team, but it's very seldom there aren't six or eight other players who also deserve the honor. Yesterday's sports hero is like yesterday's newspaper. There's a new one coming tomorrow."*

Murray told the press he'd never replace Dudley. He was right. It was to be Murray's best season at UVA.

Hugh Morton's photo of the fake punt play against UNC. The white bandage on Bill's lip glints in the sun.

CHAPTER TEN

A Number One Pick in Football and Love

DECEMBER 7, 1941, WAS A SUNDAY. BILL TOOK THE TRAIN TO WASHington to watch Sammy Baugh and the Redskins. Griffith Stadium was sold out. Bill had a three-dollar ticket.

The announcements started during the second quarter: Admiral so and so, please report to the team office—Captain so and so, you have a phone call—Major so and so, please contact your superior officer. The announcements came about every twenty seconds, just long enough to complete one and start another. In the stands, it was eerie. People looked at each other. Military men whose names weren't even called began to leave their seats.

The news was blacked out during the game—the Japanese had struck Pearl Harbor and declared war on the United States. The city was blacked out that night. When Bill returned to Charlottesville, there wasn't a light showing.

In January, Bill and a couple of teammates went to Washington and signed up for the Naval Air Corps. They returned to Charlottesville and awaited the call. Bill never discussed the decision with his parents. When Jewell Dudley later asked her son why he chose the Air Corps, he told her he wanted to come back in one piece or not at all.

The headlines were grim. Singapore fell to the Japanese. American forces held out, but were overwhelmed on the Bataan Peninsula. America was reeling and back on its heels. Was America's West Coast vulnerable? Nobody knew where this new war was headed.

Life went on, even if it was surreal. At the end of January, Bill found himself in Lynchburg, there to escort actress Ruth Hussey for the premiere of *The Vanishing Virginian*, a biopic about a former Lynchburg attorney named Robert Yancey. Hussey was in the early years of a long Hollywood career and coming off the hit film *The Philadelphia Story* with Cary Grant, Jimmy Stewart, and Katharine Hepburn. Her publicity agents wanted a Virginia connection. Who better than the state's most famous athlete?

It was an all-day and evening affair, including an afternoon motorcade before thousands of fans and a late dinner dance. Bill, his twenty-three-dollar suits a distant memory, spent the hours with Hollywood on his arm. Hussey found his courtly manner attractive. She invited him to escort her in New York at another upcoming event. He went.

In February, Bill went to New York to accept the fifth Maxwell Award. He was the youngest player to ever receive the trophy. Bert Bell, president of the club, sung his praises and brought the boy to the podium.

"Is this really me you're talking about?" Bill began. He went on to praise the coaching staff and his teammates. It was the best-balanced coaching staff in the country, he said, and nobody seemed to notice that the Cavaliers were a better team for them. Bell liked the homespun, aw-shucks kid. He was genuine. Who could have known what the two would come to mean to each other?

The East-West Shrine Game was moved from San Francisco to New Orleans that year. A Japanese air attack on the West Coast was possible. The game was played to a tie. It could have been called The Mud Bowl. Bill threw a touchdown pass and had four interceptions, some in ankle-deep water. He was voted the game's outstanding player.

The NFL draft was held in February. Frank Murray knew George Halas, who owned the Chicago Bears, and wrote Halas after the 1941 season—Murray had a back who would make a good pro. But, Halas didn't need a back. He passed the tip on to Art Rooney, who owned—along with Bert Bell—the Pittsburgh Steelers. Bell recalled the boy at the Maxwell

Awards. That, and the tip from Halas, seemed to be enough. The Steelers made Bill their first-round draft pick of 1942. The draft in those days isn't quite the circus it is today. For Bill, it was just another day.

"The Steelers didn't call on draft day. When they did contact me, all they said was 'We drafted you.' Nobody mentioned anything about being the number 1 pick."

The news came as a surprise. To Bill, it bordered on meaningless. In 1942, professional football was the minor leagues compared to college football. To grasp the difference, you only need to look at Pittsburgh in that era. Jock Sutherland's University of Pittsburgh team was covered nationally. It even made the Bluefield paper every weekend of every fall—before and after the game. The Panthers would get pregame coverage on the sports page. There would be a lead headline on the sports page and a two-spread inside after the game. The professional Steelers might get a few paragraphs and a data summary after a game.

Bill: "Of course, I knew about the University of Pittsburgh, but I didn't know a thing about the Steelers. I knew a little about the Washington Redskins. We used to go up and see them play, but I never knew anything about the rest of the league because it just didn't enter my mind. College football and the bowl games, were the big thing."

But, there it was—a job offer. Everything was up in the air for Bill. First, there was his upcoming military call-up. Then, there was the question—did he even want to play pro football? Was it even a real job? With the war, did any of it really matter?

Soon, all the other boys who signed up with Bill got their orders. Bill never heard from Washington. The days passed. It looked like the Steelers would be the only job offer he had until he got called up. He made a verbal commitment. "I probably would not have played if the war hadn't come along. I probably would have just gotten a job somewhere."

The final dance weekend at Virginia was always big. Exams were over. It was time to let go. Bill, who had not yet signed a contract with the

Steelers, checked coats at the last dance. It was good, quick money. When your shift ended, it was off to the dance floor.

The night was full of possibility. Bill idled on the side of the dance floor talking with new Cavalier captain Ed Suhling and Bobby Watts, his friend from Lynchburg. For the rest of his life, Bill would happily replay what came next for anyone who would listen.

"All of a sudden this little girl dances by. My eyes bug out."

Suhling caught the moment. He nudged Watts.

Watts: "You like that?"
Bill: "Oh, yeah."
Watts: "Do you want to meet her?"
Bill: "You know her?"
Watts: "She's from Lynchburg. Come on."

An introduction followed. She was beautiful and classically so. She had a dancer's bearing and grace on the floor. She was bright and cheerful and gracious. Conversation was easy—the smallest things delighted her and she voiced her pleasure in a sultry alto burnished by the inflections of the patrician South. She was approachable but reserved. She was elusive, but she wasn't coy. She smoked and she didn't care who knew it. She had no clue who Virginia's newest football star was. She was sixteen. Bill Dudley never had a chance.

"I started dancing with her. Other boys tapped in, but I made sure I got the final dance. I said, 'Youngster, if you are still around after the war, I'm going to look you up.'"

The moment was never far from his mind and he replayed it countless times for the next four years. In the rush of the moment, he never got her name.

On graduation day, Bill wasn't handed a diploma. He was short six credit hours. This time it was Spanish.

CHAPTER ELEVEN
The Benefits of Smoking in the Window

THEY DIDN'T GROW TOO MANY HOTHOUSE FLOWERS IN FORT SMITH, Arkansas, during the beginning of the twentieth century. It was still, in spirit anyway, a frontier town.

The Arkansas River lies at the city's western limit. On the other side of the river, Oklahoma was a territory until 1907—a refuge for criminals and rough customers. Later generations would know Fort Smith as the embarkation point for John Wayne and friends in the movie *True Grit*.

Fortunately, Ray "Dutch" Leininger wasn't looking for a hothouse flower when he met and wed Mary Elizabeth Hendricks. He was looking for a genuine helpmate. After graduating from the University of Arkansas, he tried his hand at semi-pro baseball, got a law degree through a correspondence course, and was ready to settle down.

Mary Elizabeth "Inde" Hendricks was of good Fort Smith stock, and she was a beauty to boot. The Hendricks clan were early settlers and were now well-to-do. The family owned the first car dealership in town. She was a skilled homemaker and she was able to meld the fading frontier culture with American modernity.

They met and wed. Dutch built Inde a house of stone, taking a truck or horse and wagon out on evenings and weekends and returning with as much fieldstone as either could pull. He piled the stone on a hilltop lot overlooking the emerging city. The lot was on Elizabeth Lane, given to Inde by her father on a street he named for her. When the pile got big enough, Dutch's stonemason told him he was ready to build. The home is still there.

65

In 1925, Inde gave birth to their first daughter, who was also named Elizabeth. The bill for the hospital stay was $58.35.

Dutch got a big break in 1929. He was offered the position of factory superintendent at Blue Buckle Overall Company in Lynchburg, Virginia. It would be a hard choice, leaving the family and stone house behind. Dutch decided to go have a look. It was a three-day drive if you could keep it at 45 on state two-lanes.

The interview took a day. It was followed by a couple of weeks or so of Dutch and the factory staff trying each other on for size. He would stay. Inde loaded up their belongings and children—there were two daughters now, sister Mary had come along—and followed.

The era before World War II was a high point in the American garment industry. Factories established to fill the needs of World War I remained open after the war. In the northern states, the industry attracted immigrants. The sewing machine had been around for about seventy-five years. It was a teachable skill that didn't require literacy. In the southern states, a factory floor was staffed by row upon row of women before sewing machines.

Dutch knew his business. When a wholesale buyer informed Dutch that he'd chosen another, cheaper supplier, Dutch invited the man to Lynchburg. When the buyer arrived, Dutch took him down to the floor, measured the man for a pair of overalls, pulled a bolt of denim, cut out a pattern, sat down at a sewing machine, and made him a pair, explaining at each step the cost of goods and demonstrating the time and labor.

When he handed the dumbfounded buyer his custom overalls, Dutch told him to go see if his competitor could really do it for less. He kept the account.

Dutch got another correspondence degree, this one in Industrial Management. Blue Buckle was a union shop and advertised it. By all accounts, Dutch was a highly regarded manager. Blue Buckle thrived. Dutch never became a lawyer.

Blue Bell did contract work for the major catalog retailers of the era—JCPenney, Wards, and Sears. When Blue Bell was bought by Carroll Rosenbloom, later owner of the Baltimore Colts, he was influenced by Dutch's management technique. Bill Dudley believed that "Carroll bought Blue Bell to get Dutch."

By the late 1930s, Dutch was a successful businessman and the Leiningers—there were three daughters by now—were a prominent Lynchburg family.

Dutch was a Buick man, the bigger the better, and two-toned like his shoes. He was always short. Now he was also round. Men of a certain age can still recall watching from the sidewalk as his long, cool Buick eased into the Holy Cross Catholic Church parking lot. Out would step the fabulous Leininger sisters—all hats and gloves and purses and shoes matched up just so with today's dress—to glide like tall ships to the door.

Youngest daughter Dot was Fabulous in Training. There were many churches on the block, so it was an ecumenical show. It was enough to turn the most diffident of lads into a mouth breather.

Like the Bluefield Dudleys, the Leiningers were a busy family. Dutch had been director of the Southern Garments Manufacturers Association. Locally, he worked with the Community Chest, the Salvation Army, the Chamber of Commerce, and other civic groups. He led the formation of Lynchburg's first Child Care Center.

Like the Bluefield Dudleys, the church was central to their lives. Dutch, a lifelong reader of religious texts, organized Lynchburg's first Christian Doctrine Discussion Club.

The Leininger household also shared the frugality and discipline of the Bluefield Dudleys, only to a different degree. Dutch and Inde counted dollars and cents instead of pennies.

Bad girls got "the switch." It was an elaborate punishment. Dutch would pick their switch—a thin branch from a tree or bush—and the girls watched while he whittled it clean with a pocket knife for modest lashes across the legs, with Inde all the while wringing her hands in the background. After the punishment, Dutch would apply a salve and explain the rights and wrongs of the moment.

Oldest daughter, Elizabeth, now called Libba, was a good student. Her great skill was pen and ink drawing. Her great gift was her way with people. By the time she was in high school, she could mingle agreeably in any company. Women were attracted to her. Men were dazzled.

It would later come in handy over a lifetime of running interference for Bill Dudley. Now, it was a ticket to travel. So many schools were single sex in the pre-war era that elaborate procedures designed to deliver dance partners to all-male schools were long established. It was all very formal. On dance weekends, the young women would board trains—sometimes with chaperones, sometimes in groups—and register in off-campus boarding houses upon arrival. There, they would await their dates and there they would be returned upon curfew. Young men and women could be together in the living room only.

Libba traveled the East Coast from the Carolinas to Princeton as a high school student. By the time she met Bill at age sixteen, she was a remarkably young doyenne.

Her first shot at college was short-lived. Smoking wasn't permitted at St. Mary of the Woods in Terre Haute, Indiana. Libba didn't want telltale smoke in her dorm room, so she opened the window and sat on the sill, which it turned out, was not a clever place to hide. She didn't get the switch, but she did get dismissed. She landed at Randolph-Macon Woman's College in Lynchburg.

It was one of the best things that ever happened to Bill Dudley.

CHAPTER TWELVE
The Sun Rises in Pittsburgh

IN 1942 PITTSBURGH, THE SKY COULD BE BLACK AT 9:00 A.M. THE STEEL mills worked around the clock. That, and the soft coal burned for residential heat, darkened the sky. Men who worked downtown would take a second white shirt to change into at noon. Women who shopped in white gloves found them to be gray. It didn't matter; Pittsburgh steel supplied the Arsenal of Democracy. In 1941 the national unemployment rate was still a Depression era 9.9 percent. In 1942, it was 4.7 percent. In Pittsburgh it was lower. There was a war to win.

Just as today, Pittsburgh in 1942 was a sports town. Forbes Field was built in 1909, the same year the Pirates faced Detroit in the World Series. Two of the best Negro League baseball teams—the Crawfords and the Grays—were there. Jock Sutherland's University of Pittsburgh program was a college powerhouse.

In 1941 Pittsburgher Billy Conn, a light heavyweight boxer, etched himself into boxing lore when he said "What's the use of being Irish, if you can't be stupid" after he outmatched heavyweight Joe Louis for twelve rounds, went for the knockout in the thirteenth, and allowed Louis to K.O. him instead.

When Bill and Sheb Dudley stepped off the train on a hot, dark August day in 1942 and made their way to the nearby Steelers office at the Fort Pitt Hotel, neither was on familiar ground. The Dudleys weren't bumpkins, but they were untraveled. They'd never seen anything like the Fort Pitt. It was big and ornate and commanded the corner of Tenth

Street and Penn Avenue, on the edge of Pittsburgh's "Golden Triangle." Famous for its themed Norse Room, with its vaulted ceiling and artworks made entirely of tile, the Fort Pitt was considered one of the most elegant hotels in the city. Bill and Sheb climbed the grand staircase to the Steelers' second-floor office. Bert Bell, who owned the Steelers along with Art Rooney, awaited them.

"I didn't know anything about Pittsburgh," Bill said. "The sun, it's dark. All the steel mills were in full blast. You couldn't see the sun for the smoke."

Bert Bell was a football man. He quarterbacked the University of Pennsylvania team to the Rose Bowl in 1917. After service in World War I, he coached college football and was a co-founder of the Philadelphia Eagles. He sold that team to buy a share of the Steelers. He would later go on to be the NFL commissioner.

Art Rooney was an all-round sports guy and a first-rate athlete. He played football and baseball and he boxed. He was an organizer and a promoter—he founded a semi-pro football team when he was a teenager. Rooney and Bell were instrumental in developing the first NFL draft in 1936.

The Steelers shared an office with the Rooney-McGinley Boxing Club. It was said they had a desk with two drawers, one for football tickets and another for boxing tickets. The football franchise was nine years old. The team began as the Pirates. In 1940, the name was changed to the Steelers—they were almost named the Puddlers—but there was never a winning season under either name. The Steelers were 1-9-1 the season before Bill and Sheb walked into the office.

The Dudleys didn't know what to expect. The name Rooney would someday be understood across the nation to stand for excellence. In 1942, Art Rooney was just a well-known Pittsburgher. What would become the exceptional Rooney football dynasty was yet to begin. Nobody, including the Dudleys, Bell, and Rooney, knew it would start with the small young man on the other side of Bell's desk. Rooney was sick of losing.

Art Rooney: "It's terrible. It's something you hate to think about, even. You hide it and people say, 'That Art Rooney, he's a good loser.' I'm not.

We had a house rule no one could mention football until Tuesday after we got beat on a Sunday."

He blamed himself. He didn't keep his thumb on his coaches and he put his energy into handicapping horse races. "If I had started out paying much attention to it, we could have won. It wouldn't have been hard. I had these other businesses. And maybe I spent too much time at the race track."

The team was a financial burden, especially during the Depression.

"You had two thrills," said Rooney. "One came Sunday, trying to win the game. The next came Monday, trying to make the payroll."

In 1942, the Steelers had another problem. They were losing players, coaches, and staff to the military. The league had already lost about 150 players to the military. College stars were going, too. The Steelers could field five of their twenty draft picks. There almost wasn't a 1942 Steelers. Rooney made it known he thought there probably wouldn't be a 1942 season and that was okay with him. The war effort was more important. He considered forfeiting the franchise. Washington Redskins owner George Preston Marshall was later to take credit, over and over and over again, for talking Rooney out of it.

Bell and Rooney didn't know what to expect that August day, either. The kid from Virginia certainly wasn't a shoo-in. They never scouted him. They drafted him on the suggestion of George Halas, who also never scouted him. After the draft, the oddsmakers said Bill was overrated as a collegian. They predicted he'd be an NFL flop. There was also his size. Bill showed up at Bell's office at 5'9" and 165 pounds. But it wasn't a blind date. Bell had met Bill at the Maxwell awards ceremony and he liked what he saw in the kid.

The going rate for a first-round draft pick in 1942 was $10,000. Four years earlier, Rooney scared the pants off the other owners when he offered first-round draft pick Whizzer White, a future Supreme Court justice, $15,000, thereby bumping up the price across the board. Sitting in Bert Bell's office, amateurs Bill and Sheb knew nothing of this. Since recovering from his breakdown, Sheb had rebuilt his career. In 1941, he made $5,000. He told Bell his son ought to make at least that. There must have been a third drawer, because everybody later said Bell couldn't get the contract out of it fast enough—11 games, $500 per game. No pay for exhibitions.

Bill never regretted the deal. It was what it was. "Dad was happy as a pig in slop when I signed for five when I could have gotten a minimum of ten. Hell, they signed Whizzer before that for $15,000. He was just a father trying to help his son."

There was no ceremony to the process and it didn't take long. It was a one-page contract. When it was signed, Bell wanted a word with his new young charge. It was a gravelly voiced lecture Bill never forgot. Bell sized up the moment for Bill. He had just signed a contract that paid him in three months what a successful man might make in a year. Bell then warned—never forget that professional football is only a brief interlude in a man's working life.

Bill: "He said, 'Playing pro football is fine, but it is only a means to an end, it is not the end in itself. This can get you some money to buy a house or whatever, but you must prepare yourself to do something else.'"

Bill didn't join the Steelers until ten days before his first pro game, so he missed the exhibition games. He missed practice because he played in the College All-Star Game against the Chicago Bears. The Bears won 21–0 and Bill broke a finger. The otherwise unremarkable game established the most repeated bit of Dudley lore. "Bullet" wasn't a bullet. As a pregame stunt, the College All-Star backs were pitted in a footrace the length of the field. Bill came in fifteenth, second to last.

As many times as that story has been repeated, it rarely includes the fact that Bill beat the field to the 20.

When he reported to camp in Hershey, Pennsylvania, the guards at the gate wouldn't let Bill in. They thought he was a fan trying to sneak into the camp. They couldn't believe he was a football player.

The guards should have checked Bill's bags. In those days players provided their own helmets and pads. Bill brought the equipment he used at

Virginia. NFL teams did provide shoes, which was a good thing—Bill's were still in the trophy case at UNC.

Like Bell and Rooney, head coach Walt Kiesling had no fixed expectations about Bill. He was just a kid, but he arrived in camp in playing shape and he aced Kiesling's system. "Kies" was a huge man—he tipped the Toledos at 280—and the genial buddy of Rooney. Kiesling ran the Notre Dame Box offense, which is a modified single-wing offense. It featured a balanced line and a tighter backfield. The wingback position that Frank Murray liked to spread wide at Virginia is brought in behind the line. The backfield arrangement resembles a square, hence the name. A coach typically goes to that formation if he lacks a true triple-threat back. Kiesling didn't know he had one.

There was also the problem of Bill's style—the sidearmed throws, the odd gait, the pendulum kicks.

"In the backfield, he squatted behind center like a duck," Art Rooney said. "The coaches tried to change his style. They insisted it was impossible to get a proper start from such a position."

There was also the fact that the kid wouldn't shut up. He preached to the players, exhorting them on the field and off. To Kiesling's surprise, the pros accepted the kid's leadership. Bill went into camp as the number 2 tailback behind Andy Tomasic. Bill came out of camp the starting tailback.

There were thirty-three men on the roster and eighteen of them were rookies. The oldest player, eight-year veteran Armand Niccolai, was thirty-one. The rest were in their twenties. They quickly became a close-knit team. The football season would last three months. The players knew they would go into the service and into a war afterwards. Some would go before. Among the Steelers, Bill was tagged with the nickname Beefy. "Beefing" was a popular wartime idiom that usually meant complaining. In Bill's case, it meant preaching and exhorting his teammates. He got into the game as a frustrated runt and played his way from there into college stardom. "I had to prove that I belonged there," he said. "Every play. Every down." He expected the same from his teammates:

I can't stand a ballplayer that doesn't put out. There's no reason for a ballplayer to hang back at any particular time, particularly when they're getting beat. That drives me up a wall!

If every person on the ball club puts out to their best ability, you're gonna win some ball games even when you're outclassed. You're gonna get the job done doing the best you can or you're not gonna get it done at all because you're doing it half assed.

There is no worse feeling than to know some of the ballplayers are quitting on you, not putting out.

Beefy roomed at the Fort Pitt Hotel with three linemen—center Chuck Cherundolo, left tackle Elbie Shultz, and right tackle John Woudenberg. He liked to maintain good relations with linemen, for obvious reasons.

The Steelers opened the season at home against cross-state rival Philadelphia. Like most NFL teams, the Steelers played in the city baseball stadium. It wasn't elegant. "I had a big hole in the floor in front of my locker," Bill said. "Our dressing room at Virginia was much better."

The field was marked off with the goalpost in the dirt near home plate. Baseball infields weren't grassed until after World War II. Sometimes the pitching mound was cut down. Sometimes it wasn't cut all the way. A smart football player might create a downhill run for himself.

Pittsburghers, including the press, didn't expect much from the Steelers in 1942. The team had a good line. Cherundolo was one of the best centers in the league—perhaps the best—and key to Kiesling's single wing. They were strong at guard and tackle. But three of the four starting backs were rookies. Plus, the Steelers always lost. Everybody knew that. The press had heard about Rooney's change of heart about winning. They'd believe the results when they saw it.

The team started off its tenth anniversary with a thud. The preseason was awful. The Steeler training camp was forlorn. They didn't have enough players to scrimmage. The new players weren't there. All five college recruits played in the All-Star Game and arrived late.

The Steelers suited up only sixteen players for an exhibition against the Cleveland Rams—who were in last place in their division in 1941—and lost 35–6. The thin squad was demoralized before the game started. Rooney brought in more players and filled out the roster. A 40–20 exhibition loss to the Chicago Bears followed, but that was the Bears. Everybody lost to the Bears. Bill sat out that game. Along with his finger, he had sprained an ankle in the All-Star Game. "Rigor Mortis was making a bid for a playing position," wrote Chilly Doyle in the *Pittsburgh Sun-Telegraph.*

Bill met Rooney for the first time when Art visited training camp. The Steelers had new uniforms. A reporter asked Rooney what he thought of the green jerseys. "I think the different jerseys are swell but the boys in 'em are still the same old Steelers."

His new kid recruit would make Rooney eat his words, and they would taste just fine. Art Rooney carried a little notebook around with him. He could quote Steeler attendance. A ticket cost between three and five dollars. He needed 13,000 in the stands to break even. So far, that hadn't happened much. When attendance was reported to the press, the Steeler office might throw in 5,000 extra, just for looks. It appeared the 5,000 mystery fans would be showing up again this season.

Or maybe not. The Steelers attracted 13,349 for the home opener with Philadelphia. Pittsburgh scored early in the game on a 44-yard Dudley run and late in the game on a 24-yard Dudley to Don Looney pass. The Pittsburgh pessimists weren't disappointed, though. The Eagles won 24–14.

Chester Smith, sports editor for the Pittsburgh Press*: "The cash customers aren't going to stand too long for a team that plays with its head up for the first two minutes, waits for the last two before returning to life and is thoroughly inept the intervening 56 minutes. The play looks suspiciously like gold-bricking, lack of conditioning, poor management or a combination of the three."*

Bill's first touchdown was a breakaway run. He threatened several more. A block here. A block there. It could have been different. And there was Bill's all-around game. People noticed. Bob Higgins, head coach of Penn State, was at the game. "I was glad I came. For a few minutes I expected to see, for the first time, a man throw a pass to himself."

The press observed that Bill did a large share of the playing and a larger share of the talking. Yet another nickname emerged—Bill the Beefer.

After the game, Bill went to Rooney in the dressing room and told the boss not to sweat. The team, Bill told him, was going to win some games. Rooney had heard this before. "Our team looked hopeless and I was resigned to another long, bleak season. But Dudley came to me in the dressing room and told me not to take it to heart. 'This club's going to win some games, Mr. Rooney,' he said, and from the tone of his voice I knew he had no doubt about it. As for me, I passed it off. I had heard the same thing from a hundred players before, but it never turned out that way."

Rooney had another visitor after the first game. Team captain Chuck Cherundolo needed a word with the boss. Cherundolo liked this new kid, but he behaved oddly between plays. He talked to himself as he came back to the huddle.

Art Rooney: "It later developed that Dudley actually wasn't talking to himself. He used to break through the line and make different feints at the linebackers to determine whether they moved better to the right or left. If they moved better one way, Bill would cut the other way. He was mumbling this information to fix it in his memory."

Cherundolo would become Bill's best friend on the team.

The Steelers traveled to Washington, DC, the next week to face Sammy Baugh and the Redskins. They lost 28–14. Once again, a loss was followed by enthusiasm. This time it was fueled by Dudley heroics. He was carried off the field in the first quarter with an ankle injury. He got taped up, went back in the game, and returned a kick 84 yards for a touchdown on his first play. It was the first Steeler kickoff return for a touchdown in six years.

The *Pittsburgh Press* became a Dudley convert: "Overshadowing the bitter disappointment of players and coaches was admiration for their sensational recruit, halfback Bill Dudley."

The Steelers had scored four touchdowns in two games—one on a Dudley run, one on a Dudley pass, and one on a Dudley kick return. The fourth TD was set up by an 11-yard Dudley pass and a 23-yard Dudley gain late in the Washington game.

"He's the best back we had since I came to Pittsburgh in 1937," Walt Kiesling said. "When they carried him to the sidelines during the first quarter against Washington, I hurried over to talk to him. There were tears in his eyes as he reported his ankle was hurting plenty. Yet before the period was over he was begging me to put him back in. He has a knack of picking openings almost before they develop. He's a good punter, fair on defense and should develop into a far better passer."

The sweetest praise came from The Boss, Art Rooney, who also managed to use the occasion to take a shot at the Press Boys.

"Whizzer White couldn't carry that boy's shoes. Dudley is easily the finest back we have had in our 10 years in the league. Bill has the old college try to go along with his ability. His great comeback after being carried off the field in the first quarter would have made front page headlines in every sports section of the country had it happened in a college game. Yes, he's tops in my book."

The press was taking a shine to the boy. After the Washington game, a sportswriter had his picture taken with Bill. When he later presented the photo to Bill, the young star asked the sportswriter to autograph it. The press boys marveled. He was as approachable, they said, as a high school freshman.

Bill went home to Bluefield after the game. He had gotten a call from his father. The draft board was after him.

The war was never far from anyone's mind. It affected every little thing. Even if you wanted to ignore it, the coffee and gas rationing were there to remind you every day. Night football games were forbidden. Also, Americans for the first time were adjusting to something called

Daylight Savings Time. By September, Bill still hadn't heard from the Navy.

The year started out well for the Japanese. Island by island, they took over the Pacific Rim. In February, the American defenses in the Philippines collapsed and President Franklin Roosevelt ordered General Douglas MacArthur to evacuate. In April, the Japanese overwhelmed American and Filipino forces in Bataan. In May, Corregidor surrendered to the Japanese. Would Australia fall?

The Nazis had Europe. Now they were advancing. German troops invaded North Africa. Hitler ordered the occupation of Stalingrad in Russia.

By fall of 1942, America had recovered from the sucker punch at Pearl Harbor. The Sleeping Giant was awake and on the prowl. In summer, the US Navy halted the Japanese advance at the Battle of Coral Sea. A month later, they handed the Japanese their first major defeat at Midway. The world didn't know it then, but America would control the Pacific from that day forward. In Europe, Major General Dwight Eisenhower was appointed commander of US forces. In October, British and American forces landed in North Africa. In November, a million Russians breached German lines.

The bad guys weren't losing, but they weren't winning, either. Everybody was itching to get into the war.

Bill: "I wanted to kill Japs. I know it sounds terrible to say it today, but that's what we all wanted to do."

In the massive drafting, recruiting, and inducting effort following Pearl Harbor, Bill Dudley was just a sheet of paper. He'd been shuffled aside.

In Bluefield, Bill contacted his local draft board and enlisted in the Army Air Corps. He didn't know what the Navy problem was, but he knew he couldn't straighten it out in a month of Sundays. He didn't even try. He later discovered the problem was his age. He was too young to enlist in the Navy without his father's signature. His papers were put aside.

The Army had no problem with Bill's age. A week after he committed to the Army, he got a letter from the Navy. They wanted him in the Naval Free Flight Program in North Carolina and they wanted him to play football for Navy. It was too late. He was in the Army now. He was to report in December.

Back in Pittsburgh, Bill had good news for Rooney. Bill could finish out the season. When Bill ran into Kiesling in a restaurant, he had good news for him, too. It could be a winning season. The team was picking up and would be tough to handle for the rest of the season.

Kiesling: "Frankly, I wasn't as sure as Bill appeared to be. We had the Giants, Dodgers and Eagles coming in a row, and they all promised to be set to rub it in."

There wasn't much cause for optimism. The Steelers were on a losing streak. They lost their last two games in 1941 and lost both exhibition games and the first two regular-season games in 1942. Kiesling was still searching for an offense.

Maybe it was the losing tradition. Maybe it was the bad start of the season, but Kiesling, Bell, and Rooney apparently couldn't grasp what Bill, the lifelong student of the game, recognized about the team. It was the mental game again. Bill understood football and the men who play it on a different level. He saw things.

He understood that, along with their good line, the Steelers had a talented backfield. Sure, they were rookies, but, along with Bill, they had another triple-threat back—Curt Sandig could run, pass, and punt. He was a good receiver. Andy Tomasic could run and pass. He was a good punt returner. Fullback Dick Riffle was a powerful runner and could return kicks. Joe Hoague was a reliable rusher off the bench. It was just a matter of spreading the ball around. As tailback, he could do just that.

Kiesling wasn't like Shearer or Murray. He didn't go in much for one on one. Bill did most of his football talking with the Steeler backfield coaches. Bill also felt he could lift the team. He did. The veterans listened to him. They even got worked up. He lifted them as Kiesling had never seen. Bill's message came from the heart and he delivered it throughout his life.

None of us are perfect but each has the ability within himself to do just a little better—a little more. You hold the key. Will you lock the door of life and throw away the key or open it wide with renewed strength, effort and knowledge? You can be better than you are—humble in spirit with sincerity of purpose exemplified in faith and trust in your fellow man and God Almighty.

Kiesling saw it pay off in the next game. The Steelers, at home in Forbes Field, faced the New York Giants. The Steelers beat the Giants 13–10. The spectators included 4,000 Junior Commandos who had collected fifteen tons in a scrap metal drive. Bill was still limping from the Redskins game. He gained 135 yards and had two kickoff returns that made him the league leader in return yardage.

With Bill lame, the ball did indeed get passed around. Hoague scored on a 3-yard rush in the second quarter. Sandig scored on a 4-yard rush in the fourth. Armand Niccolai missed an extra point. The press began to notice what Bill already understood, including Chilly Doyle of the *Sun-Telegraph*:

The toast of grid fans of the Greater Pittsburgh sector are Bill Dudley and Curt Sandig, a pair of feather-footed halfbacks who with clever ball carrying and other triple-threat tendencies have transformed the down-trodden Steelers. As one Steeler official remarked, "Bill and Curt complement, as well as compliment, each other," and many of their victims will support the statement.

Bill went into the game limping and came out with a gash on his face and a broken nose. The press boys wanted to know how he felt about the pro game. How did it compare to the college game?

"In the pro game there are no weak spots. That's the big difference I've noticed. I have found you can't relax for a second among the professionals. I have played about 50 minutes of each Steeler game this season, and I've had to be on my toes all the time."

It was bittersweet for Rooney. He won the game and lost money at the same time. His little book showed attendance was 9,600. But, his little book would improve. The game was a turning point. The players were ecstatic. It was a win.

Next up was Brooklyn. The Dodgers led the Eastern Division and were favored to win before 17,689 fans at Ebbets Field. It was a running game for both teams. The Steelers never completed a pass. They won on a 7-yard Dudley rush in the second quarter. From there it was a defensive struggle, which turned out well for the Steelers—a substitution error in the fourth quarter put Bill and Curt Sandig out of the game, scuttling the Pittsburgh offense.

Kiesling told the New York press boys to avoid making judgments. "Dudley wasn't himself today. He was handicapped by an injury on the inside of his left knee. No, he wasn't running like he can. Of course, he did all right but don't base his performance on today's first showing in New York as an indicator of his ability."

Two wins in a row. Bert Bell had owned or co-owned a team in the NFL for ten years. This was his first two-in-a-row. The press boys began to notice. The threesome of Dudley, Cherundolo, and Sandig made the *Sporting News* weekly all-star team.

The next week was an away game in Philadelphia. The Steelers avenged their home opener loss and beat the Eagles 14–0 in front of 12,500 fans. Sandig scored on a 39-yard run. Riffle scored on a 1-yard run.

The Steelers had won three in a row. Even in wartime, this meant something in Pittsburgh. It was all so new, winning. A win for the Steelers in the upcoming rematch with the Redskins would mean Pittsburgh was tied for the lead in the Eastern Division. Art Rooney noticed when he picked up the tab after lunch with his staff.

"Even if I hadn't seen it with my own eyes, I would know we were on a winning streak because my coaches are eating better than I can ever remember. It is a sure sign. When they putter around with a sandwich and a salad, it is a cinch we're not doing so well, but when they hand the menu back to the waiter and tell him to bring it all with a cup of coffee, old Steeler University is in the groove."

Chauncey Durden wrote: "Thanks to Dudley's inspirational play, the Steelers, instead of playing the doormat role they've played in years past, are second in the Eastern Division standings. For once the Pittsburghers have had something to cheer about and they've cheered themselves hoarse over Dudley and the Steelers."

Art Rooney's little book looked pretty good the next week. The Redskins came to Forbes Field, and it was a record crowd. Ropes were spread around the outfield to hold an overflow of guests from the military. Unlike the Philadelphia rematch, the Redskins made a game of it. Washington won 14–0.

Once again, the Steelers could have won it. Pittsburgh had the edge in most of the statistics. More first downs—14 to 7. More yards rushing—113 to 67. More yards passing—134 to 126. Several Dudley runs—one breakaway for 52 yards—put the Steelers in scoring range against the Redskins. None were converted. They just couldn't cash in. The Washington defense had Kiesling's playbook nailed. The Steeler offense struggled. Bill was the leading ground gainer with 103 yards, but he lost 38 yards when he was smothered again and again behind the line of scrimmage. Kiesling used three different passers when he went to the air in the second half. The worst: A field goal was blocked and resulted in a Redskin touchdown.

The streak was over. But the Dudley breakaway threat was still scaring coaches. After the game, Washington coach Red Flaherty had a word for those preseason oddsmakers who labeled Bill a flop. "Bill Dudley is the greatest rookie back ever to play professional ball. He's the kind of fellow who can go for a touchdown every time he gets hold of the ball."

Art Rooney had never met anyone quite like Bill, but the boy was familiar all the same. The two were twenty years apart, with so much in common.

Both were unassuming men who were born into small coal country towns. Both were exceptional athletes who played above their weight. Both were men of faith—Rooney a Catholic and Dudley a Protestant. Both liked action—as with the Dudleys, the Rooney family business was being busy. Each was a man who other men deferred to.

Rooney introduced Bill to horse racing. He took him to the golf course. He took him along on public relations visits. They visited an orphanage together. He took him to Oney McManus's bar. Today, we might say they hung out together. In that era, they said Dudley "loafed with the boss."

Bill: "Other than my own father, I respected Art Rooney more than any man I ever met."

The relationship was close enough that Bill wasn't too surprised when Rooney asked for some advice after the Washington game. Should he fire Kiesling? The content of the question, though, was a surprise. Rooney and Kiesling were friends.

I said, "No, but he's not going to give you a winner." Kies just didn't have the mind to be a head football coach. A successful coach wins games, but he's also a special breed. It's the way you handle people and their response to you—to your philosophy.

"The average football coach knows what he needs. A good coach knows what he needs to win. You can give another coach the same talent to work with and he won't win. If a good coach has a weak position, he'll camouflage it and then try to improve on it. He'll fill the spot with someone who can at least do a half ass job, because he'll do a half ass job every play rather than do a good job one time and a lousy job two or three plays later that can hurt you. A successful head coach could be a successful executive of any corporation."

Kiesling stayed. The Steelers won their next four games. The Steelers beat the New York Giants 17–9 at the Polo Grounds before 19,345 fans. The game featured a Dudley 66-yard run and a Sandig 64-yard punt return.

The first streak wasn't a fluke. The players believed in themselves and the team. There was an air about practice, which was moved to afternoons in hopes of clearer skies and cleaner air.

Bill: "We had a lot of fun. Pittsburgh in '42 was probably one of the most fun years I ever had. We'd work out from one to three o'clock in the afternoon, and it was just overcast all morning long."

The sidelines of an NFL game weren't patrolled by security guards in those days. It was loose. Journalists mingled with players. Rooney sat on the bench with his clenched cigar. Suddenly, the Steeler sidelines were getting crowded. Everybody wanted to be in on the wins.

They beat the Detroit Lions 35–7 the next week in Detroit on touchdown runs by Dudley, Sandig, and Riffle; a Dudley pass; and a Dudley fumble recovery.

The Steelers then beat the Chicago Cardinals in Forbes Field, 19–3. Rooney's little book was happy. Attendance was 20,711. The Steelers took a break from the NFL schedule the next week. They played a military squad, the Fort Knox Bombardiers, in a fundraiser to build a USO canteen near the railroad station in downtown Pittsburgh.

A rematch with Brooklyn followed the next week. The Steelers beat the Dodgers 13–0 on a lousy day. A heavy rainstorm turned Forbes Field into a bog and limited attendance to 4,719.

For the four-game streak, the Steelers outscored opponents 84–19.

Going into the final game against Green Bay in Milwaukee, a win for the Steelers would have tied them for the division lead with the Redskins. The Packers had Don Hutson, a kicker and wide receiver who was on track to win the MVP for the season.

The Packers won 24–21, surviving a Steeler rally. The score was 10–7 going into the fourth quarter. The Packers scored two quick touchdowns. The Steelers answered with two touchdowns on a Dudley run and a Dudley to Martin pass, but the clock ran out. The difference was a Don Hutson field goal.

For the season, Bill ended with 696 rushing yards on 162 attempts. He passed for 438 yards and had 24 yards receiving. He returned 20 kicks for 271 yards, 11 kickoffs for 298 yards, and 20 punts for 271 yards. He punted 18 times for 572 yards. He scored six defensive touchdowns with three interceptions and three fumble recoveries.

He led the league in rushing. He was voted All-Pro in the same backfield as Sid Luckman, Sammy Baugh, and Andy Farkas. He was runner-up to Hutson for MVP and ahead of Sammy Baugh. That he was also Rookie of the Year was almost an afterthought.

The Steelers finished 7-4, good enough for second place in the division. The little book showed the franchise made money for the season. The players got a bonus check—$165 for second place. It was the first winning season for Pittsburgh. For the Pittsburgh fans, it was "what if?" A good field goal instead of a blocked one in the Redskins game would have put the Steelers in the championship game against the Bears.

"As it turned out, Dudley was right," said Walt Kiesling. "I think he had a lot to do with it, too. Of course everybody knows what he has done on the field, but I mean, the players like him and listen to him."

Ches Smith wrote, "The year 1942 would go down as the year pro football found a happy home in Pittsburgh."

There was one more game to be played. The Redskins beat the Bears in the championship game. Now, an All-Star team would face the champion Redskins in a postseason charity game. Bill, Cherundolo, and John Woudenberg of the Steelers were starters on the roster. The game raised $75,000 for the Merchant Marine Seaman's Benefit Fund. About $90,000 in war bonds were sold.

The All-Stars won 17–14. The All-Stars had never beaten the championship team in any NFL season. The pundits were quick to point out, though, that Sammy Baugh didn't make the game and was replaced by Andy Farkas. Farkas, it should be noted, was no slouch as a football player. This wasn't your average sleepwalk-through-the-playbook All-Star Game—fights broke out—even though the players were unpaid.

The All-Stars scored first on a 98-yard Dudley interception return. He gave the crowd their money's worth. It was a jump pass. Every club had the play, but the Redskins liked to use it that season. Bill saw it coming. Merrill W. Whittlesey described the play in the *Washington Post*:

Farkas took the ball from center, stepped to the line of scrimmage and leaped with his arm cocked for a jump pass. He whammed the ball toward Bob Masterson, but Dudley crouched in front of the Redskin end and grabbed the ball.

Dudley cut to his right and was off on a beautiful run, one of the greatest touchdown jaunts of the season. The former Virginia All-American outdistanced the Redskins who were closest as he cut to the sideline, passing Masterson and Zimmerman who gave futile chase.

Bullet Bill looked sure to be caught around midfield but he had a sprint in reserve and by this time he picked up blockers. Around the 25, two or three Redskins nearly caught him, but as they swerved in to cut him off he waited for them to get by and neatly cut back to midfield and finished his run by falling directly between the goal posts. He must have covered 140 yards and was so tired he fell into the end zone. The crowd roared for five minutes and gave him a great ovation as Coach Hunk Anderson took him out of the game. The All-Stars pounded him and pumped his hand until he begged off.

After the season, Tex Mayhew, the Steelers trainer and a former pro player, would recall that College All-Star sprint from the beginning of the 1942 season. "I've seen a lot of players with more ability than Bill Dudley, but I've never in my life seen one with more determination when he has the ball. When he was with the college all-stars they had a foot race among all the backs. He finished fifteenth. But they weren't carrying a football. If they'd let him carry the pigskin I'd wager he'd come in first."

The best football team Pittsburgh had ever seen dispersed to military duty around the country. The team would never reunite. All of the Steeler players who entered the war survived it, but it was the end of a football career for many.

Art Rooney: "I'm sure that if the war hadn't come along, Dudley would have led the Steelers to the championship. He was that good and he made everyone else who played with him that much better."

CHAPTER THIRTEEN

America's Best

AFTER THE 1942 SEASON, BILL WENT HOME FOR CHRISTMAS. Everything had changed. Everything was changing. Brother Jim was already in the military. Brother Tom was heading there. Sister Margaret was married and gone. Her husband was in the Navy. Marshall Shearer was back in the Navy. The war was ever present on the home front—bond drives for money, and scrap drives for metal, rubber, and rags. "Victory Gardens" adorned every yard. Women were mobilized for the war effort and took over jobs that were formerly men-only.

Gasoline rationing was a month old. Shoe rationing would follow. The national unemployment rate was 1.9 percent and the Depression era Works Progress Administration was dismantled. In Washington, the final doors, hinges, and nameplates were added to the world's largest office building, the Pentagon.

The tide was turning. Two epic battles filled the news—Guadalcanal in the Pacific, Stalingrad in Russia. In February, Japanese forces evacuated Guadalcanal. Hitler was stalled in Stalingrad. He ordered German troops there to fight to the death. They didn't. The German 6th Army surrendered.

Meanwhile, the Allies began bombing the Italian mainland. In March of 1943, the British RAF began bombing German targets.

Bill had one more game to play as a civilian. The Norfolk Shamrocks—a minor league team in the Dixie League—had called. A post-Christmas fundraising game against the Camp Lee Soldiers was scheduled. The game was in Richmond. Would Bill lend his name to it? He did, and 14,000 fans followed. He gave them their money's worth, playing the inconsequential match as if it were a Steelers' game.

Hank Wolfe, the Virginian-Pilot: *"Dudley's name is magic. Virginians and servicemen will show up in full force wherever he plays."*

Dick Williamson, Richmond Times-Dispatch: *"The Bluefield Bullet, fresh from a spectacular rookie season in the National Pro League, 'made' the game here. Not only because he broke away for two touchdown runs, but also because his determination was able to inspire a little fire into the rest of the players. It was a case of Dudley delivering or the whole thing being a flop."*

It took about a year for the Army Air Corps to turn a recruit into a pilot. Bill entered basic training in Miami after the All-Star Game. It didn't start well. He and another recruit were horsing around on the train and a window got knocked out. It was just the kind of thing a drill sergeant could use to dress down a football hero. It didn't matter.

Bill: "Basic training was getting up in the morning, exercise, falling in line and all that stuff. I was already doing that before I got there."

The drill sergeant wasn't stupid. He used Bill to win the base touch football championship for his squad and gave Bill a few hours of leave in return.

By March, Bill was on his way to the College Training Detachment at the University of Florida. It was a classroom environment for basic learning—Morse code and radio communications. From there it was pre-flight school at Randolph Field near San Antonio, Texas, which was known at the time as The West Point of the Air.

In August, Bill was sent to Aviation Cadet School in Stamford, Texas, near Abilene. Sometimes he learned the easy way. Sometimes he learned the hard way.

I was there in Stamford, Texas, for my first flight lessons. My first landing, solo flight, you know, I came in and just greased it in. My instructor, a fellow by the name of Curley, was sitting on the side and he said, "Go around and give me another one."

Well, I was flying high. The next time I came in for my landing, I realized I was going too fast. I lowered my flaps and tried to cut down my speed. I hit the ground and bounced 40 feet in the air and accelerated and stayed up. I went around again. I landed and the instructor gave me a look, and said, "You thought you were pretty hot after that first landing, didn't ya'?"

I said, "Yes, Sir." He said, "Well you learned the most important part about flying an airplane. As long as you have power, you're in control. You lose power, you've had it. I didn't have to tell you you needed to go around again—you just reacted."'

In Stamford, Bill ran across a soldier from Lynchburg. Bill wanted to know about a Lynchburg girl he'd met at a dance. He started to describe her. He didn't make it halfway through the description. They talked about the girl. Bill at last found out her name. He said he'd look up Libba Leininger when the war was over.

Bill: "He said, 'She's probably not going to be around when you get back. She won't last long.'"

You can ruin a man's day. You can ruin a man's week. But that one ruined a man's war.

Then it was on to Ellington Field in Houston for advanced training in twin-engine flight. Bill received his second lieutenant's bars in March 1944. It seemed to Bill like everybody was in the war but him. The same month he got his bars, Bill read that movie star Jimmy Stewart was leading bombing missions over Berlin. He wanted in, too. While he was in Houston, Bill got in touch with a former frat brother at Virginia.

Bill Crumm flew the bomber "Jack the Ripper," the first plane to drop the bombs on Berlin. I found out he was going to take a B-29 group to the South Pacific and I was gonna try to get with him. He came into Houston. We got along fine. He had received my letter to go with him and he said, "Bill, I would love to take you with me, but you've been declared essential to the war effort."

I said, "What?" He said, "You're gonna go to Randolph Field and play football this fall." I said, "You're kidding. They haven't said a word to me about it." He said, "That's where you're going and I can't do a thing about it."

Declaring someone essential to the war effort was the military's way of keeping a soldier stateside. It meant they had other uses for you.

Crumm was right. It was back to Randolph Field for Bill. He was to be a bomber pilot flight instructor. It wasn't what Bill wanted. He wanted to fly a P-38 Lightning, a twin-engine fighter aircraft that was as versatile as Bill. It was used as a bomber—it could dive bomb or fly level—and a reconnaissance craft. It was also a long-range fighter escort. P-38s made reconnaissance flights and were radar pathfinders for larger bombers. The plane was used in evacuation missions, ground attacks, and night fighting. If you flew a P-38, you were in the war.

Bill: "I would have given anything to fly an airplane into Japan or Germany. It just wasn't to be."

The war changed that summer. On June 6, 1944, the Allies—150,000 men—stormed the beaches of Normandy on D-Day and they weren't thrown back into the sea. Two days earlier, Allied forces marched into Rome. Two weeks later, US naval forces performed heavy air raids on Guam and defeated the Japanese fleet in the Battle of the Philippine Sea. In July, US Marines raised a flag over Mount Suribachi during the Battle of Iwo Jima. American troops secured Saipan. The good guys were winning.

South Texas is about as different as it gets from the coal country hills of Virginia. The horizon stretches as far as you want and in those days it was full of empty. If you fell asleep at the wheel, you just rumbled along the plains until you woke up and steered back onto the road. When it wasn't hot and sunny, it was warm and cloudy.

When Bill returned to Randolph Field that summer, he found the place thick with football players. He was about to join the best team he would ever play for.

Frank Tritico's career winning average was 100 percent. He coached one season and never lost a game. His team outscored opponents 508–19. Tritico's previous coaching experience consisted of some sideline work at the junior high school level. When he was handed a team of nine professional players and the cream of college recruits, he knew, and his players knew, he was in way over his head. It didn't matter.

Wartime football was different. The game was the same, but the leagues were changed. Military brass loves winning football games almost as much as they love winning battles and wars. Now the brass could draft the best players and put them where they wanted. They knew this wouldn't last forever. They created their own league of camps and bases and airfields. The military teams would play each other and also play college teams. All-Star military teams would play NFL teams in Bond Bowls. At Randolph Field, they assembled the best.

The Ramblers were a sensational team. The roster included triple-threat back Pete Layden, a Texas boy who played for the New York Giants; running back Bobby Cifers, who was drafted by Detroit before the war; running back "Tippy" Madarik, who was already a Lion; receiver Don Looney, who played with Bill for the Steelers; Notre Dame's "Dippy" Evans, who would play for the Bears after the war; Baylor's Jack Russell, who would play for the Giants; Texas A&M tackle Martin Ruby, who was drafted by the Bears before the war; tackle Walt Merrill of the Brooklyn Dodgers; running back Johnny Goodyear, who Bill faced in two 1942 Redskins games; and Bill Dudley.

Along with Bill, the Rambler backfield was deep in top-flight backs. The press labeled the quartet of Evans, Madarik, Layden, and Dudley the "Four Thunderbolts."

The Randolph boys coached themselves. Bill and Layden built their own scouting network with Art "Tonto" Coleman, a football coach in Abilene who Layden knew. Then Bill and Layden set up their own system.

Pete and I were roommates. We'd get a scouting report from Tonto, who'd tell us what the Hell's going on. Coach Tritico would just go out there and give us an offense and a defense. We changed half of it once we got into the game because we all knew what each of us were doing. It was something. Everybody on the team knew more football than Tritico, but we liked playing for him. He was a pistol.

It was like sandlot football. The players loved it.

We had communication. We were undefeated when we played Second Air Force in New York. It was our last game and it was our only close game. I knew that our right end could get open, but it had to be a deep pass. As we get back in the huddle—Burruss was his name—he said, "Bill, I can get open." I said, "I know you can, but I can't throw it that far." Old Layden says, "Oh, Hell, I'll throw it." I said, "Alright." And so we called the play, Layden threw it about 50 yards and Burruss goes in 15 yards for the score.

The Ramblers played home games in San Antonio. They knocked off Abilene Field 67–0 in the home opener. They defeated college power-houses Rice, Texas, and Southern Methodist by an average of 47 points. Bill was averaging a first down every time he carried the ball.

Texas scored a touchdown against the Ramblers on October 7. The Randolph boys wouldn't allow another score—including a shutout of an undefeated Charlie Trippi–led Third Air Force Team—until December 10, when they faced March Field in Los Angeles.

In the meantime, Bill had a job to do. He instructed pilots and flew in the mornings and practiced football in the afternoons. He took his job—like he took all jobs—very seriously. He sometimes instructed the instructors who were instructing him.

One time, I'm with my instructor in the right seat getting my advanced training. He was flying the airplane. And we take off and we are about a couple of hundred feet in the air and a flock of birds hits the fuselage and the lieutenant takes his hands and puts 'em over his face. Leaves the damn wheel. And the plane starts going down. And I grabbed the wheel, gave it full throttle and pulled it out. He just looked around and said, "Thanks, Bill." Then we came down 'cause one of the birds knocked a hole in the wing. I was not a hot pilot, but I was a damned good instructor.

Military life agreed with him about as much as it could for anyone who was there by necessity. Sometimes, though, the Dudley temper collided with military protocol. Here is what it looks like when a captain crosses the wrong lieutenant.

I had this captain that I was given to teach. He had flown twenty missions and was back to learn to be an instructor. Twenty missions and never had a scratch or anything.

There's a procedure you go through when you lost an engine. I was gonna show him. I explain the standard procedure—what we're gonna do that day, how I'll do it. I gradually trim the ship up. I pull a prop. Instead of going through the standard procedure, he put both throttles to the firewall—the plane goes up, and I say, "Captain, I got it!" He says, "Like hell you have, lieutenant. After flying all these missions, I'm not gonna get killed by some freshman." I said, "Captain, I have it!" He said, "NO, YOU DON'T!"

With that, I backhanded him and he said, "I'll have your ass." I said, "Fine. Let's go in."

So, we get in and I call the Major in—"We got a problem, Major." The captain has calmed down a little bit. The major says, "Bill, have a seat—I'll be with you in a few minutes." So, he takes the captain in and they go through whatever he told him. They come back out and he says, "What's your take on it?" I told him, "Frankly I got control of the airplane. It's my ship. I went through the things he didn't do and so forth." The major said, "He told me about the same thing, but tell me something, did you have to hit him?"

I said, "Major, what would you have done?" He said, "Well, I'll give him to somebody else and just forget it."

It was part of his training. He had a procedure he had to follow—things had changed. What that pilot did when he was overseas wouldn't work on that twin engine bomber. We spent a lot of time on procedure. If you lost an engine on takeoff, you're gonna crash if you don't do the right thing—same thing on landing.

The Ramblers faced their toughest opponents in the final two games of the season. These wouldn't be shutouts. The Ramblers traveled to Los Angeles on December 10 to face the March Field team. The Flyers were 7-2-1. Bill knew the team well. The Flyers had an early opening game that season—a Treasury Bond fundraiser August 25 against the Redskins—and Bill was loaned to the Flyers for the game. He had his usual spectacular breakaways that day before 50,000 fans at Memorial Coliseum, but the 'Skins gave March Field their only loss, 7–3.

Randolph Field beat them 20–7 on a Dudley to Goodyear 20-yard pass, a Dudley interception that set up a score, and two Dudley quick kicks. Bill was named Outstanding Player of the game. And he made a friend.

While at the hotel, I get a phone call from Don Ameche. He got in touch with me and wondered if I would visit with him. So he came out to practice one day and we talked and he said he was considering starting a ball team out there. But more important—did I think I could arrange for his sons to be on the field for the game? I said, "Mr. Ameche, I don't know, but I'll talk with the coach." When I mentioned it to Tritico, he was in high cotton that it was Don Ameche and said no problem.

Ameche was at the height of his early movie career. After the war he faded from Hollywood stardom, only to return for a rekindled career and an Oscar nomination in the 1980s. In 1944, he was a household name. Five years before, he had the title role in a biopic that became a classic—

The Story of Alexander Graham Bell. For a time, Americans referred to the telephone as an "Ameche."

He and Bill hit it off. Ameche was of Hollywood, but he wasn't Hollywood. He was pretty much the same off screen as on. He wasn't self-absorbed. He was a family man. He and his wife, Honey, had six children. Two were adopted. The man was easy company at cocktail hour and suppertime. Bill and Ameche would remain friends the rest of their lives.

The season-ending game would be the only real test for the Ramblers. The Second Air Force Superbombers out of Colorado were 10-3-1 going into the game, the tie a 0–0 contest against March Field. The Superbombers outscored opponents 507–57. They had triple-threat back and future college Hall of Famer and NFL star Glenn Dobbs, who once punted a ball 87 yards in a University of Tulsa game. Dobbs knew the Ramblers. He led them to a 9-1 season the previous year. The Superbombers also had college backfield stars Ray Evans of Kansas and Johnny Stryzkalski of Marquette. The game was billed as the Treasury Bond Bowl. It was also billed as the Army Air Force Championship. The *New York Times* reported:

> *One of the authentic great teams is Randolph Field, loaded to the wings with professional college veterans, and none greater than Bill Dudley, the heavy-duty left halfback who was an All America at Virginia and then an all-league sensation with the Pittsburgh Steelers, and better today than ever.*
>
> *Here is a team, No. 1 in the service field, that stands comparison with Army, the national college champion, and the Giants and the Packers, one of whom will emerge as National League champion tomorrow on the same ground. The Ramblers, in fact, may be better than any of them.*

Snow kept attendance low—although 8,356 attended—but the game still raised about $80,000 through underwriters. Before the final game, Henry H. "Hap" Arnold, Commanding General of the US Army

Air Forces, got both teams together. "When I was at the Point, I always wanted a good football team. Now I've got four of the best in the states. Some of you all have been complaining about not going overseas. Believe me, within about a month after this season, we're gonna all be overseas. Go out there, have fun, play your asses off."

It was a sloppy field in the snow. The Superbombers won on the ground. They outgained the Ramblers 302–134 rushing. The Ramblers won in the air. The Bombers were 4 of 11 passing for only 30 yards. The Ramblers were 5 of 6 for 56 yards, but two Rambler passes were for touchdowns.

The Ramblers won, 13–6 on a Layden to Burruss 47-yard touchdown pass set up by a blocked punt by Russell, and a Dudley to Goodyear 3-yard pass. Bill had one of his patented 90-yard kickoff returns, only to have it overturned by a holding penalty.

Army finished that season 9-0, playing college teams, and was ranked number 1 in intercollegiate play by the AP. The Ramblers were ranked number 3 behind Ohio State. Navy was fourth. The story at the time was that Army didn't want to risk their ranking by playing the Ramblers.

"There were rumors we were going to play West Point. They had Doc Blanchard and Glenn Davis and they were real strong. The story I got was that head coach Red Blaik didn't want any part of us."

Bob Considine of the *Washington Post* considered the Ramblers to be the best team in the country—college, service, or pro. So did Art Daley of the *New York Times*. For Bill, it looked like yet another mythical championship.

For the season, Bill had 640 yards rushing, including touchdown runs of 47, 48, 50, 59, and 67 yards. He passed for 520 yards and ten touchdowns. He kicked seven extra points. The Touchdown Club in Washington called Bill's name again. He was named the service MVP. He was selected for the GI All-America team by the Associated Press.

Once again, one of the best teams Bill would play on was dispersed, never to reunite. "General Arnold was right," Bill said. "We were all shipped out after the last game."

High spirited Randolph Field Ramblers: Everett Elkins, Dippy Evans, Pete Layden, and Bill Dudley. COURTESY OF THE LYNCHBURG MUSEUM SYSTEM

Two weeks after the last game, the Germans launched a surprise attack on advancing Allied forces, mostly Americans, in the Ardennes region of Belgium, France, and Luxembourg. The ensuing Battle of the Bulge in heavily forested terrain would last a month and it would be the biggest and bloodiest fight of the war, but the lights were already turned out for the German army. It was just a matter of time for the Nazis. They were out of men. The Luftwaffe was destroyed.

CHAPTER FOURTEEN
Luckily, There Was Baseball

BILL WAS SENT TO SEATTLE AND THEN SHIPPED TO SAIPAN—IN JANU-
ary 1945. There was a ten-day stop in Hawaii for maneuvers. When the
Marines seized Saipan, Guam, and Tinian in the summer of 1944, they
secured the Mariana Islands, which were near enough to Japan to launch
missions. A B-29 had an operational radius of 1,600–1,800 miles. Japan
was 1,400 miles away.

It is 45 square miles of tropical paradise, unless you're a soldier in a
war. Then, it's just a lonely dot in the Pacific. Bill would be stationed there
until the end of the war, attached to the 20th Air Force. What was at the
time the world's largest airfield was carved out of the island. The runway
ended at a cliff, which came in handy for Bill and other pilots.

*B 29s—sometimes they had a tendency for the engines to heat up.
That's the reason pilots kept them low over the water before they
started to climb to keep their engines cool from the water. When you
took off of Saipan, you took off a kind of cliff—the first thing you did
once you got off the island, you lowered the nose to get down on the
water and make sure the engines were cool before you started to climb,
especially with a load.*

Back in the States, the first stirrings of postwar America appeared.
The sense that the war was being won became an awareness that it was
soon to be over. After four years of deprivation, Americans were ready to
move on into a much-changed world. New yearnings surfaced.

On the islands, there were different yearnings. Nobody was leaving until the thing was over. The war dragged on. Every soldier knew that, back home, the world was moving on while they stayed put. It was exceedingly hard on Bill. That last dance at UVA seemed so long ago, and "she won't last long."

I wasn't doing any missions. I flew a lot of inner island bland stuff for one reason or another. I was just trying to do my job. I still instructed, but I had to struggle to keep my flying time in. I flew my plane. I did my job every day. But inside, I couldn't wait until it was all over. I just wanted it to be over.

When he had time, Bill would get a plane and fly to Tinian. Bob Crumm was there, the only link to his former life. Luckily, there was baseball.

The Army Air Force had put together three teams representing bombardment wings. The 58th Wing was based at West Field on Tinian, the 313th Wing at North Field, Tinian, and the 73rd Wing on Saipan. It was a morale booster. The airmen could watch and be in the company of some of their favorite players. And what favorites:

Future Hall of Famer Enos Slaughter and three-time All-Star Howie Pollet of the Cardinals; future Hall of Famer Joe Gordon and teammate Johnny Sturm of the Yankees; All-Star Birdie Tebbetts and Billy Hitchcock of the Tigers; Chubby Dean and Buster Mills of the Indians; Stan Rojek, Chet Kehn, and All-Star Lew Riggs of the Dodgers; Taft Wright, Dario Lodigiani, and Stan Goletz of the White Sox; Nanny Fernandez and Max West of the Braves; Mike McCormick of the Reds; and Tex Hughson of the Red Sox, along with twenty-eight other pro and college players. They were there to play ball and do double duty as flight and ground crewmen.

When the 73rd Bombardment Wing Bombers found out that football star Bill Dudley was on the island, they brought him on as a utility player.

It was a snap for the same engineers who built the world's largest airstrip to construct a few ballfields. All they needed was someone to give them the specs. It was like having a portable stadium. Carve the field out of the jungle, build up a mound, lay down some bases, and play ball.

The fields were dirt. Seats were made of bomb crates, of which there were plenty. Bomb crates also made good fences. The teams realized quickly that the crate fences could be adjusted, depending on who was pitching and which team got to the field first.

The three teams played a twenty-seven-game round-robin series. There were 12,000 spectators at the opening game in July. Games were played on Saipan, Tinian, and Guam. One early series was played at Iwo Jima.

All three teams had good, major league pitching. The games were played all out, like a pennant was on the line. There was the occasional fight. Dustups were common, especially with the star players.

Enos Slaughter and I got along fine. He played full steam. He stole second base in a game and came in spikes high. Joe Gordon was playing second. Gordon says, "Dammit, Enos, what's wrong with you? Coming in here spikes like that?" Enos says, "Joe, when I steal a base it's mine. I don't care if it's in New York, St. Louis or here in the islands. If you don't like it, get the hell out of the way." Gordon just shook his head and went back to position.

Bill played the same game he played back in Bluefield. He got on base. Bill's unorthodox playing style extended to baseball. When he played the outfield, he fielded fly balls with a running basket catch, taking in the ball waist high, a decade ahead of Willie Mays.

Bill: "I'd catch a fly ball and the other dugout would start yelling 'Run with it, Dudley! Run with it!'"

Introduced by Americans in World War I, baseball was especially popular on Saipan and Tinian. Not only did locals play the game, but so did their Japanese occupiers. All told, the league played before about 180,000 soldiers, sailors, and Marines. The Japanese stragglers who watched from the surrounding jungle—and they were there—weren't counted. The spectators were all male.

Bill didn't remember "seeing a single woman on Saipan, Tinian, or Guam."

The Nazis surrendered in May 1945. Relieved Americans celebrated Victory in Europe—VE Day. By August, the scuttlebutt on the Marianas was about one topic: How would the Allies finish off Japan? There would be no surrender. Would there be an invasion? Estimates were that it would take a million men to take the island. The boys were not privy to that number, but they knew an invasion would be big. Still, they weren't seeing that kind of buildup. One day in August, Bill did see a ten-foot-long, 9,700-pound clue as to how the war would end:

> *I was playing baseball with the Saipan team on Tinian. We're riding in a truck and all of a sudden we looked over there and saw this great big damn bomb. Didn't know what the hell it was at the time. It was about a hundred yards away. Saw it being wheeled on one of these crates they carry bombs on. I said "Look at that big thing!" We wondered if there was a plane with a belly big enough to hold it. It was a tremendous thing compared to other bombs we had seen. Of course we knew after it was over—didn't know it was the atom bomb at the time—I just knew it was a damn big bomb. Turns out, I saw them load the atom bomb on a plane, although I didn't know what it was at the time.*

The bombings of Hiroshima and Nagasaki ended the war in the Pacific. Now, Americans could celebrate VJ Day. Years later, Bill was making a public appearance and he was introduced as a war hero. He came to the podium and told the audience he was going to dispense with his customary opening humor and set the record straight. "I flew one mission over Japan as a copilot on a B-29. It was a supply mission when the war was just about over. We didn't see an enemy plane the whole trip. I wasn't a hero."

After the A-bomb was dropped, it was just a matter of time before the Japanese surrendered. It was time to get in line to go home.

Officers accumulated points based on time served, missions flown, time overseas, and other requirements. Once you got enough points, you were eligible for dismissal. Those with the highest points got the first offers of release. Bill was on Saipan and had enough points to get out. He filed for release in August 1945. The Japanese surrendered on September 2. Bill got his orders to leave right after. Finally, he was on his way back to the States.

When Bill landed in Hawaii, he saw a major he knew from Randolph Field in the airport. There was a quick conversation.

> *Major: "Hello, Bill."*
> *Bill: "Hi, major."*
> *Major: "Where ya' headed?"*
> *Bill: "Home. I've got enough points to get out.*
> *Major: "See ya' later."*

Later that day, an orderly approached Bill. Lieutenant Dudley had orders to get to the commandant's office, ASAP. Bill arrived at the Hickam Field office and the commandant sat him down.

> *The Commandant said, "Lieutenant, I'll make this short. I understand you have enough points to get out. I can put you on a ship that will leave in three days and dock in New Jersey in six or seven weeks. However, if you agree to play four or five games for us, I'll see you are flown directly to the separation center the day the last game ends." I said, "I don't have much of a choice, do I?" He said, with a little smile, "Oh, yes you do."*

When Bill left the commandant's office, there was the major, sitting on a sofa.

Major: "Bill, how'd it go?"
Bill: "I think you already know."
Major: "I'll see ya' at practice this afternoon."

The major coached the team. His Army Air Force All-Stars included several former Ramblers. One of them was Jack Russell, who gave Bill one of his favorite wartime playing stories.

Charlie Justice was playing for the Navy. Jack Jacobs punted for us and our end, Russell—a hell of a good football player, about 6'2" 225—he was lumbering along about eight or ten yards ahead of me going down the field. I'm behind him and I see Justice is gonna catch it rather than try to make a fair catch, and I yell, "Russell, hit him, he's gonna catch it!" And Russell turned on the damn speed and he hit Justice about the time the ball got there. The ball went one way and Justice went the other. Well, I see Charlie when we played together for Washington in '50 and he looks at me and says "You son of a bitch, I can still hear you saying, 'Hit him Russell, he's gonna catch it!'"

The Army Air Force All-Stars won all five games, including a win over the Navy Stars on a Dudley 30-yard rushing touchdown before 45,000 servicemen at Pearl Harbor.

Bill: "We beat the Navy All-Stars. That's all they really wanted."

In the dressing room after the final game, Bill looked up to see the same orderly who nabbed him five weeks before. His orders were to wait for Dudley, give him anything he wanted, and drive him to his plane right after the game. A deal is a deal.

The war changed so many things, but it produced, within Bill, an unexpected change of heart. The racial makeup and the race relations in prewar Bluefield were no different than any other small town in the Upper

South. Bill lived a mostly segregated life, parallel to, but at an arm's length from, black people. His parents' attitudes harkened to another century. Jewell wouldn't allow black people in her home.

The University of Virginia was all white when Bill attended. The 1942 Pittsburgh Steelers were all white. Although the NFL was integrated in its early years, no black players were in the league after 1933. It would be 1946 before Woody Strode and Kenny Washington re-broke the color line and played for the Los Angeles Rams.

Bill would later confide to Art Rooney Jr. that the war altered all that for him when he played and worked alongside black men for the first time.

Art Rooney Jr.: "Bill was a son of the south and that's what he knew. He played with black players for the first time in the service. It opened him. He told me the experience got him to see black people as human beings. He came to understand the south in a very much different way."

It was a change that Bill embraced and grew with for the rest of his life.

Bill Dudley spent every day of his life in a hurry. Even when he was standing still, he leaned forward. After he retired from football, he got in a bigger hurry. His secretary of forty years kept a separate file drawer for his traffic tickets. Bill had a years-long agreement with an auto body shop—same day service on dings and fender benders—so his wife wouldn't find out about them.

Travel for Bill was a constant after he left football. His insurance business required travel. He traveled for his retirement duties with the NFL and the Hall of Fame and for personal appearances. He was a walking, or perhaps traveling, contradiction. He couldn't stand to be late and he rarely left himself enough time to get there on time.

People who drove Bill to the airport all relate the same story. He rushed from his house to the car and rode in grim silence, ticking off

Bill (right) with a teammate at baseball practice on Saipan during World War II.

the seconds—and woe to the driver who failed to fill up the tank before picking him up. Upon arrival at the airport, he made a Pony Express stop—one leg out the door while the car was still moving. When the door to the airport slammed behind him, the car would still be rocking from his exit.

If there was ever a man who needed his own airplane, it was Bill Dudley. He left the service a good pilot, expertly trained, and he could afford it. So, why didn't he?

Bill: "I thought about buying a plane once. I thought about flying commercial at one time. Then I got married and after that, I didn't think about it anymore."

Then again, perhaps a private plane was just too extravagant for Jewell Dudley's son.

CHAPTER FIFTEEN

$1,000 Per Game and Bad Romantic News

B꯫ILL WAS DISCHARGED FROM THE ARMY AIR FORCE AT FORT MEADE, Maryland, in October 1945. He went home to Bluefield. Again, everything had changed. Both brothers survived the war. Jim, who served in the Army infantry, got shot up in France and lost an eye and had some shrapnel in his neck. Tom was a pilot in Australia. He got through it without a scratch.

The word "normalcy"—coined by President Harding after World War I—returned to the language, but there would be no return to the old normal. America was the new global superpower, but Americans weren't interested in power. While the rest of the world picked up the pieces, Americans worked. The postwar economic boom they started was nothing like the world had ever seen. It began a period of prosperity that ran unabated for three decades.

Americans had been through all the reality they needed. *Life* magazine described the country's mood: "If the songs a country sings are any indication of its mood, the U.S. last week was lolling in an amorous, sentimental daze. On dance floors and radios were heard such plaintive queries as 'Why don't you surrender?' and such pleas as 'Linger in my arms a little longer, baby.'"

Few things make home seem more special than a bunk in a barracks. Men came home from the war, oh, so ready for a house and a family. The fuse on the baby boom was lit.

While the rest of the world rebuilt, Americans played again. In October, baseball attendance hit a record 10.3 million. The nation watched as number 1 Army beat number 2 Navy in college football. Professional football, meanwhile, was hanging, if not by a thread, than by a string.

Art Rooney wanted to close down the Steelers after the 1942 season. There wouldn't be enough players. The Steelers would be bad again. He was right. Bert Bell talked him out of it. They could find a way. Although what followed was comical in its desperation, Bell was more right than Rooney.

In 1943, the two Pennsylvania rivals merged—the Philadelphia Eagles, a team Bell started, and the Pittsburgh Steelers, a team Bell co-owned. They became the Steagles. Walt Kiesling split coaching duties with Greasy Neale. To just about everyone's surprise, they had a winning season—5-4-1—even though they allowed more points than they scored.

It was the first winning year for the Eagles. On the field it looked like semi-pro football, which was what it was. Everybody skimped—the players did their own laundry. The merger ended after the season.

Winning didn't make it easy for the players. Win or lose, they were scorned. During World War II, there were twenty-one different draft classifications in four categories for men aged eighteen to sixty-five.

If a man was a father, and the child was born less than nine months after Pearl Harbor, he would be a low-priority choice. If a man worked in one of the many war industries, such as making weapons, he could be deferred. If he was a clergyman or a farm laborer, or if he worked in a field essential to defense or had already served, and on and on.

If a man was physically unfit, he was deferred and labeled 4F. The military had its own logic about who was and wasn't fit. A man could fail a medical exam because of flat feet or ulcers.

If you were classified 1A, you were drafted.

Most people understood only two of the classifications: 1A and 4F. Nobody wanted to be 4F. The most cruel wartime burden a man could bear stateside was to be labeled a "slacker," a man who avoided military service.

Still, you could fail a medical exam and at the same time be capable of playing football. Two Steagles were partially blind. Two were partially deaf. Others had bad knees or flat feet. The public, especially in steel industry Pittsburgh—a critical war industry if there was one—didn't understand this. The players were ridiculed.

It was a matter of perception, really. Future Hall of Famer Bill Hewitt—a tight end and the last player to refuse to wear a helmet in the NFL—played for the Steagles. He quit the game in mid-season. He couldn't take the ridicule anymore. He was thirty-four. Future Hall of Famer Sam Baugh, who was twenty-seven when the war started, was deferred because he ran a cattle ranch in Texas that provided beef considered essential to the war effort. His 1943 season is commonly remembered as one of the best in NFL history.

You could play for the Randolph Field Ramblers and be a hero. You could play for the Steagles and be a goat. The irony wasn't lost on Bill. "After the Rice game (with the Ramblers), there was a quote in the paper that we made our contribution to the war effort. 'Cause we had a football team? I don't know."

In 1944, the Steelers merged with the Chicago Cardinals. The Card-Pitts were relentlessly awful. Kiesling split coaching duties with Phil Handler. They lost all ten games. Sportswriters referred to the team as the "Car-pits."

A week after Bill left the military, the Steelers called. There were four games left. He could finish the season for $1,000 per game. Don Ameche also called. He now owned the shares of the Los Angeles Dons he'd told Bill about earlier in the war. Did Bill remember his offer? "Meech wanted me to play for the Dons. I told him that I had told Mr. Rooney I'd play for him if I came back from the war."

Bill arrived in Pittsburgh on a Monday. He started against the Chicago Cardinals that Sunday. The press boys wondered if Bill, who still liked maintaining friendships with linemen, thought a back should be paid $1,000 a game. "Sure, if the linemen are, too," Bill replied.

Walt Kiesling was gone, replaced by Jim Leonard. The Steelers were 1-5 going into Bill's first game of the season. Pittsburgh beat the Chicago Cardinals 23–0 at Forbes Field on a pair of Dudley touchdowns and Dudley extra points. The headline in the next day's paper read: "That Man Is Back."

The Cardinals win was the last for the 1945 Steelers. The team finished 2-8 for the season. Bill scored every point for the rest of the season and led the team in scoring for the year. Even at 2-8, Art Rooney's little book was happy. Attendance would never go below 13,000 again.

Bill signed a contract for the 1946 season—$1,000 per game—and went home to Bluefield. It was time for unfinished business.

The first call Bill made when he got out of the Army was long distance to Lynchburg, Virginia. (Note to younger readers: If you don't know what long distance is, ask somebody with gray hair.) There was great news and good news and bad news. The great news: Libba Leininger wasn't taken—she *did* last long enough. The good news: She remembered him. The bad news: She was booked up for the rest of the year.

Bill: *"You had to get on the list early."*

He got on the list. He'd faced big odds before. Now, he just needed an opportunity. This time, though, he couldn't get it by taking another year of Home Ec.

But he could take a course in Spanish. In four weeks of play in the late fall of 1945, Bill had made about double the average wage for American workers for a year. It bought him time. He needed nine hours to get his degree. His senior year Spanish hadn't been so bad. Maybe, this time it would work. He had time for a spring semester. In January of 1946, Bill moved to Charlottesville. Libba Leininger was sixty miles south attending Randolph-Macon Woman's College in Lynchburg.

The Libba list was a long list. Bill had his first date with Libba in February. He thumbed a ride and was picked up by a Lynchburg boy. They talked.

Bill: *"I'm Bill Dudley."*
Driver: *"You the football player?"*
Bill: *"Yeah."*

Driver: "Why are you going to Lynchburg?"
Bill: "I have a date with Libba Leininger."
Driver: "Whoa, boy, you're keeping some class company, ain't you?
She's attractive as hell."
Bill: "I know."
Driver: "Good luck. You'll need it."

When they first met, Bill was nineteen and Libba was sixteen. People speak today about "exceeding expectations." Bill's expectations were towering when he knocked on Libba's door five years later. They were exceeded when she opened it. The poise, the charm, the wit, the easy personality, the independent streak were all there and improved with time. She was a jaw-dropping beauty.

For the next seventeen months, Bill Dudley engaged in an agonizing game of cat and mouse, except it wasn't a game to him. His mind was made up. It was made up before he knew her name. It had been made since that first turn on the dance floor back at UVA. Her mind was anything but made up about anything. She was spinning. Wherever she turned there seemed to be another man on bended knee.

He and Libba dated throughout the late winter of 1946. He saw her at least twice a month. A typical date was dinner at the White House Restaurant—"Virginia's Finest Eating Place"—in downtown Lynchburg, followed by a dance at Oakwood Country Club.

Bill hit it off with her parents. He talked baseball with Dutch—the former semi-pro couldn't get enough of the tales of Enos Slaughter, Joe Gordon, and Birdie Tebbetts. Her parents knew who he was—the Steelers didn't make headlines in Lynchburg, but the Ramblers did—even though Libba was only vaguely aware of his football career. She knew that he was well known, but that was about it. She wasn't a fan of football in high school and went to a few college games as social occasions. She probably never watched a complete play.

Bill thought things were going well. The parents liked him. There were so many shared values. Bill was lucky in sports and lucky in war. Could he be this lucky in love? No. Libba came up to Charlottesville for final dance weekend and dropped an anvil on him. She said she was going to marry Paul. Paul. Who was Paul? Bill didn't know Paul. Had Libba mentioned Paul? He didn't think so.

Bill: "You are?"
Libba: "Yes."
Bill: "I guess that about does it."

Emphasis on "about." When you are low on options, the only real option is determination. "She won't last long," "Good luck, you'll need it," "Whoa boy, you're keeping some class company, ain't you?"—these were the voices of surrender. Bill would have nothing of it. In his mind, Libba Leininger was fair game until a wedding band was slipped on her finger. He didn't hide his intentions.

In July, Bill passed through Lynchburg on his way from Bluefield to Steeler training camp. A glance at a map will show that it was a detour. He stopped and called Libba. He was told she was attending an engagement party at Oakwood. He called Oakwood and got Libba on the phone. After a few moments of chatting, she put Paul on the phone. Bill was his usual blunt self. "I congratulated Paul. Then I said, 'I'll tell you another thing. If I can beat your time, I will.'"

Paul was warned, and at his own engagement party, no less. Bill had a season of football ahead of him. Libba was going into her senior year in college. For Bill, there was little left to do but pray, which he did.

CHAPTER SIXTEEN

1946: A Hall of Fame Season

PITTSBURGH IN 1946 HAD A PROBLEM. IT LOOKED JUST LIKE PITTS-
burgh in 1941. The Arsenal of Democracy was retired, but the sky was
still dark at noon. The terms "pause button" and "on hold" had yet to enter
the language, but postwar Americans would have no trouble understanding the concept. For five years they'd put everything into the war effort.
The home front had to wait. Now the waiting was over. Cities across
the country breathed in the postwar boom. While the rest of the world
rebuilt, America built. They needed steel. You couldn't make enough of it.
Pittsburgh, meanwhile, risked choking itself on its own success. The city
could supply the steel, but it wouldn't thrive if nobody wanted to live there.

Richard King Mellon spent the war as a cabinet secretary in Washington. When he moved with his wife, Constance, to Pittsburgh after the
war, they realized they'd never get anybody to come to work there unless
the city was cleaned up. Mellon formed an alliance with the Irish Democrat bosses and Mayor David Lawrence and rammed clean air ordinances
through city council. It wasn't popular. People were forced to stop using
coal in fireplaces. It worked.

It was just a beginning, but it catalyzed a Pittsburgh renaissance. The
stage was set for downtown to be brought back to life. Buildings were
leveled, including the slum where Mayor Lawrence was born. Pittsburgh
was showing it could reinvent itself.

The Steelers, too, were reinventing. After the 1945 season, Art Rooney lured Jock Sutherland to coach the Steelers. It was a coup—Rooney had tried to nab the famous coach before and failed. Sutherland was a legendary college coach at the University of Pittsburgh. From 1924 to 1938 he coached the team to five national championships and four Rose Bowls. Pitt was 111-20-12 under Sutherland. When Pitt de-emphasized the football program in 1938, he quit.

He coached the professional Brooklyn Dodgers to winning seasons in 1940-41. The Dodgers were second in their division both years. He then entered the war as a lieutenant commander in the Navy.

He was also a dentist. As an All-America college player he played on Pitt's 1917 undefeated team, which was known as "The Flying Dentists." The team sometimes started dental students at every position.

He was tall, good-looking, and reserved. He was humorless. He was formidable. The press boys called him The Dour Scotsman. Rooney didn't care how dour he was. Football is a coach's game. Rooney meant it when he said in 1942 that he was sick of losing. He'd promised Pittsburgh a winner. The war was over. It was a new beginning. A man like Sutherland could make good on the promise.

For the first time in Steeler history, the Pittsburgh fans had high expectations before the season started. There were plenty of reasons. They had Sutherland. He was local and the fans knew how good he was. Chuck Cherundolo, Andy Tomasic, and Bill Dudley were returning from the 1942 team.

The backfield was loaded with talent. Along with Dudley and Tomasic, the Steelers had triple-threat backs Johnny Clement, Merl Condit, and Charlie Seabright. They could all rush, throw, and kick. They could all return kicks.

Condit was an NFL All-Star before the war. Seabright, a blocking back and quarterback, and Clement, a tailback, were rising stars. Both had strong rookie seasons in 1941. Both were back in the game for the first time since the war started. They had Steve Lach, Bill's former

All-America rival. Fullback Tony Compagno and end Val Jansante were the only unknowns at skill positions.

Steeler fans were also concerned. Sutherland would run the single wing. The formation was passé. The raw power football of the single wing had given over to the spread formations and finesse game of the T-formation. The oddsmakers had the Steelers winning two or three games, even with Dudley at tailback.

Then again, Sutherland was the acknowledged master of the formation. A variation of the single wing was named after him. The Sutherland Single Wing used a different backfield formation—the tailback and the halfback were both triple-threat positions. It was less power and more finesse. If you had the talent, it would work. He had the talent.

Bill got in his car to go to Hershey, Pennsylvania, for the start of practice and drove straight into the Dour Scotsman's doghouse. "I got a letter to go to camp. And I don't remember whether it said practice started on a Monday morning or just report Monday. I didn't get there on Monday until 12:30 or 1:00, so my first practice was Monday afternoon."

In 1942 the Steelers practice schedule conformed more or less to the Pittsburgh pollution schedule. The team practiced in the afternoon sunlight, such as it was. Bill assumed it was the same, even at the Hershey training camp. It wasn't. Sutherland called a morning practice. The first practice was over when Bill got there. Bill apologized. He made no excuse. The mistake was out of character for him. Sutherland refused to accept the apology.

Sutherland may have been a dour Scotsman, but Bill was a blunt Dudley. Neither was a diplomat. Bill was later told that Sutherland thought Bill's selection as military service MVP had made him a prima donna.

If Sutherland considered Bill a prima donna, it was an opinion formed from within. Bill Dudley was not an unknown. Sutherland lived in Pittsburgh in 1942. He saw Bill play many times. He read the press accounts. He was Bill the Beefer, not Bill the Diva. "That wasn't my attitude and everybody knew it," Bill said. "He just wouldn't give up on it. He was that kind of man. He wanted all to know he was boss and nobody could mess with him. "

The two went sideways and stayed there. Nobody really knew why. Things never got better. Jock made it known around the league that Dudley was hard to handle.

Bill: "Jock hurt me a lot with some other coaches in the pros. I got along real well with all the college coaches I ever had. I got along with Kies. I never had any problems with coaches. I did what I was told, just like I did with Jock. But, Jock, of course, didn't like, quote, the Star System."

Perhaps it wasn't just that Bill was a star. He took up with Art Rooney right where he'd left off—at the racetrack, at the golf course, at card games—wherever the action was. Bill was the favorite of The Boss. Rooney named a racehorse Bullet Bill. Jock was just an employee.

Sutherland didn't run his trademark formation. He ran a classic single-wing formation with an unbalanced line. The only adjustment he made was at tailback. He positioned Bill for a deeper snap. Sutherland was banking on raw power. Games would be won in the fourth quarter. A disciplined offense would wear down a defense. It was power football. There was no subtlety in this offense The defense knew where the runner was going.

Jock will tell you—"I'll tell ya' where I'm coming and I'm gonna beat ya'"—and that was his philosophy. He designed the blocking around a hole and figured our men were gonna outman theirs. And that's what happened quite often. When they outmanned you, they kicked the living shit out of you. That was it in a nutshell. He was very successful in the past. Why change?

Practices were as rough as they were tedious. The players ran compact wind sprints designed to grind a formation into a player's muscle memory. They seemed endless.

It was all drills. Military precision drills. There wasn't a team in the league that drilled that way. The linemen had their steps. The backs had their steps. Two steps, cut. Four steps cut. Six steps cut. Eight steps pivot. Again. Two steps, cut. Four steps cut. Six steps cut. Eight steps pivot. Again. If we do it long enough and hard enough, we win. That was the theory.

It was something like Pavlov's dog. You heard a number, you reacted. It didn't matter how tired you were, it was automatic.

The squad also scrimmaged every day. Bill didn't particularly like the grueling regimen, but he didn't question it.

Jock knew what it took to win in his fashion. There are football coaches who know what it takes to win and some who think they know what it takes to win. Jock knew. Jock knew that if he could get his people to do things his way, by the end of the ballgame his team would be in better shape than the other guys.

The workouts were a brutal reality, but the theory was just a theory.

The Steelers faced the Chicago Cardinals in the home opener. They beat the Cardinals 14–7 on a Dudley to Seabright pass and a 1-yard run by Compagno, plus two Dudley extra points. By game's end, Sutherland's strategy was obvious to Bill. Sutherland had three triple-threat backs. He used one of them. Bill touched the ball on almost every offensive play. He kicked and punted and returned kicks and punts. He played safety. He never left the field.

Something was becoming obvious in Art Rooney's little book. It was a sellout crowd of 32,951 at Forbes Field. Every home game sold out that year.

The Steelers traveled to Washington to face the Redskins the next week. The Steelers tied the game with a scrambling comeback in the fourth quarter. They entered the final quarter down 14–0, the tie coming on a 17-yard pass from Clement to Jansante and a 1-yard Dudley touchdown run.

Next up was the New York Giants. The Steelers lost at home, 17–14. They had two scores on a Dudley pass and a Clement run. The Steelers started the season 1-1-1. It wasn't supposed to be this way.

The fans were restless. Then the second Sutherland vs. Dudley incident happened. For Bill, this one cinched it. The relationship never recovered.

And then one afternoon, we were out there practicing. I never was a good passer. I was average in the pros. He (Sutherland) came down and I was pissed off because I'm not hitting the receivers. And he came over and made a statement like "What's the matter?" And I said something like, "Well, sir, if you'd put different color uniforms on defense, it might help." The defensive backs had the same uniforms as we did. And he said, "Are you coaching this football team?" And I said, "No, Sir." And he said, "You'll take orders just like anybody else." I said, "Yes, Sir."

And I went to him later. He said I wasn't blocking and tackling the way I should be. I was upset. I had tears in my eyes. I told him, "From the time I was in high school I've always played all out. No one ever accused me of not doing my job. I was never called anything but a team player." And I said, "Sir, if you don't want me, then trade me," because I had never been talked to like that before, and every coach I had played for knew that I was putting out all the time and I didn't ask for any favors.

But then he said the other ballplayers resented my attitude. That was a big surprise to me. And I said, "If that's true, then let's trade me." The Doctor kind of passed over my suggestion that he trade me, but I said, "I'm serious. I'll talk to Mr. Rooney about it tonight." I went to Mr. Rooney, but he just glossed over it, too.

That's one thing that I never heard from anybody. I'd heard that sometimes I would be right forceful during a ball game, but never, to my knowledge, in all the time I played ball did I know anything like what Jock said. I urged ballplayers to play. I didn't get on anybody for mistakes. I always had a good relationship with the ball players. They were my bread and butter! For a running back particularly.

Bill went to Cherundolo. Was Jock telling the truth? No. The boys felt the same about Bill as they had felt back in '42. Bill smoldered. Sutherland lied to him and it was a petty little lie at that. Bill had a code and it didn't include lying.

The first incident happened at a closed training camp. This second one happened at an open practice. A reporter caught it all. "There was this one writer there who completely blew this thing with Sutherland out of proportion," Bill said. "Because he happened to be at practice that day. And that was his story."

This was all new to Bill. He'd always had cordial relations with the press boys. Now, he was on the backside of a bad story, the kind of melodrama that is catnip for sportswriters. The story changed Bill. He remained cordial, but he kept to himself. Over the season, writers would press him. Why didn't he ever give them a story? His answer: He didn't want to.

You learn not to talk around certain reporters. I had a writer tell me, "Bill, I'm just like you." I said, "No, you're not." He said, "Yes, I am. I get paid for what people read in my column." I said, "I'm paid to perform on the field. You're gonna write about what I do on the field. My work is a public exhibition." And he said, "Yeah, but your mind isn't." And I said, "That's exactly right and I intend to keep it that way."

Bill couldn't escape Sutherland even when he went home. They both roomed at the Pittsburgh Athletic Club downtown. The bellhops told him that this annoyed Sutherland.

Doc lived there, too. He wasn't married. He wasn't chummy with ballplayers. He wanted professional distance. He was arrogant—very ramrod stiff. We both took our meals there. He never spoke to me the whole time. I think he thought I was taking his turf.

Bill Dudley loved talking football with coaches. He envied Sid Luckman, who worked closely with George Halas in Chicago. When

Bill tried it with the Pittsburgh coaches in 1946, he was rebuffed. With Sutherland, a suggestion amounted to an insurrection.

You could spend all day playing armchair analyst about Jock Sutherland. The man had an ego, but that's not unusual for a head coach. It's a requirement. His position with the Steelers, though, put him in new territory, ego-wise. Read press accounts of the University of Pittsburgh teams when Sutherland coached there and you'll see the first reference to the team is invariably "Jock Sutherland's University of Pittsburgh Panthers." But these weren't Jock Sutherland's Steelers. They were Art Rooney's Steelers or they were Bill Dudley's Steelers. Jock ran a distant third.

Football was all Sutherland had. He was unmarried. He had no family. He seemed friendless. He was austere to the point of being farcical—players accused him of putting oatmeal in the water at practices to discourage drinking. Compared to the cigar-chomping Rooney and the electrifying Dudley, he was just another guy in a suit. And maybe he knew football was leaving him behind.

What if Bill was wrong in 1946? What if Jock didn't know how to win in the postwar era? George Halas and his boys killed the single wing in 1940. It was just a matter of time before Sutherland's signature offense went away. The single wing was power football, sure, but it didn't produce as many points as the T-formation. And producing points is, after all, the whole point of an offense. Taken in that context, Sutherland's maniacal drills looked more like death throes.

The Steelers needed a win for themselves and for their fans. Next up was the Boston Yanks. The fans got their victory. The Steelers won 16–7 on two Lach touchdown rushes and a Dudley field goal. It was another sellout at Forbes Field and a record crowd. Portable bleachers were brought in to handle the throng.

The up and down season continued. The Steelers lost the next week to Green Bay 17–7. The Steelers' only score was on a 31-yard Dudley run and Dudley extra point.

Then it was back to Boston. The Steelers rolled over the Yanks, 33–7. It was 7–6 Boston at the half after the Steelers scored on a Condit run. It was all Dudley in the second half. He scored on a lateral from Compagno from the Yanks 23, an 80-yard pass reception from Condit, and a 38-yard rush.

It was another record crowd at Forbes Field the next week when the Steelers faced the Redskins. The comeback tie game earlier in the season had the fans tasting a win, and they were hungry. The last time the Steelers beat the Redskins, Bill Dudley was a senior in high school.

The fans were also coming for the Bill Dudley show. Nobody had seen anything like this one-man backfield. Each home game that year set an attendance record, beating the previous week by about 2,000 paying customers.

They were coming to see something unique in football. Sure, there were triple threats and there were versatile ballplayers, but Bill was playing fifty minutes or more per game. He rushed. He passed. He caught passes. He kicked and punted. He returned kicks and punts. He kicked extra points. He led the league in interceptions. He was playing the modern equivalent of eight players on offense, defense, and special teams. Bill was the league standout. Even so, Sutherland was telling the press boys that Dudley was two years away from his peak.

There was the anticipation. You never knew when Dudley would pop one loose for a long one. Every rush, every punt and kick return, every interception—and there was an average of one of those per game. What we would today call multitasking made for a crowded pregame warmup for Bill. He described his routine:

After church I'd go to the ball park and then get taped up. For a one o'clock game I'd be on the field by noon if I could. You had to loosen up—kind of a routine movement. You'd do some exercises and things. Whatever the coach wanted. Then I wanted to catch a punt or two and kick a punt or two. Same with kicking. I wanted to do some passing. I never felt like I was pushed going from one to another, but I never stopped to take a breath, either.

Players had their routines in the locker room before the games. Some guys would hang their clothes up the same way each week, things like that. Me, I always packed extra socks because I couldn't get a shoe to fit. That was about it.

I personally was always thinking about the game—who we were playing, about the scouting report, constantly reminding myself that a certain team likes to do this, or do that when this happens. All that stuff was going through my mind. That was what I believed would help me to do my best to win a game.

For all his military precision on offense, Sutherland turned Bill loose on defense. He played pretty much the way a free safety does today. Steve Owens, the Giants coach in 1946, rated Bill the best defensive back in the league. Bill had, Owens said, a knack for knowing where the ball was going.

I had pretty much a free hand back on defense most of the time. I had people I was supposed to cover, but if he didn't do anything I could release and play the ball. I knew what was going on in the game. I just had to ask myself "what would I do in this situation?" And I was a damn good tackler.

My job was to tackle 'em. If they get by the line of scrimmage, you gotta tackle. It's not your job to beat somebody up—it's your job to get 'em to the ground. And to do that, I was taught you gotta get in close to the runner. You've gotta get in close to him to bring him down.

Sometimes the only way to get to the man is to leave your feet, but once you leave your feet, you've got no control over yourself. So, I was taught in high school to always go through the man. And I believe that's still taught today. Good tacklers do that—go through the man.

I tackled most people around their thighs. If you look at a man's feet or his head and shoulders, you're not gonna be able to tell what it's gonna do.

If you watch various backs running, you see the differences. Those with speed will try to put it on as soon as they feel like they can make a break. Others will not go all out until they know they are in the clear.

(Hall of Famer George) McAfee was the hardest runner for me to bring down. He ran straight up. He had a hell of a start and stop. (Hall of Famer Don) Hutson, I never knew what he was going to do once he had the ball. (Hall of Famer Marion) Motley was tough to bring down. If you try to tackle him above the waist, he'll give you a biggy (forearm). I'd get a hold of him and he'd drag me for three or four yards while I yelled for help.

He (Motley) was 245 and I was 170. In one game I had to pull him down 11 times unassisted. He gained a lot of yardage, but he never scored.

(Philadelphia Eagle and Hall of Famer Chuck) Bednarik was the hardest tackler in the game. We're playing in an All-Star game. He says, "You pick up the end, I'll pick up the back." Bednarik had a running start on the receiver, Tank Younger, swinging out of the backfield. Younger came across for the pass, Bednarik had a five-yard start and floored him. He got up and gave me a "hee-hee-hee." I said, "Do that to me and I'll kill ya'."

Next year, I'm returning a punt for Washington, playing Philadelphia. I was just about to hit the out of bounds line when all of a sudden, whooosh, two knees go flying by my helmet. Chuck came back and helped me up. He said, "Almost got ya', didn't I?"

The fans at the Redskins game got their money's worth. Bill intercepted a Sammy Baugh pass in the first quarter and returned it 81 yards for a score. The Steelers were ahead 7–0 at the half. Steve Lach iced it in the fourth quarter with a 5-yard touchdown run. Baugh later scored on a 1-yard rush for the Redskins, but Washington ran out of time. It was Pittsburgh 14–7.

The Steelers were 4-2-1 and on a win streak. Things should have been looking up for the players. They weren't. Sutherland's brutal preseason drills continued through the playing season. The team was worn down. They considered Sunday a day off. You only had to play a football game. Sutherland was more taskmaster than motivator. He alienated players.

There wasn't the esprit de corps of 1942. Jock didn't care about anything other than winning or losing a ball game. He didn't give a damn about the ball players. Charlie Seabright, for example. He treated Charlie like dirt and Charlie was a damn good blocking back.

I respected Jock, but I didn't like him. I thought he was arrogant. Looking back on it, I think Jock was a real SOB when it came to trying to get along with everybody. If he hadn't been the head coach, I think some of the ball players would have kicked the living shit out of him.

Bill was wearing down, too. Defensive linemen keyed on him. Sutherland's offense telegraphed where the ball was going. When the snap came to Bill, the defensive line shifted. There was usually more than one brute waiting when Bill got to the hole. That second Redskin game was brutal. Bill bruised his kidneys, which led to another confrontation with Sutherland:

I couldn't run and I needed to get heat treatments. We had a good trainer and good facilities when they would let you use them.

I told the Doctor, "Doc, I can't run." He made me stay out on the practice field. I wanted to excel, and I was willing to spend the time in practice, but if you're injured—if you aren't full speed—you can't practice properly. It doesn't do a bit of good to run a play at half speed. If you can't run it full speed, you can't get your timing down.

And he gives me this false speech. As far as I'm concerned he was the most insincere man I saw in my life. It was so artificial, him giving me this pep talk.

The next week we were playing Detroit. I got one treatment before we played Detroit.

Sutherland had lied to him early in the season. For Bill, that was it. He would never trust him again. "It's awfully hard to see a man like this—he would get emotional and you damn well knew it was a put-on. He'd come over and put his arm around you and you knew it was phony."

The Lions were a middling team, 3-3-1 going into the game. The Steelers lost 17–7 playing at Detroit. The Steelers' only score was a 10-yard Dudley rush.

Bill: "He (Sutherland) kept me in. And as a result, I couldn't cut and Detroit ended up beating us. No way they should have beaten us. I gained six yards the whole game. On defense I let a boy run by me and catch a pass and go ninety-two yards for a touchdown. I couldn't play, really. If he had let Clement play and let me rest, we would have been alright."

The Steeler offense was scoring. They just weren't scoring enough. After the Detroit game, the team watched film, which provoked yet another blowup with Sutherland.

I score from about ten yards out on a play going up the gut. And so, we get to the play on the film and we're looking at the play. All the coaches had seen the film before. When I was going into formation for the TD, I saw my guard give me a motion, pointing, to go on his inside. Which I did. There was a hell of a hole there and I almost fell through it.

Thank God I scored, because I would have caught more hell than I did. We're looking at the film and Jock says, "Bill, what play was called?" And I said, "226." And he said, "Where did you run?" I said, "228, where there was a hole." And he said, "Would you mind telling me why?" And I said, "No, Sir, just look at the guard giving me a motion." Well, everyone started laughing and Jock just cut it off like that. The guard was a boy named Nick Skorich. If he couldn't block the way he was supposed to, he gave me a signal. I always had good relations with my blockers.

Jock was only concerned with the play that was called. Every time I lined up to run a play, I would run my head back and forth across the field, number one to keep from telegraphing, but number two, it gave me a good idea about where the linebackers were. It might tell me that I might have to cut in a bit quicker or swing wider, or get to the outside quicker or things like that.

Bill ran Sutherland's offense, but Bill was an innovative player. He was improvisational and a student of the game, and he was frustrated. He was anything but mechanical, and he was getting tired of hitting holes that weren't there. Sutherland's theory wasn't working. His precision drill single wing wasn't wearing down opponents. It was wearing down the Steelers. It gave Bill yet another nickname. Bill was no longer Beefy. He was now called Flat Top by his teammates and by other players in the league, because he was creamed so often in the Steeler single wing.

Bill: "In 1946, I figure I played about three years of football in one year."

Size matters when two men meet head on. Bill was small for any era—his Hall of Fame ring fit inside Bronko Nagurski's. When Bill hit a hole that was closed, it was a pop gun against hydraulic power. A few seasons later, as the Steelers still clung to the single wing, George Halas summed it up for Rooney. "You do kick the hell out of the opposition physically, but the opposition is still getting the points and beating you. Remember, the other team takes that beating once. Your team takes it every week."

After the Detroit game, Bill told Cherundolo—his best friend on the team—he wouldn't be back in Pittsburgh the next season. The Doctor didn't care for him. They both knew that, but Bill also knew Sutherland didn't care about him.

The Steelers next faced the Eagles before 38,882 fans at Forbes Field. They got more Dudley heroics. The Eagles were up 7–0 going in the fourth quarter and had the ball on the Pittsburgh 32 when Bill intercepted a pass and returned it 44 yards. A Dudley pass put the ball on the Eagles 1 yard line. Steve Lach took it in. A 14-yard Dudley field goal iced the game. Even with the up-and-down season, the division title was still up for grabs. The Steelers were in second place with only two games remaining. The next game against the first-place New York Giants would be a big one.

The trip to New York was more than just an away game for Bill. It was also an opportunity to connect with Libba. These kinds of moments were rare and precious during football season.

During the war, AT&T discouraged long distance phone calls. The network couldn't be expanded in wartime, and it couldn't handle the growing load. Not so in 1946. A long distance call was expensive and it required a switchboard operator to complete, but you could do it. Bill Dudley was making $1,000 per game. He had plenty of nickels to slide into a pay phone. When he had the opportunity, he called Libba. "If I can beat your time, I will."

In one call, Libba dropped the news that she and her mother wanted to go trousseau shopping in New York. What a coincidence. Bill would be in New York the weekend of Thanksgiving. Why not shop that weekend? It was arranged. Bill met them for lunch. Bill had game tickets for them. Paul wasn't there.

The Giants game was close and exciting, but the Steelers lost 7–0. When he left for Pittsburgh, Libba saw him off at Grand Central Station. What did she think of the game? She remembered hearing his name called, but that was about it, and it was enough for Bill Dudley. They made their farewells and it was back to football.

The Steelers lost another close one to the Eagles, 10–7, and that was it. They were 5-5-1. Few numbers better describe mediocrity for a season. But a mere ten-point swing in the last two games would have given the Steelers the division title. There was so much promise at the beginning and so little spark at the end. The Steelers were drained.

The fatigue was understandable, but something else was wrong—the Steelers weren't winners when they needed to be and could have been. It wasn't that Sutherland didn't understand the pro game. He had two good seasons with Brooklyn. How could he fashion a weak offense out of so much backfield talent? Why did he alienate his players? Why the maniacal repetition of drills?

Nobody knew in 1946 that Jock Sutherland was suffering from a malignant brain tumor. In later years, Bill understood this as a partial answer to the riddle.

I think that the Doctor was beginning to have some effects from the brain tumor. In practice sessions, he was known to be very strict in the running of plays. We were running a new play he gave us in practice. He stopped the play and came up to me and said, "Who taught you to do it that way?" I said, "Sir, you did—you just did it yesterday." And he looked at me and started to get on me. You see, the Doctor was beginning to have lapses of memory. I don't think there's any doubt that the sickness that killed him more than a year later already had begun. But of course he didn't realize it. The assistant coaches were so dominated by him they didn't say anything. There was one, though. His name was Mike Nixon. And I said "What about it Mike?" And Mike said, "Bill's right, Doctor." Well, Jock turned around and walked right off.

In the final game against Philadelphia, Bill suffered a knee injury. It would be the first time that football sent him to the hospital. "Cherundolo snaps the ball and I punt—and he's blocking instead of going downfield," Bill remembered. "The defense player gave him a shove. Cherundolo hits me and I'm lying on the ground and he lands on my leg. All internal ligaments were torn."

His knee was repaired in Pittsburgh and a friend drove Bill back to Bluefield. They stopped in Lynchburg, a detour again. Libba was, unsurprisingly, still engaged. In Bluefield, it was time for a hard choice. Bill had already told Cherundolo he wouldn't return to Pittsburgh. Saying it was one thing. Doing it was another. The facts on the ground didn't look good.

It was one of those "what if" situations. You don't know how much you would've played that next year. And you don't know how well your knee would have stood up with all the stress. The single wing, it's all cutting—and I knew that the knee was damaged to the point that it would never serve me well again for that kind of cutting.

My knee would swell up and then I would have to stay off it. And from what I'd seen of Jock's attitude in '46, if that had happened in '47, I don't think he would have put up with it, would have let me rest. He didn't let me rest when I hurt my back.

If I went back, there would be problems. I wasn't going to change and he wasn't going to change. There was no use in torturing myself to go through all that again. There would be divisions and Mr. Rooney would end up in the middle.

He wasn't going back, period. His personal feelings couldn't enter into it. In March of 1947, Bill sat down and wrote the hardest letter he would ever put to paper.

Dear Doctor:

Since the close of our season I have had a long and continuous debate with myself as to whether or not I should play another season with the Steelers. In view of the very fine treatment from Mr. Rooney, the excellent support of the Pittsburgh sports writers and editors, and the very high esteem in which the Pittsburgh fans seem to hold me, it was a difficult decision to make.

As you probably know, Doctor, I was inwardly unhappy throughout most of the past season. This unfortunate and distressing situation had its beginning in Hershey, Pennsylvania. Our personalities clashed there rather seriously, as you will recall.

You are a great Coach and I admire and respect you very much as such and also as a very fine man. But individually our personalities and natures seem not to click together.

My life so far has been wrapped up in football. At the same time it has been developed from childhood—both at home and in school and in church—in a happy vein. So, to be unhappy is a real punishment and I shall not undertake another chance of inward heartaches and unhappiness. To do so could easily provide opportunity for great embarrassment and injury to you, Mr. Rooney, the club, the public and myself.

Such being the case I have decided it best not to attempt another season. If you and Mr. Rooney wish to trade, sell or release me, of course that is your privilege. In such an event I would appreciate your advising me of your intent. Meantime I have made tentative arrangements for my immediate future activities.

I want to leave with you and Mr. Rooney my very best wishes for a continued successful operation of the Pittsburgh Steelers, and my everlasting gratitude to all of those connected with the sport including the fans for their fine treatment and support of me. I shall in no way make the content of this letter public or discuss it generally with other parties until such time as you think it wise or best to do so.

Sincerely yours,

Bill Dudley

Bill never consulted Rooney before writing the letter. He never talked with Rooney about a trade after the letter. He never notified the press. His "tentative" plans weren't tentative. He already had a job as a coach at Virginia. The extraordinary 1946 season notwithstanding, he quit.

The relationship between Bill and Sutherland was far more complex than the narrative of the Dour Scotsman vs. the peppery star the press boys played up. Bill admired and disliked and pitied and scorned Sutherland in a circle of emotions that never stopped spinning. If Sutherland wanted to break Bill, he failed. He didn't break him; he made him. Bill said it more than once, "Jock Sutherland made me MVP."

But, for Bill it was never about winning awards. Sutherland was the only coach Bill had in the pros who Bill thought was capable of delivering a championship. A championship was the reason Bill played the game. To Bill, being named MVP didn't mean you were the best. A championship, and only a championship, did. Winning one was the reason he played the game.

When I was a kid I dreamed about being on a championship team. It never worked out. I wanted to win. I loved it. But a championship. There's a camaraderie that exists among all ballplayers. I've noticed, particularly at All-Star squads or Hall of Fame gatherings, that if any of the boys ever played on a championship team, there's camaraderie there that you don't get anywhere else.

I never thought about winning trophies or awards. The honors I get, well, they're here today and gone tomorrow.

But Bill also thought Sutherland—great coach that he was—blew it.

Doc didn't have to play me that much. Johnny Clement was a pretty good runner and a better passer than I was. He was a big tall kid. He could see the field better than me. If Jock was so good a coach, why didn't he let Clement play more offense in passing situations and not tire my ass out playing both ways? Now, don't get me wrong, I got MVP because I played all those positions, but if he'd played Johnny Clement more, we would have won.

Worse, Sutherland forced Bill to choose between himself and Art Rooney. Bill hated leaving Pittsburgh. He always had fan support, but Pittsburgh was special. Pittsburghers were loud and loyal. He loved the fans and the fans loved him. "Probably, no other player in our long history in Pittsburgh ever captured the imagination and hearts of the fans as did Dudley," said Art Rooney.

Bill Dudley was incapable of holding a grudge or nursing resentment, but he never got over the missed opportunity of Pittsburgh. Put him in a formal interview situation and ask Bill about Sutherland and you'd get, "I always respected him as a coach." Ride shotgun with Bill while he's doing 85 on I-66 and you'd get, "The son of a bitch was a phony." Bill never told Sutherland what he thought of him. Bill held his tongue, not an easy thing for a Dudley.

"Near the end of the season of '46, Ernie Bonelli walked off the field and told Sutherland 'Stick it up your ass, Doctor,'" Bill said. "I wish I had done that, but I thought too much of Mr. Rooney."

When an issue is unresolved, there always seems to be one more thing to say. Fifty years after Bill wrote his letter to Sutherland, he sent a letter to Tim Rooney, Art's youngest son. Here's a portion:

Even with all the differences in 1946, there was a lot more that went into my decision in writing my letter to Dr. Sutherland. I believe all of you in the past have received a copy. Your father was probably, outside of my father, the finest man I ever knew. We had a great relationship and I firmly believe to this day that if I had gone back in 1947, it would have been a horrible year, causing divisions because the "Doctor" could not carry your father's shoes as a man, person or

*anything else. One of these days, maybe in a visit, I will be glad to go
into the whole season. Looking back, I am convinced the brain tumor
that eventually killed Jock was bothering him in 1946. I don't know
how many more years I will be around, but just wanted to reiterate
my feelings for Pittsburgh and your family.*

Jock Sutherland dangled a championship in front of Bill and then
took it away. He gave Bill Dudley his best season and his worst season
in the same season. A half-century later Bill Dudley was still spinning.

Bill won his second league rushing title with 604 yards. He led the
league in interceptions with 10 and in punt returns—385 yards on 27
attempts. He also led the league in lateral passing, a statistic that is no
longer used, but a telling one nonetheless. A lot of things can go wrong
with a lateral, especially if it isn't designed into the play—something
that would later drive Bill nuts as a coach. If you don't know what to
do with a football once you have it, you have no business attempting a
lateral.

It was a Quadruple Crown. Sam Baugh won a Triple Crown in
1943, leading the league in passing, punting, and interceptions. Steve Van
Buren did it in 1945, leading in rushing, scoring, and kickoff returns. A
quadruple had never been done and would never be repeated.

Bill also passed for 452 yards. He caught passes for 109 yards. He
returned 14 kicks for 280 yards. He punted 60 times for 2,409 yards.
He made two field goals. He recovered 7 fumbles. His ten interception
returns totaled 242 yards.

He led the Steelers in scoring—48 of their 136 total points. He
kicked their only two field goals. He was named the NFL's Most Valuable
Player. It was a performance for the ages.

In later years, Bill would say it was impossible without Cherundolo.
At center, he was the most important lineman in the single wing. Bill
thought he was the best center in the league. Cherundolo—who Bill
always wanted to be considered for the Hall of Fame—was the only
Steeler who played more minutes than Bill.

Bill, forever the student of football, was right about Clement. He and Steve Lach led the Steelers to an 8-4 record and their first-ever postseason game in the 1947 season. Sutherland dispersed rushing duties among six backs. It was downhill for Pittsburgh from that season. The Steelers were the last team in the NFL to abandon the single wing, dropping it in 1952. The Steelers wouldn't have a successful franchise again for twenty-four years. They had five winning seasons between 1948 and 1972.

Jock Sutherland's behavior became more erratic during the 1947 season. He was found, wandering and confused, in a field in Kentucky in the spring of 1948. A few weeks later, he died after undergoing surgery to remove his brain tumor.

The Steelers of 1946 had better players and a better coach than the Steelers of 1942. The Steelers of 1942 were a better team.

Walt Kiesling was inducted into the Pro Football Hall of Fame in 1966. Sutherland is in the College Football Hall of Fame.

CHAPTER SEVENTEEN

Heartache to Hero in Ninety Days

FOR ALL THE TRAUMA OF THE 1946 SEASON, BILL WENT HOME FEELING a little wind at his back. The weekend in New York with Libba was encouraging. Libba could shop whenever she chose. A train left Lynchburg for New York every day. Why did she pick Bill's weekend? Was it because of, or in spite of, it being Thanksgiving? Where was Paul? Why did she go out of her way to say goodbye? Did she want just one more look? Was *any* of it really a coincidence?

Bill was too lame to drive home after the 1946 season. A friend drove him. On the way to Bluefield, they stopped in Charlottesville, where a doctor examined Bill's knee. They drove on to Lynchburg—again a detour—and spent the night. Bill managed to work in a visit with Libba and then it was on to Bluefield. He was there only a day when the phone rang. It was Libba. Would he like to come to Lynchburg and escort her to the Junior League dance? Paul was traveling on business on the West Coast. The dance was at Oakwood Country Club. They would be chaperoned by her parents. "I came to Lynchburg and took her to the dance," Bill said. "I stayed at her house and had a delightful time with her parents. We stayed up 'til 3 a.m. over coffee and drinks. The next day I said, 'Can I see you again?' She said, 'No.'"

Bill went back to Bluefield, yo-yo'd again. From there it was on to Charlottesville to work on his degree—Spanish again—and to talk with Art Guepe about coaching the Cavaliers. Guepe took over head coaching duties at Virginia in 1946, when Frank Murray returned to Marquette. Bill would need a job that fall. When he revealed to Guepe his decision to retire from the Steelers, Guepe hired him as a backfield coach. Bill would begin during spring practice at the end of the semester.

It was a long distance call from Charlottesville to Lynchburg. Bill kept slipping in the nickels. During a call in February, Libba lifted the anvil she dropped on him almost a year before.

Libba: "I may be having second thoughts."
Bill: "About what?"
Libba: "Marriage."
Pause.
Bill: "Oh, can I see you?"
Libba: "Yes, but we can't go any place."

Chuck Yeager made headlines in October 1947 when he broke the sound barrier. It could well have happened seven months earlier when Bill Dudley borrowed Art Guepe's car and drove to Lynchburg after that call, arriving with the same set of goosebumps he started with.

For the next three months, Bill pressed his case. He and Libba saw each other, but avoided public appearences. Again and again, they met at the Leininger home. They sat and talked. The wedding plans progressed. In March, Bill mailed the letter to Sutherland. He told Libba about it and about his new job in Charlottesville. The wedding plans progressed. Bill abandoned his Spanish studies. He wore out Art Guepe's tires and Route 29 between Charlottesville and Lynchburg. The wedding plans progressed.

It was two weeks before the wedding. The invitations were out. Gifts were arriving at the Leininger home. Libba's trousseau linens displayed her new monogram. It was all set except for one item. Libba walked into her parents' bedroom one night. Dutch and Inde sat up in bed. Libba had some news. She wanted to break the engagement.

It didn't come as a complete surprise. The Dudley boy had, after all, been sitting on their porch for the last ninety days. So, it wasn't time for panic. It was time for a deep breath, which both Dutch and Inde Leininger took.

Bill and Libba announced their engagement a month later, on July 4. They were married twenty-five days later—Bill Dudley wasn't going to give anybody enough time to beat his time. Inde put a new wedding together in short order. Part of the task was daunting—disposing of the old gifts, developing a new guest list. Other parts were simple—Libba already had the dress.

Bill's only remaining hurdle was a trip to Bluefield, where he made it plain in as gentle a fashion as a Dudley can state his mind, that he was marrying a Catholic and that was that.

It was a very small wedding in the parlor of the Leininger home. It was followed by a big party at Lynchburg's handsome Boonsboro Country Club. A half-century later, Bill's son, Jim, would observe that of all the photographs of his father out there, the ones taken on his wedding today are unique—that it wasn't possible for him to look happier.

Bill: "It was the culmination of waiting, hoping, and praying. I always thought I had a pretty good relationship with the Lord. I knew I wanted her. He knew it. I might as well ask for it. I prayed for her and I got her."

Nine days after the wedding, Coach Gus Dorais of the Detroit Lions came to Charlottesville. He wanted to talk football with Bill. The Lions were coming off a bad season. They won one game in 1946. Dorais wanted to switch from the Notre Dame Box to the T-formation. He could use a man like Bill. The team was owned by Chicago department store executive Fred Mandel, who had already gotten the bidding rights for Bill and was ready to go high. It wasn't the trade Bill expected.

The Steelers didn't approach me after I wrote my letter. I think that Mr. Rooney wanted me back. But I don't think Jock wanted me back. Unfortunately I was treading on his ground because I did have a good reputation in Pittsburgh and I was proud of it. People would yell for me, you see. And the Doc didn't like that.

They almost had a trade worked out with Philadelphia and Washington, but it didn't materialize. It was my understanding they (the Steelers) didn't want to trade me to anybody in the East. That was standard procedure because they didn't want to play (in the same division) against me. You don't trade your good ballplayers to someone that you are gonna have to face a couple of times a year. I think Sutherland thought, "He's not so good I can't do without him. Just trade him out of the division and I don't have to work with him." So they traded me to Detroit.

I was very much surprised when I was traded to Detroit. I felt sure I would be traded to somewhere, but Detroit? And then the first thing I knew—I didn't get a call from Pittsburgh to say I had been traded. I got a call from Detroit saying that I had been traded to them. And I remember telling Dorais on the telephone that I had had this injury and I didn't know how my knee was going to hold up.

Dorais wanted to meet the man who retired after an MVP season. Were the Jock Sutherland stories true? Was Bill a Little Napoleon who would try to run the team? Would he alienate the other players? He also wanted to size up the knee problem. He came to Charlottesville.

The two hit it off. Dorais was a fatherly type of coach. He didn't see in Bill anything resembling Sutherland's description of him. He offered Bill a contract contingent on the condition of Bill's knee. A doctor the team used in Los Angeles would have to bless it.

Bill had contingencies, too. He was newly married. This contract was for two. Bill was a long way from the kid who sat across the desk from Bert Bell. He wanted a three-year, no-cut contract for $20,000 per year and he wanted a $5,000 signing bonus. There was another bonus. The trip to Los Angeles to see the Detroit team doctor would double as a honeymoon. Bill would be the highest paid player in the NFL, ever.

This was new—a waiver of the injury clause. This is routine in a modern player's contract. In 1946, if a player was unable to compete, the team could release him. Bill would be paid if he played or not.

If the player contract wasn't renewed at the end of three years, Bill was guaranteed a coaching position at Detroit. This was also new. "They didn't issue those kinds of contracts very often," Bill said.

The Lions agreed as fast as Bert Bell did in 1942. The trade was made. When the news broke, the press boys didn't know where to start. Who trades an MVP? Why? And the contract—that much? Guaranteed? Three years? No cut? A signing bonus? A coaching job? The rumors flew. One had Rooney offering to rewrite Bill's Steeler contract and pay him $20,000 per year. They said that's where Bill got his number for the Lions. Another had Bill, upon learning he was traded to Detroit, crawling back to Rooney and begging for reinstatement, only to be rebuffed. Meanwhile, Sutherland tossed a few poison darts during an interview with the *Pittsburgh Post-Gazette*.

I know for a fact that a few of the boys would not have returned to the squad if Bill had rejoined us this year. When they heard the news that he had signed with the Detroit Lions, one of them remarked, "Well, Detroit got itself another coach."

It would be sixty-eight years before another NFL team traded the league's leading rusher before the following season, when DeMarco Murray left the Cowboys for the Eagles in March of 2015.

For his part, Bill understood. It wasn't personal. He never talked with Art Rooney about the trade. He never publicly or privately asked to be traded. Bill knew that Art Rooney had spent years trying to get Sutherland. Rooney couldn't choose between the two and Bill wouldn't ask him to.

If Rooney had let Bill retire, the Steelers would not have gotten any players in return. It was a big trade, and it took two weeks to nail down. On August 6, the Steelers traded Bill, along with tackle Jack Dugger, to the Detroit Lions for halfbacks Bob Cifers and Paul White, plus the rights to Michigan tailback Bob Chappuis and a first-round draft choice for 1948 that was used to take Bobby Layne. "It was like losing one of my own sons," Art Rooney said.

Bill lost his favorite owner and his favorite team and his favorite town. "People ask me which team was my favorite and I have to say Pittsburgh. It's where I played first, and where I made my reputation. People remember me better here. When I come in—and this doesn't happen in other places—somebody will pick me out of the crowd. I can be standing in front of a hotel here, and someone will holler out to me 'Hey, Bill, what the hell are you doing in town?' I've always felt at home in Pittsburgh. When I first came, being a Southerner, I was a stranger. And, so to speak, they took me in."

Guepe let Bill out of his contract at Virginia. Guepe's brother needed a job anyway. Libba and Bill sub-leased their new apartment in Charlottesville. Bill's agreement with the Lions was verbal. He didn't sign a contract until he got to training camp. However, Dorais paid the $5,000 bonus in Charlottesville. It was time for a honeymoon.

"I would not have played if I didn't have that contract," Bill said. "I discussed it with the athletic director at University of Virginia. And I discussed it with Coach Guepe, who hired me. That was the only way I would have returned to football with a guarantee of a no-cut with money."

Along with the bonus, Mandel threw in a car—a good one was about $1,500—a gesture that wasn't all that unusual for Detroit players. Libba and Bill picked out a convertible and drove cross country to Los Angeles— one at the wheel while the other suntanned in the back seat.

The knee examination required two appointments over the course of a week. Libba and Bill filled the time with Don and Honey Ameche, and also looked in on jockey Eddie Arcaro, who Bill also befriended during the war. When they visited the Ameche home, Libba noticed two things—the house was huge and many of the rooms were unfurnished. The Ameches explained that they wanted space for their kids to ride their bikes and trikes.

The knee passed the test. Bill could play. It was back in the car and straight to training camp.

The Rooney/Dudley friendship outlived the moment and lasted a lifetime. Twenty years later, Bill sent a business letter to Art Rooney. He closed it on a personal note:

You showed a young 20-year old kid a lighted pathway of life. An employee/employer relationship became a friendship, strong and silent. You gave me an opportunity to play pro ball in its early years. Bossman, you made it all possible. You provided the trust, faith and inspiration in an owner who cared. Deep down I know that God knows what Art Rooney meant to Bill Dudley.

In three months Bill Dudley went from forlorn and single and out of the NFL to the happiest man on the planet. What does the top of the world look like? For Bill, it was the open highway through his convertible's windshield—the woman of his dreams behind him, basking in the sun, and all his.

Off on a California honeymoon in a Detroit Lions convertible, 1947

CHAPTER EIGHTEEN
Time for a Jacket and Tie

DETROIT IN 1947 WAS AMONG THE WORLD'S PREMIER INDUSTRIAL CIT-ies. In Detroit they didn't say "among." Motor City didn't produce a single car for retail sale during the war. Now, everybody in the country wanted one. The economy boomed. The city was transforming into a modern, glass and steel metropolis. They got rid of the streetcars and built massive highways. Suburbs sprouted. The population reached its peak—nearing two million—during the three years Bill played for the Lions. It was one of the largest metro areas in the country.

Along with the skyscrapers, the city had its Gilded Age mansions and tree-lined boulevards. It was called The Paris of the West. The one thing it didn't have was a good football team. The Lions were 1-10 in 1946. Was that about to change? Chauncey Durden wrote:

> *Bullet Bill Dudley, professional football's highest paid performer, now gives Detroit Lions fans something to roar about. The 25-year old crackerjack back-of-all-gridiron-trades draws down a reported $25,000 per year salary, regardless of possible sidelining injuries. Dudley, a former U. of Virginia and Pittsburgh Steelers star, is the original money-back guarantee.*

When Bill and Libba rolled into Alma, Michigan, for training camp, he was once again late for camp. This time it wasn't a mistake—they were delayed by the medical exam in Los Angeles. Again it was misunderstood—this time, though, by the players.

Bill had a new reputation. It didn't sit well with the boys. They had read about the Sutherland vs. Dudley feud in the papers. They didn't know these accounts were one-sided. How could they? Bill never discussed the matter with the press. Sutherland did and he could be venomous. Would Bill try to run the team? Would he even play full-time?

On top of that, Bill brought Libba to training camp. That wasn't done. At least, it wasn't done before. Bill had it cleared by the Lions—of course they cleared it because he said if she wasn't there, he wasn't there—but the players didn't know that. It looked like a prima donna move. The players were quartered in a dorm at Alma College. Libba stayed a few blocks away. She had a room in a boarding house well within visiting distance.

Finally, there was the contract and the bonus and the car. It was an eye-popping package. The average wage for an American in 1947 was $2,850. The Detroit ballplayers were paid better, but not at the Bill Dudley level. He knew what he was getting into: "Oh yeah. When I went to Detroit, I was asked a question, 'Bill, don't you think some of the ball players resent the amount of money you make?' I said, 'I can't control that. The only thing I can do is to try to show up and do my work.'"

Which he did. Although Bill knew and liked two players on the team—Tippy Madarik from the Randolph Ramblers, and Bob Westfall from the Army All-Star team—Bill knew he had to win over the players on his own. "I guess the fellows needed to be shown I was alright."

He knew only one way to accomplish that—play like he always played. He settled the matter at the first exhibition game at Battle Creek. Coach Dorais had excused Bill from the game. Bill played anyway and at one point came out of the game with a nasty gash on his lip. He had it stitched up on the sidelines and went back in. That, and the fact that he practiced like he was trying to make the team, was enough for his teammates. At the end of camp, they voted Bill team captain. He got every vote, but one—his own. He was elected captain all three years he played there.

Gus Dorais was a solid football man. He was an All-America quarter-back at Notre Dame. For years, he and teammate Knute Rockne were credited with inventing the forward pass in the 1913 season, although it had been legal since 1906.

They weren't the first overall, but Dorais-to-Rockne was the first high-profile passing combo. In a 1913 game against Army, Dorais was 14 of 17, passing for 243 yards and three touchdowns. His 40-yard completion to Rockne was record length. Army didn't know what hit them. The game changed college football. Dorais went on to be a successful college football coach—he had a .672 winning percentage between 1914 and 1942—and is in the College Football Hall of Fame. He'd coached the Detroit Lions to losing seasons through the war years.

The 1947 season was to be his last as a coach, although he was only fifty-six. The season was preceded by a family tragedy.

Bill: "Gus had a child drown right in front of him about a week before training camp started. His wife saw it, too. Gus didn't recover from it. He just wasn't into coaching the whole season. It affected the season and probably cut short his life. Gus was just there. He was never the same man I met in Charlottesville."

Frank Murray always said Bill would have been one of football's greatest receivers if he didn't have to throw the ball, too. It was time to see if Murray was right. In the Dorais offense, Bill would still be in position to carry the ball, but he was also the man in motion and pass receiver coming out of the backfield. Bill threw only four passes in 1947. Receiving exploited a new Dudley talent and it lowered the wear and tear on his body, which was a good thing—his knee was never 100 percent that year.

His devotion to his marriage stayed at 100 percent and never dipped. Libba had Bill fully housebroken early. He was a willing participant. He had roomed the last nine years with football players and soldiers. The old habits died fast.

Libba rarely heard the word "no" in her home. Unlike so many postwar couples, they didn't buy a house. Not that they couldn't afford one—

the average price was $6,600—but the children of Dutch Leininger and Jewell Dudley weren't ready to spend that kind of money. Bill had a three-year contract. It was long for football, but short in the lifespan of a mortgage. They lived in a motel apartment.

Libba joined the Junior League and soon her southern charm drew the attention of Amy Whitehead, wife of prominent Detroiter James Whitehead. The Whiteheads became good friends. They introduced the Dudleys to the Country Club of Detroit in affluent Grosse Pointe. Bill was now a very long way from his twenty-three-dollar suit.

The jacket and tie conventions of the University of Virginia served Bill well in Grosse Pointe. The grace and poise that made Libba the toast of Lynchburg worked even better. Coupled with Bill's newfound fame, they won over Grosse Pointe. Bill was no longer loafing with the boys.

Bill: "If you have Libba out front running interference, it's hard not to succeed."

Lions owner Fred Mandel wasn't Art Rooney. He didn't try to be. He did, though, go out of his way to keep his players happy. The team threw parties where players drew raffle tickets for cars. The training facilities were first rate. You didn't have to wait for a heat treatment. The players were well equipped.

The Lions started out limping and never got to full speed. The season started with three away games. The Lions were out of Pittsburgh's division, but Bill's first game of the season was in Forbes Field.

At the coin flip, Detroit captain Dudley watched as Jock Sutherland came off the bench and joined them at midfield. Sutherland shook Bill's hand and wished him well. It was a show. The fans loved it. Bill thought it was hogwash.

The Lions lost a close one, 17–10, and there was little satisfaction for Bill when the locals cheered his 30-yard touchdown reception. One cheering fan, though, meant something. Jewell Dudley traveled to Pittsburgh to see her son play. It was the only game Bill recalled her attending, but according to Libba, she should have seen more, because Libba "never saw her get so excited."

The second game was a 45–21 drubbing by the Chicago Cardinals. In game three, the Lions finally got a win, beating the Boston Braves 21–7 in a contest that was all Dudley. Detroit scored twice in the first quarter on a 64-yard Dudley pass reception and 41-yard Dudley interception return. Bill threw for a touchdown in the fourth quarter.

Dorais was listless. The win didn't lift him. By week four, he was done. On the train to game four in Chicago, he delivered what is surely the least stirring pep talk in the annals of football.

Bill: "Gus gets us together and he says, 'We're here to play the big bad Bears. We're going to get the hell kicked out of us, get back on the train, get drunk, go home and get fired.' He didn't get fired until the end of the season. Otherwise, that's what happened."

He didn't take Gus to heart. On the first Chicago possession, he returned a punt 84 yards for a touchdown. On the first Detroit possession, he got his second concussion.

When I came to I didn't know where I was. I asked the guy sitting next to me on the bench, "Where are we?" He said, "Chicago." I said, "Who are we playing?" He said, "The Bears." I said, "Am I married?" He said, "Yes, to Libba. Now shut up and let me watch the game."

I looked at game film the next week. They guy who hit me was a friend of mine. I played with him in the service. Name was Davis. In those days, the tape we used came in boxes. Davis had one of those boxes taped around his arm. It was like concrete. He hit me upside the head. God, I was mad.

When the Bears came back to Detroit (later that season), we ran the first play at him. I didn't try to make yardage. I threw both feet at his face, but I missed him. He said, "Whoa, Bill. Let's talk after the game is over." After the game he said, "I felt real bad about Chicago, but you didn't deserve to be on the same field as us and you were beating us. Coach (Hunk) Adams read us the riot act on the sidelines. He said, 'You're supposed to be so tough and so mean. If you don't take out the first person you hit, you'll answer to me.' You were the first person."

Now, a great majority of players are kind-hearted. They're some that I think try to injure you. It's not that they really want to personally hurt you. They think, "If we get him out of the game, we stand a better chance of winning the game."

A lot of people tend to miss tackles when they try to hurt the runner. They're trying to hit 'em up high and really knock the hell out of 'em. But there are very damn few people in the game that have the ability to try to injure somebody and at the same time make the tackle. Most the time they try to injure a player when somebody is already holding him, and they're going in there as the second man or third man.

I never hurt anybody.

Forearm clubbing was banned two seasons later in college ball. NFL rules later prohibited it.

For the rest of the season, the Lions had two wins, beating the Giants 35–7 and the Redskins 38–21. The rest of the games weren't even close. They finished 3-9. Gus got fired. Mandel sold the club.

Murray may have been on to something. Bill played in nine games and caught touchdown passes in seven of them. For the year, he caught 27 passes for 375 yards. For the first time, he wasn't his team's leading rusher. He rushed 302 yards on 80 carries. He passed for two touchdowns. He returned punts for 182 yards and kicks for 359 yards. He punted for 657 yards. He was third in the league in all-purpose yardage. He led the team in scoring with 66 points. He was named the NFL's Defensive Player of the Year.

A news article at season's end addressed Bill's salary. The minimum wage in 1947 was forty cents an hour. Was a football player worth that much more? The reporter compared the Detroit gate receipts for 1946 and 1947. There was a $60,000 increase. The writer concluded that having the league's most feared punt and kick returner and interception artist, even on a losing team, was a bargain.

In 1947, the Yankees beat the Dodgers and Jackie Robinson in the first televised World Series. Major League Baseball and the National Hockey League both set up pension plans in 1947. Television and unions. At the time, the two events seemed unrelated to Bill. This would change a decade later.

After the season, it was back to Charlottesville to pick up the abandoned Spanish studies. Three credit hours down, three to go. When Bill and Libba returned to Detroit in the fall, they needed a bigger apartment. There was a baby on the way. But, first, there was a trip to Hollywood.

Columbia Pictures had contracted Bill to play himself in a seventy-minute film, *Triple Threat*. The plot: An egotistical college football star gets a shot at the NFL. He almost blows the chance and loses his girl, too, until his attitude changes.

It starred Richard Crane, a leading man in B-movies who went on to serials—he became Rocky Jones, Space Ranger—and TV westerns. It also starred Gloria Henry, who would become familiar to many as the mother of Dennis the Menace in the 1960s TV series. There was tough-guy character actor John Litel. There was also Mary Stuart, who later spent forty years on daytime TV's *Search for Tomorrow*. The soap plot married her four times. She ended with the character name Joanne Gardner Barron Tate Vincente Tourneur.

The real draw, though, was a cast of many genuine football stars, including Sammy Baugh, Steve Van Buren, Tom Harmon, Paul Christman, Sid Luckman, Charlie Trippi, "Indian Jack" Jacobs, Johnny Clement, "Boley" Dancewicz, Bob Waterfield (who was married to actress Jane Russell), and Bill Dudley. They all played themselves in walk-on roles. Hollywood didn't impress Bill: "It was ten days on the set. Libba and I went out there. It was a farce. The so-called star couldn't run from here to the door. I never saw the movie. A friend of mine saw it on the late, late, late, late show and said it was the worst movie he'd ever seen. We got $1,500 and a vacation."

When he returned to the team in 1948, Bill understood his situation in Detroit. It can take years to build a winning program. Bill figured the Lions were five years away. He had two years left on his contract. Edwin Anderson of Goebel Brewing Co., and Lyle Fife, owner of Detroit's Fife Electric Supply Co., bought the team in January for $165,000. Bo McMillin was brought in to coach, bringing Bill's relationship with Marshall Shearer full circle. McMillin was a College Hall of Fame coach with a 140-77-13 record. He wouldn't fare as well in the NFL.

"He knew football, but he could not communicate with the pros very well even though he had played pro ball," Bill said. "I think it boils down to personality. McMillin could not make the transfer—I don't know why, but it just wasn't there. He brought his line coach from Indiana, but he wasn't a good line coach in the pros, and other teams were setting up both defensive and offensive coaches."

If nothing else, the 1948 season would sound different. Officials began using whistles instead of horns.

The team struggled. McMillin had conflicts with players—not including, interestingly, Bill. The team never got off the ground and never got out of the cellar, two apt cliches, and ended the season 2-10. Bill was injured much of the season—bruised ribs, a shoulder separation, and a bad toe. He couldn't get his shoe on. Like other players of the day, Bill functioned as his own equipment manager. He cut the shoe and put a pad in it.

He was out for five games, but he led the team in scoring. In seven games he caught six touchdown passes. He caught 20 passes for 210 yards. He returned kicks for 210 yards. He punted for 825 yards. He had his lowest rushing total—97 yards—ever.

But the spectacular plays kept coming. In one game, he silenced the crowd at Tiger Stadium when he performed a back flip to catch a pass that was thrown behind him.

Along with the new whistles, there were other firsts in 1948. It was the highest-scoring season in NFL history. The average score per game was 46.48 points. The record would stand for sixty-five years.

Plain leather helmets were becoming history, replaced by plain plastic helmets. In Los Angeles, a Rams halfback named Fred Gehrke painted a horn on each side of his new plastic helmet. The rest, if not history, is helmetry.

For the first time, Bill didn't return to Virginia after the season. Bill and Libba's first daughter, Jarrett, was born in December. Telegrams poured in from across the country. Only a year and a half before, Bill was single and ready to ditch the game. Today, he was a family man with a salary that made headlines.

A new team, a new town, a new wife, a new child—it was time to harken to the advice Bert Bell delivered when Bill signed his first contract. Bill needed to begin a career outside the game. By 1948, paychecks in the NFL were big enough that working the offseason was a choice. Some players did. Some didn't. Bill worked for the Ford Motor Company. It was the Bluefield Dudley in him. He couldn't just sit there.

Some ball players would not take a job for less than what they were earning, which I never did understand. And so I worked in their (Ford) farm division and traveled from Detroit to the farm area and worked on farm tractors.

My job was to teach in the mechanic school. Mechanics would come in from all over the country. We'd start on a Monday. We'd take a Ford tractor apart and put it back together again. It took a week.

It must have been quite a job interview. Throughout his life, Bill never owned a tool, which meant he hurled borrowed tools to the floor on those too-late Christmas Eves when he had to assemble a bicycle or a doll's house. Again it was the Bluefield Dudley determination. He mastered the tractor.

There were other changes in his life. He was becoming more than a sports figure. He was becoming a celebrity.

Toots Shor was the legendary owner of a legendary restaurant in Manhattan that attracted America's biggest celebrities in the 1940s and 50s. He referred to it as a saloon. He was a big man—his saloon career started as a bouncer—and he held his friends close. Shor didn't defer to celebrities. Fame didn't guarantee you a table. If he didn't like you, you waited in line, no matter who you were. If he liked you, he was a loyal friend and admirer. People he liked, he called "crum-bums." Jackie Gleason was a crum-bum. Charlie Chaplin was not. After Don Ameche introduced Bill to Shor, Bill Dudley became a crum-bum. Pay attention to the classic film *White Christmas* and you'll hear Bing Crosby, a crum-bum, give the restaurant a plug.

Professional football was growing in the public mind. Bill's MVP season in Pittsburgh put him above the horizon and into the public eye in a way that could never have happened before the war. His move to Detroit and his headline-making salary put him into rarified air. He was famous and it was okay with him, sort of.

Bill: "Everybody likes to be known, to be spoken to. It's nice getting a good table at a fancy restaurant. But, what does that have to do with life?"

If he arrived alone at Toots Shor's saloon, Toots seated him with another sports figure or celebrity—Bill got to know Joe DiMaggio, among others. If he arrived with Libba, they got a prominent table. Onlookers looked and photographers snapped. Bill and Libba often went out with Bob Waterfield and Jane Russell. The photo boys shot Libba as much as Jane, a source of everlasting delight for Bill.

They were high times. A night out in Florida with the Ameches turned into a weekend in Havana. Tommy Dorsey cooked a late night breakfast in their kitchen. A decade after he stopped playing, Bill took his daughter, Becca, into P.J. Clarke's, the famous Manhattan bar, and he was greeted at the door: "It's been a long time, Mr. Dudley. Good to see you back."

Bill had a good season in 1949. He was healthy. He played all twelve games and showed the old Dudley form, including one of his patented punt returns—67 yards for a touchdown against Green Bay.

But it was a good season with a struggling team. Detroit went 4-8. They were losing close games. McMillin's relations with the players soured.

For the season, Bill led the team in rushing with 402 yards. He caught 27 passes for 190 yards. He returned kicks for 246 yards. He punted for 1,278 yards. He led the team in scoring with 81 points.

It was contract time. If the Lion's didn't renew Bill's contract or trade him, he could exercise the coaching option. They traded him to the Redskins. "If I didn't play, they would keep me on as a coach and pay me a salary of $12,500. When they traded me to the Redskins, I think it was because McMillin was afraid I might want to exercise the coaching option. He didn't want to have anything to do with that. He didn't want to feel like he had to hire me. And I can understand that."

With the Washington trade, it was back to Virginia for Bill and Libba. There was another baby on the way.

Bill was right about rebuilding the Lions in five years. It took four. After Bill was traded in 1950, Buddy Parker succeeded McMillin and Detroit picked up Doak Walker, Bobby Layne, and Leon Hart. When the Lions won back-to-back championships in 1952-53, they had four Hall of Fame players on the roster. Bill had missed another shot at a title.

The Anderson and Fife consortium sold the Lions in 1963 for $4.5 million.

In the spring of 1950, Bill received his diploma from the University of Virginia. He took on Spanish and won.

CHAPTER NINETEEN

Sam Baugh, Yale, and the Desire to Be Ordinary

If the South had a home team in the 1950s, it was the Washington Redskins. Owner George Preston Marshall controlled the radio rights for most of the South and was early to embrace television. Southern Railway's flagship passenger train, the "All Pullman" Crescent, pulled into Union Station every Sunday morning, midway in its New Orleans to Newark route, packed with fans.

When Bill sat down with Marshall to discuss his standing after the Detroit trade, Bill needed some persuasion. There was so much up in the air. Bill was losing interest in football. He had a family. His brother, Jim, wanted him to consider a career in life insurance. Although he and Libba hadn't really settled in Detroit, he could work for Ford again. "Marshall and I got to talking. I told him I didn't care if I played or not. Marshall was expansive. He was always expansive. He said, 'You're gonna like it here, Bill. This is my sole business. This is my only income. We run it like a business.'"

Bill signed a two-year contract. It was a pay cut—to $12,500 per year—but the Redskins had one thing that made it worthwhile for Bill. They had Sammy Baugh.

Sam Baugh was the best football player I ever saw. I know people will differ with me on this, but I watched him play and I played against him and I played with him. I learned from him. Modern quarterbacks, I don't think there is any comparison. They might throw the football better, but Sam did everything. He had a rifle for an arm. He was a good punter and an excellent safetyman. He was a better runner than most people gave him credit for.

He was tall and nimble, so he could move around and see. He was a great competitor. If Sam Baugh made up his mind to win a game, you knew you had a chance. He'd get you closer than anyone else could. He was the epitome of success.

I can see him now, coming back to the huddle. You could tell he saw something over there and he'd design a play in the huddle. A pass pattern or a running play. He'd say, "You do this and you do that. Let's go." If you weren't in the play, he'd say, "You just mess around out there." In other words, get out of the way.

In the NFL, I dropped only one forward pass I could have caught and it was from Sam. I was wide open. The defensive back was five yards off me. Sam hits me with a perfect pass in the chest. I dropped it. The defensive back came up and said, "Bill, I never thought I'd see that." When I got back to the huddle, Sam was laughing.

There are Old South towns and there are New South towns. New South towns look different from Old South towns—more glass, less brick. Old South towns feel different—more tradition, less aspiration. An Old South town seems smaller than a New South town, even if it's bigger. Lynchburg, Virginia, is an Old South town.

In 1950, it was the fifth-largest population center in the state after Richmond, Northern Virginia, Tidewater, and Roanoke. But it was still small enough for the local paper to publish a five-column headline: "Bill Dudley to Build House in Lynchburg."

It was an easy choice for Bill and Libba. They had considered Charlottesville, but Lynchburg was Libba's hometown. Bill had friends in Lynchburg. There was a commuter train to Washington—the Crescent made a stop there. And the Dudleys needed a house instead of an apartment. The family was bigger.

Little Bill Dudley was born in December 1949. He arrived prematurely while the Dudleys were visiting in Bluefield. The baby had to stay in the hospital until he reached six pounds. It was an anxious stay in Bluefield. Hospital policy forbade parents from spending the night in the building. No amount of persuasion from a distraught mother could overcome the rules. Little Bill eventually gained his weight and was released.

In Lynchburg, Bill and Libba moved in with Libba's parents, found a place to rent for a bit, and then decided to build, giving the *News & Advance* their scoop.

Life in Lynchburg also fulfilled what Bill's son, Jim, would later describe as a "desire to be ordinary." Bill had been a celebrity since that Navy game when he was seventeen. "He never had a chance to not be idolized," said Jim. "The trappings of supreme accomplishment didn't seem to appeal to him. He'd seen things at the top that didn't appeal to him—unsavory things you have to put up with to get and stay there."

Bert Bell might as well have been whispering in Bill's ear. The football money will stop. Then what? Bill wanted a regular job, a regular house, and a regular family. You could do that in Lynchburg. It was big enough to allow him to make a living. It was small enough that Lynchburgers would eventually quit noticing him.

Bill rented an apartment in Washington with Sam Baugh. He would commute by train during the season. They were easy roommates. Both were clean livers. Both were quiet at home. Both lived football during the season and lived life in the offseason. If Baugh had a vice, it was pinball. Bill always said the man couldn't walk past a machine without playing it. If there were a football stat compiled for roommates, Baugh/Dudley would be the champs, hands down. Lifetime stats combined:

Games: 255
Yards rushing: 3,382
Yards passing: 25,268
Yards receiving: 1,383
Yards punting: 22,549
Punt return yardage: 1,614
Kick return yardage: 1,743
Field goals: 66

Extra points: 122
Interceptions: 54

It was another season of change. A new child, a new team, a new town, a new house, and a new rule. For the 1950 season, the NFL adopted unlimited substitution. Every team knew it was coming—the league experimented with it in 1949—and had already developed separate offensive and defensive teams and schemes. The day of the specialist had dawned. The two-way, triple-threat back was on his way out.

Players could now develop narrower sets of skills for specific positions. They could also develop their bodies. A two-way football player was an endurance athlete, and looked it. They played at their natural weight. A shirtless Bronko Nagurski reveals the physique of a modern tri-athlete or, to keep it in the era, Johnny Weissmuller in the early Tarzan films.

What football needed now was a player who could deliver extraordinary bursts of strength and speed for intermittent rounds of plays. Could a player today bulked up with thirty or forty extra weight-room pounds even go a full sixty minutes? We'll never know.

Now football needed players with highly developed single skills, especially kickers or punters. As training and positions became more customized, the NFL team roster limit grew from thirty-two in 1950 to fifty-three (with a game day roster of forty-five) today. It was the end of the triple threat back. Unlimited substitution may have been a factor when the rebuilding Detroit team traded Bill. "When the game went one way, coaches didn't know what to do with me."

The one-way game took Bill out of the flow of game.

The biggest thing that people don't realize—if you're just on offense or just on defense, you're not actually active more than 15 to 30 minutes during a whole game. You don't get to know the opponent. If you're playing just one way, you don't get to know them. If I'm just playing offense, then I don't get to know any of the offense players we play against. You never see 'em hardly.

Bill expected a good season for the Redskins. He was in a backfield with Baugh; Charlie "Choo Choo" Justice, just drafted after an All-Star Military and College Hall of Fame career; and Rob Goode, the number 8 pick in the 1949 draft. Bill no longer needed persuasion from Marshall. He was ready to play. His knee was back.

Bill: "I had a good start and good cut and good balance. Coach (Herman) Ball was a real student of the game, and excellent tactician. We started out like we were going to have a pretty good team, but it turned into an average year."

It was worse than average. The Redskins were 3-9 in 1950. They walloped the Baltimore Colts in game one, 38–14, and then lost the next eight games. Only two of the games were close—a 21–17 loss to the Giants and a 24–21 loss to the Giants. Baugh was thirty-six.

Still, the Dudley legend was burnished. The second to the last game was played against the Steelers on a wet and muddy Forbes Field. In the first quarter, Steeler Joe Geri kicked a 60-yard, coffin corner punt, headed out of bounds at the Redskin 3 yard line. Bill beat the ball to the 3, put his toes on the line, reached across, and brought the ball in. He eyed the nearby official. Yes, he was inbounds. He faked to the middle and went up the sideline as the Washington blocking formed. The Steelers never knew what hit them. It was a 97-yard touchdown return.

Art Rooney: "I noticed some kids sitting on our bench had jumped up and were running alongside Dudley, cheering 'Go, Bill, Go!' They were my own sons.

"People came up to me and said, 'Your sons are cheering against the Steelers.' I said, 'No, they're cheering for Bill Dudley.'"

Bill: "I had some of my best days, peck on wood, on muddy fields. The number one thing to remember about weather is that they've got the same conditions you do. On mud you gotta run a little more flat footed—you can't get up on your toes, because you can't get your trac-tion with just your toe in the mud. And it didn't affect my speed—I was slow anyway."

For the year, Bill rushed for 339 yards and caught 22 passes for 172 yards. He returned punts for 182 yards and was 31 for 31 in extra point attempts. He led the team in scoring. He had two interceptions.

The All-Star Game returned to the NFL in 1950 after being suspended since the 1942 game. The game was renamed the Pro Bowl and the format was changed. The stars didn't play the season champions. The league was now divided into two conferences that played each other. It was a close game. Bill's American Conference team, coached by Paul Brown, lost 28–27, but the fans witnessed Bill crawling for a touchdown. "In that era if you were knocked down, you could get back up and run. You had to be tackled. I caught a punt, the blocking set up and I went down the sidelines. I see Paul Brown running with me. He was outrunning me. I was knocked down at the two. I crawled over."

When Bill played in Detroit, Libba attended home games. Bill rode to the stadium early with other players. She followed him to the stadium later, taking in the game with other players' wives and girlfriends, and waiting for him outside the locker room after the game. There she had the pleasure of watching her husband work his way through a crowd of female autograph seekers until he arrived at her. She taught herself the game, using a book.

Now, in Lynchburg, the home games were a train ride away and there was a toddler and a baby in the house. She could still watch the games, though. There was something new—the Redskins games were televised.

During the season, Bill spent most of the week in Washington. He took the train home after the Sunday game and returned Tuesday for practice.

The next season got off to a rotten start. The Redskins lost the first three games in 1951. After a 45–0 rout by Cleveland, Marshall fired Herman Ball and replaced him with former Washington star Dick Todd. To Bill, this was just the Marshall style. "George Marshall was a micromanager. He didn't believe in getting coaches he couldn't tell what to do. He called the shots. He ran the thing."

Under Todd, the Redskins were 5-4 for the rest of the season. The biggest win was a 31–21 defeat of the Los Angeles Rams, who went on to win the NFL championship.

Bill had a great year kicking. He nailed 10 of 13 field goal attempts for a 76.9 percent average. He didn't start a game, but he rushed for 398 yards and caught passes for 303 yards. He returned punts for 172 yards and kicks for 248 yards. He punted for 942 yards. He led the team in scoring.

Bill was thirty-one. It was "then what?" time. "I had no agreement with Washington beyond the two years. They really weren't talking to me. I'd developed some bursitis in my knee. When that acts up, you can't run. I was going to get out of football."

Then, he got a call from Herman Hickman at Yale. Was Bill interested in coaching the Yale backfield? Yes. Then it got complicated.

Herman hired me in May. In July, he gets fired. Jordan Olivar was the new coach. He didn't know me from Adam. At our first meeting, he didn't know the line coach, either. Hickman had just hired him, too. Olivar was a good head coach. He said, "We don't know each other, so let's get started on the right foot. Anything that happens at any time—training camp, regular season—it's my decision. It's not yours. It's not (line coach) Joe's. It's Coach Olivar's."

Olivar was Bill's kind of coach. He was a no-nonsense football man who compiled winning seasons in eight of the next ten years at Yale, including two Ivy League titles. Yale went 7-2 that year, outscoring opponents 240–120, and providing the Ivy League with a moment that angered Harvard men for the next fifty years.

The final game of the season was Yale vs. Harvard. It was a blowout. Yale had just scored a touchdown and was ahead 40–14 in the fourth quarter when Olivar put the team manager, Charlie Yeager—all 137 pounds of him—into the game for the extra point. When Yeager, out of nowhere, got open on a rollout play, Yale quarterback Ed Molloy tossed him a pass for the extra point. Cries of poor sportsmanship echoed through the Crimson stadium.

The Yale Daily News: *"The diminutive Yale manager rubbed salt, pure unadulterated salt into Harvard wounds when he caught a Molloy flip for the Blue 41st point."*

What nobody knew at the time was that Olivar had promised Yeager he'd get him in a game before the season ended. Harvard was the final game. At halftime, Olivar told Yeager to suit up. It was less an insult to Harvard than a promise fulfilled to the little manager. Who knew the kid could get open?

Actually, fifty years may be too short a timespan. There may still be some Harvard men out there who haven't forgiven Olivar.

Bill got $5,000 for the season. It was a nice paycheck, but he didn't make it home much that fall. He lived on campus and made scouting trips on weekends.

The NFL came looking for a player one last time in 1953. Marshall called from the Redskins. Was Bill interested in coaching the backs? They were 4-8 under new coach Curly Lambeau in 1952. They were rebuilding. Bill went up to Washington and agreed to coach for $5,000. Then Marshall upped the negotiations.

Marshall: *"What if I want you to play?"*
Dudley: *"You'll have to pay me more."*
Marshall: *"I just want you to kick, play some D."*
Dudley: *"I'll need more money."*
Marshall: *"I don't want to do that."*

Dudley: "If we have a good year, you'll pay me an extra $1,500. If we don't, you don't owe me a dime."
Marshall: "Who makes the decision?"
Dudley: "You will. If you don't think I've earned it, don't give it to me. If you think I did, then you do."

Marshall agreed. Bill Dudley was now a player-coach. Too bad Jock Sutherland wasn't there to see it. Marshall was right, sort of. Bill was a placekicker, but he played more than a little D. He played in every game.

Sam Baugh was gone, retired at age thirty-eight. He was replaced by Eddie LeBaron. The Redskins still had Charlie Justice and they still had Pro-Bowler Hugh Taylor, Baugh's favorite receiver. Both had good seasons. Justice rushed for 616 yards and caught passes for 434 yards. Taylor had 703 yards receiving. The Redskins eked out a winning season, going 6-5-1.

For the season, Bill kicked 11 field goals and made all 25 extra point attempts. He led the team in scoring, although it was his only season without a touchdown.

He loved coaching, especially working with the rookies during games and at practice. He fit the player/coach role well. "I knew most of the players. They knew me. It wasn't a problem. I worked with the younger players. I didn't try to tell the veterans what to do."

It was barely a winning season, but it was a winning season—at one point they had a shot at second in the division—and Bill played every game. At season's end, he went back to Marshall.

The 'Skins used to hold back 10–15% of your money, in case you got in trouble or got drunk or had a bad debt. That was returned in your final check. I went into Marshall's offices and looked at my check. The secretary says, "Is something wrong?" I said, "I thought I was getting more money." She says, "Mr. Marshall is in. Do you want to see him." I said, "Yes, ma'am."

Now, Marshall always had this big desk that was set up so he was looking down on you. He said, "Hello, Bill!" He was very expansive. He said, "How's it going. You ready to go home?" I said I was. He said, "What do you want to see me about?" I said, "Do you recall our discussion earlier in the season?" He said, "About what?" I related the story to him. He said, "Do you think you earned it?" I said, "Sir, it's up to you. That was our deal." He called the secretary and had her write me another check.

That was Marshall. If you didn't ask him for it, you didn't get it.

Bill now wanted one more year on the field. He thought he wasn't used properly in either Detroit or Washington. He could have contributed more. When he looked at the upcoming Steeler team, he felt he could contribute there. But Marshall owned Bill's trade rights, even though his contract was over. Free agency for players was a long way away.

Bill: Pittsburgh tried to get permission from Marshall to let me play there in '56. Marshall wanted the sun and moon. Today, it's no problem. If you don't play for a club for a year or so and another approaches, you have the right to deal with them.

Bill dropped the idea. In an odd reversal, when the reserve clause was challenged by the players association in 1970, Bill testified against it at a Senate hearing.

Football came calling again in December when Carroll Rosenbloom invited Bill to Baltimore.

I got a call from Carroll Rosenbloom. I'd known him for some time. My father in law worked for him. He wanted to know if I would coach. I said, "What did you have in mind?" He said, "Coach the Colts." I had already turned down two coaching opportunities, but I said, "I'll consider it on a five year contract." He said, "How about three?" I said, "I have a family. I think I can do it in five years. It will take five years to give you a winner." Carroll said, "I'm thinking more in terms of three." He hired Weeb Eubank. I believe Weeb gave him a championship five years later.

I felt like I might be doing my family an injustice because you never know where you're going—there are very few places that I wanted to coach in college or pro—and you have to be willing to move and I didn't want to move because I liked Lynchburg. We started to raise a family, and the old saying goes: "You give up something you get something and you hope that what you choose to get, you get more out of."

Bill kept in touch with Sam Baugh for the rest of his life, mostly by telephone. With the exception of his Hall of Fame induction, Baugh never appeared at any NFL or Redskin functions. He refused to fly. Baugh coached briefly at the pro and college levels and took a shot at acting in Hollywood westerns. After that he retired to his Texas ranch and stayed put.

Sam Baugh: "We always wondered how he (Dudley) gained as much yardage as he did. But he had that instinct. He would do things that always amazed me, how he could get out of trouble. I admired him when we played against him. I was happy as hell when we got him."

Nine years. Nine coaches. No championships. For Bill Dudley, it was time for something new.

CHAPTER TWENTY

Elephant Hunting with a Pen

ELEPHANT HUNTERS USUALLY DON'T LAST LONG IN THE LIFE INSUR-
ance game. These are the agents who go into the business to pursue
top-tier clients only. A typical elephant hunter gets in the business,
places policies with affluent friends, and fades away when he runs out
of affluent friends.

Successful life insurance agents learn the basics of calling on people.
It's 10-3-1. You call on ten people. Three will see you. One will buy. If
you want to sell two policies a week, you have to call on twenty people.
You don't have that many friends. You have to make cold calls. "You can't
sell a man insurance by throwing a football at him," Bill said. "Insurance
is not a business where the work comes to you. I can count on one hand
the number of people who came to me asking to buy a policy."

Successful agents sweat the small stuff. You walk into a workday
with an open schedule. The phone rings. A client has noticed that her
son's middle name is misspelled on the policy. You hang up and work the
problem through the system. You call the client back: problem solved. It's
a half hour of your day. Sometimes, your entire day is made up of these
half hours. And, of course, there are days when a client dies. Big or small,
you service the clients as the issues arise.

Good life insurance agents are the opposite of the smooth salesman
caricature. They are better listeners than talkers.

Bill: "In the estate planning business, you try to make people realize they are individuals. One shoe doesn't fit all. Yours might be the same style, but it isn't the same shoe."

These are the lessons Bill learned from his brother, Jim. By 1950, Jim was an agency manager for Home Life in Richmond, Virginia. After the 1950 season, Jim approached his little brother. Football wouldn't last much longer. What did he want to do?

Bert Bell's admonition in 1942 was never far from Bill's mind. Bill had an offer to go into the real estate business in Charlottesville. It was a good company, but it was in Charlottesville and it meant leaving Lynchburg. There was coaching, but that, too, meant leaving town. A radio station in Lynchburg was for sale. He was mulling it.

Jim Dudley: "I want you to think about life insurance."
Bill: "I don't know anything about life insurance. I can't do that."
Jim Dudley: "Dammit, you haven't tried. I'll pay you whatever anybody else will pay you. But, I'm your big brother. You gotta do what the Hell I tell you and agree to do it for two years."

He had to have an office—no working out of the home—and he had to be out of the house by 8:30 every morning. Bill did what his brother demanded. "I had a lot of love and respect for my older brother. He was the best life insurance man I ever saw. He was honest. He was one of the most principled men I ever met. I did what he told me to do. It was a pretty good decision."

Life insurance is a tough business. The product is an intangible, so agents can be perceived as hustlers. For the buyer, comprehending life insurance requires confronting one's own mortality. Bill soon learned that what Jim predicted was true—some people he knew crossed the street when they saw him coming.

Selling policies to friends at startup was frowned upon at Home Life. Elephant hunting and all that. Bill didn't care. If his friends didn't believe in him, who would? He developed a sales method and used it unchanged over the course of his career. He warmed up his cold calls. He sent letters to potential customers telling them to expect a call and followed up as he worked his way through his list.

His fame opened doors. A lot of people just wanted to see what he looked like up close. Once he was in the door, though, he was just another insurance salesman. Home Life had a philosophy: offer estate planning service to anyone who would talk with you. Translation: no elephant hunters.

Home Life had a system. The agent interviewed a potential client for about fifteen minutes. A questionnaire followed—it took about thirty minutes to fill—and afterwards, the agent had a profile to work with. Work the system right and you'd get four interviews a month and make at least one sale. Bill averaged two sales. He believed in what he sold. He considered the interview and questionnaire a service.

I was convinced and still am, that I can help any man that I sit down and talk to. I can help him plan for his family. Whether he buys life insurance from me, I don't care. My older brother convinced me of that. You show them what you can do and what you're going to do and you do it. Then the business will take care of itself. I can honestly say, that once I started doing that, there were very few times where I worried about where the next sale was going to come from.

There's no fooling around. In a real sales discussion, three out of four people I talk to end up recognizing a need. Many times selling is a question of personalities, of being able to communicate. If I can't make a person see a need, I know I don't have a sale. The reverse is also true, though. But I've found that most people want to do the right thing if they only know what the right thing is."

He never talked business in social settings. He wrote the letters and made the calls, but he discovered that referrals were his biggest source of business. His clients were mostly owners of small businesses—construction, retail, and the professions—in central Virginia. His best publicity came from settled claims. If it was settled well, word got around. He considered his product important and sometimes the Dudley bluntness came into play. He could, and did, walk out on the occasional customer.

I'm convinced that anybody who is worth something should start out with a basic life insurance. If you live or die, you have a responsibility. I had one fellow who said "If I died tomorrow, it would be just tough luck on my wife and children." And I said, "What do you mean, tough luck?" He says, "If I don't have any life insurance it would be tough luck." And I said, "Well, who's responsible for taking care of them?" And he said, "Oh, someone will take care of them." I got up and said, "I'll see you later." There was no common ground, so I just left. If he didn't understand his responsibility to his own wife and children, then the point was moot.

Every insurance company has some version of The Million Dollar Roundtable—an honor for the top 5 percent of producers. If you're an agent, that's your goal. Bill grew his business, taking off each fall to play or coach football. He doubled his sales in the first three years—$300,000 to $600,000. By 1959, the year after he stopped coaching, he had a seat at the roundtable.

Smith Ferebee liked, among other things, golf and gambling. He won his first big bet by playing 144 holes of golf in a single day. In 1938, his business partner challenged him to another golf marathon—600 holes of golf in eight cities, coast to coast, over four consecutive days. That translates to thirty-three complete 18-hole rounds. At stake was 296 acres of waterfront property in Virginia.

Ferebee did it. The stunt attracted a national following. Celebrities showed up. When he finished rounds in the dark, spectators lit the course with their auto headlights. He never lost a ball. He was thirty-two. Afterwards, he went into the insurance business. By 1961 he managed the Richmond office for The Equitable.

In 1961, he thought he had a shot at another winner. Jim Dudley left Richmond to take over the Atlanta office of Home Life. Perhaps his famous brother was available. He made a simple pitch to Bill: Everybody needs a coach, including him. Bill agreed. He also issued a subtle challenge to his competitive prospect. "You're top dog in Jim Dudley's agency. You'll be half a dog in mine."

It was hard to turn down a guy like Ferebee. With brother Jim's blessing, Bill joined The Equitable.

Bill ran The Equitable office like he ran his paper route as a kid. It was full speed. Football is a full force game of dodging opponents now and stopping them later. Insurance is a gentle game of persuasion. During a football season, if Bill's team won on Sunday, he allowed himself to feel good about it until Tuesday. In the insurance business there is no season and you need to win at least twice a week to break even. Bill allowed no time for adjustment to this new game, if he even saw the need. Peggy Moody, his secretary for forty years, started working for him straight from college. He was demanding—that Bluefield hardwearing ethic was in force.

"Many a day I went home and cried," Moody remembered. "It wasn't the big errors. It was the little ones. Once I was made aware of what was done wrong, it was over. I could build on that and strive to do better. That was my saving grace."

Bill had a sixth-floor, corner office overlooking downtown Lynchburg. It was small and narrow. There was room for a desk and a chair and a filing cabinet. A visitor had to stand. Peggy Moody soon understood that there was room enough for the mercurial Dudley temper. "There were times when the phone was thrown across the room. When I was in there I tried to stand out of the way."

Bill did not like to use the personal pronoun "I." Peggy would take dictation. He would read the letter and edit out all the personal pronouns. It made for strange reading—"Will be in New York on October 3 and like to have lunch"—and a delightful little avocation for Peggy, who spent forty years sneaking the letter "I" back into his correspondence.

Bill was active in the life insurance business for fifty-three years. It put him in his third Hall of Fame—The Equitable Insurance Hall of

Fame. Salespeople lose more than they win. Bill's motivational style was a perfect fit for the job.

> Bill: "How do you know when you are doing your best? Is there a gauge other than failure? Not failure in your job, but failure to accomplish or set goals above those that you've already accomplished."

Every person who knew Bill would, sooner or later, mention his humility. It was genuine. Bill Dudley could be on stage before an adoring crowd at the Football Hall of Fame in Canton, Ohio, on a Sunday and be back in a cramped office on the phone working the 10-3-1 on Monday. In the grand scheme of things, it was all the same to him.

Insurance runs in the family: Agents Bill, Jim, and Sheb Dudley

CHAPTER TWENTY-ONE
A Charmed Household Goes Silent

In 1954, the Dudleys became a family of five when daughter Becca arrived in May, joining Jarrett and Little Bill. The charmed lives of Bill and Libba Dudley were played out in a brick and clapboard, two-story colonial home in Lynchburg. Bill had given Libba a budget. She could build the house she wanted within it.

Libba contracted the construction. Bill's only role was to withhold final payment for a year. If the basement leaked, he wouldn't pay it. It stayed dry. Libba's colonial house remained the Dudley home for the next forty years. Like so many homes of the baby boom era, it grew with the family. When the first television arrived, the basement became a TV room. A bar was added. Like the Bluefield Dudley home, there was music, this time in the form of an elaborate room-to-room audio system that was unusual for the day.

It was a small, child-friendly cul-de-sac neighborhood within walking and biking distance of Oakwood Country Club and the Leininger home. Kids and dogs played in the yards and in the street. There was even a Lynchburg version of the Tower Ground—the green acreage surrounding the Presbyterian Church at the rear of the neighborhood. There was Saturday and Sunday football and the occasional big game on Thanksgiving when the college kids came home. Bill joined in now and then.

The summer of 1954 looked bright for the Dudleys. Bill's life insurance business had doubled in three years. He had a contract to coach the

University of Virginia backfield that fall. Head coach Ned McDonald had gone 1-8 the previous season. They talked it over:

He wanted me to be the backfield coach. I said, "You don't want me." He said, "Why?" I said, "I can't help it. I have a reputation. You're the head coach. You're making a change bringing me in. If we win, I get the credit. If we lose, you get the blame." He got up and shuffled his feet and said, "Oh, hell, no." He hired me.

The summer of '54 looked bright for America. The bloody, three-year Korean War was over—40,000 Americans never returned—and the genial, competent Dwight Eisenhower was in the White House. More than half of American families owned a car and the car embodied 50s style. The bulbous postwar designs were gone, replaced by more powerful, longer, sleeker, chrome-encrusted models that showed the early hint of fins.

Women wore long, sleek, form-fitting dresses, with the assistance of a Playtex Magic Controller girdle. Almost half of American homes had a television set. *Father Knows Best* was a popular show.

If a nation can be said to breathe a sigh of relief, it happened when a vaccine for polio, often called infantile paralysis, was introduced. The nation had been terrified by a two-year outbreak of this crippling disease for which there is no cure—a virus that invades the nervous system and can paralyze a child in hours. What followed was America's first mass vaccination.

There was more money. Wages were rising. A nation splurged.

The Dudleys' first splurge was for a lawn service. Libba expected Bill to mow their new lawn. Bill expressed his lifelong loathing for the task. She told him to get out there anyway. As she watched her husband through a window—he, running and cursing behind a mower—she decided the lawn service wasn't such a bad idea.

It was a freer era for children. Jarrett, six, and Little Bill, five, had the run of the neighborhood. They could walk the three blocks to their grandparents' home. To Jarrett, home life seemed to reflect the popular reading instruction books she was given in the first grade. "I thought we were the perfect family—like Dick and Jane and Spot—only we were Jarrett, Bill, and [dog] Juno. Then we added curly haired baby Becca, our 'Sally,' and that just made it more perfect."

Within a year, family car ownership—the barometer of American affluence—spiked to 70 percent. Change was welcome. A restaurant named McDonald's opened and changed American dining. Radios broadcast a song entitled "That's All Right" by a young man named Elvis and changed American music. Disneyland opened and the *Mickey Mouse Club* made its television debut and changed American entertainment. Rosa Parks refused to give up her seat on a bus and changed American culture.

There was no end of promising days in sight.

In most ways, Little Bill was an ordinary little boy. He was nice looking—he got the best of his mother and father—and did what little boys do. As parents, Bill and Libba were a mixed reflection of their own parents. The whip hand of the Bluefield Dudleys was tempered by the firm hand of the Fort Smith Leiningers. The Bluefield Dudley penchant for open affection and expressions of endearment was not moderated.

But the little boy was also different. As he grew independent Libba warned the other children to go easy. Little Bill bruised easily. Nobody thought much of it. Maybe it was temporary.

He was a sweet, happy little boy, who from birth carried his father's first college nickname. Little Bill was never a junior.

One summer day in 1955, Libba got a call from the Boonsboro Country Club. Little Bill was extremely bruised over most of his body. He was bleeding. He'd been playing in the pool at the club. Children on the scene were questioned. Was he hit by something? Were they playing rough? No. Little Bill was taken to a Lynchburg emergency room. The doctor there wasn't sure about a diagnosis, but it could be serious. He suggested they see a specialist in New York. The tone couldn't be disguised. It was serious.

Sheb Dudley arrived in town that day. He took Little Bill to Bluefield to spend the night, returning the next day. That evening there was a family dinner in the Dudley dining room. There were gifts. Little Bill opened a package containing two pairs of summer pajamas. Jarrett got an envelope with train tickets to Bluefield.

The next day, Jarrett departed for Bluefield, Becca went to the Leininger home, and Bill, Libba, and Little Bill entered Memorial Sloan Kettering Hospital in Manhattan. They got Little Bill settled in and the rounds of tests began. The diagnosis returned quickly. Little Bill had acute leukemia. When the doctor said, "We'll do everything we can," Bill understood for the first time how serious the situation was.

Again, hospital policy denied the parents overnight privileges. It was, literally, a nightmare. Bill and Libba spent the days with the child. They were turned out in the evening and waited at the door the next morning for admission. These were cruel, agonizing nights. How could they sleep knowing their little boy was alone in a strange room with strange sounds and strange people coming in and out? Little Bill didn't even know why he was there. Any reprieve would do. Something. Anything. One evening, Bill and Libba thought Little Bill had been given one, but the moment proved crueler still. It started with a phone call. "We got a phone call one night. They said it looks like he may be in remission. Early the next morning we got another call. There was a relapse. They told us we'd better get over there."

By now, Dutch Leininger was in New York. He, Libba, and Bill made their way to the hospital. The bedside vigil lasted into the night.

It wasn't a good scene, but I don't think he (Little Bill) knew. He asked me to tell him the story of Joseph and the multi colored coat. I told him the story. He went into unconsciousness and that was it.

There were six days between the time we knew he had leukemia and his death. We had no idea when we went to New York that we might not bring him home. Thank God he didn't suffer.

Little Bill was buried in Lynchburg. Bill rode back on the same train with the little boy's body. Nida Watts, wife of Bill's friend Bobby, drove Jarrett home from Bluefield, trying to explain to the mystified girl that her brother was in heaven and would never come home again.

The once charmed household went silent. There was a black wreath on the door. Libba took to her bed and stayed there. Bill went from one bedroom to another—consoling his wife in one room, trying to explain things to his daughter in another. Meanwhile, there was a baby to mind.

Bill coached at UVA that fall, but his heart wasn't in it. The family spent Thanksgiving in Pittsburgh with the Rooneys. They wanted to get Libba out of the house—anything, really, to bring her back around.

She didn't come around. The household was cold. Libba was a hollow presence. Bill immersed himself in his work and was often absent. By the following spring, friends and family were concerned. There were two children at the Dudley home who needed parents. The parents and children who had gone different ways after that tragic family dinner the summer before had never fully reunited. It was time to intervene.

That spring, Art Rooney introduced Bill to a retreat at the Abbey of Gethsemani in Kentucky, a Trappist monastery. The Abbey welcomed guests—and still does—to stay for periods of silence, prayer, and reflection among their acres of fields and woods. There were also services, lectures, and discussions. His healing began there. Over the years, Bill would return two more times. Dutch went with him one year.

That same spring, Libba's mother, her sister Mary, and Nida Watts took her on a trip to Canada and sat her down for some reflection and some of what we would now call tough love. She still had a family, they reminded her. It was time to get back into life, or, as they would phrase it in the 50s, snap out of it. Libba returned to do just that, also immersing herself in a Catholic book study group.

For the couple, it was the beginning of the end of a long road back.

Bill: "It was life. It happens to lot of people in a lot of different circumstances. If you give the Lord a chance, He makes it easier to get from that moment. The Good Lord gave me the strength to handle the death of Little Bill. We were lucky to have him as long as we did."

To this day, Little Bill's red and white cowboy boots sit on the hearth in the Dudley living room.

When Bill and Libba were sent away from the hospital each night, they found themselves on the streets of Manhattan, alone and hungry. Dinner would be their first meal of the day. They went to the place Bill knew best, Toots Shor's. Shor put them at an out of the way table and told people to leave them alone. Years later, it dawned on Bill that he never paid for a meal that week. "It was an emotional blur. We came in. We ate. We left. Toots just took care of it. That was Toots."

Libba never forgave the people at Memorial Sloan Kettering for sending her away those nights, but there was no one to name. It was just the faceless bureaucracy we all call "They."

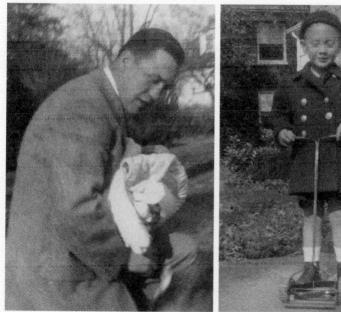

Holding infant Little Bill (left); Little Bill at age 3.

CHAPTER TWENTY-TWO

1958

THEY SAY BERT BELL WEPT AFTER THE "GREATEST GAME EVER Played"—that he knew what December 28, 1958, meant for the future of football when a cool, workmanlike Johnny Unitas led the Baltimore Colts to a sudden death overtime victory against Frank Gifford's New York Giants, 23–17 for the NFL championship.

A dozen future Hall of Fame players and three Hall of Fame coaches were in the game. Lousy late December weather kept most of the country indoors that day. The game was televised by NBC. Bell had spent years tailoring the league schedules and rules and media policies to create just this kind of game.

It wasn't rah-rah college football. It was men doing their jobs and it was a captivating thing to watch. Bell was right. It was the beginning of the NFL's rise to the top of American sports.

It was almost five years to the day after Bill told Colts owner Carroll Rosenbloom it would take that long to build a championship team. Bill was in the stands that day, too, but he had other things on his mind. For one, his family had grown again. Son Jim was still in a cradle. For another, he had been given the business opportunity of a lifetime.

The NFL Players Association wanted a pension plan. They had tapped estate planner Bill Dudley as the man to craft one.

The Players Association was officially two years old in 1958, but it was many years in the making. It would be several years more before it became the union it is today. The association was born in Hall of Famer

Dante Lavelli's basement in the early 1950s when he still played for the Cleveland Browns. He eventually brought in other players of the era—including Hall of Famers Frank Gifford and Sam Huff of the Giants, Norm Van Brocklin of the Rams, and Don Shula of the Colts—and an attorney. It was a gutsy move. You could lose your job. Some meetings were open. Others were in secret. Some players wanted their names on attendance rosters. Others didn't. Even so, the meetings continued and the numbers grew.

The headline grievance was pay for exhibition games or training camp. There wasn't any. You had to make the roster to get a check. There were other, deeper issues. An agreement like Bill's Detroit contract—no-cuts and injury clauses—was still rare. But the heart of the matter was that the owners still treated players like it was 1940. Football was changing. Football may be a coach's sport, but the fans come to the show to see the players. Every year, there were more and more fans in the stands and before television sets.

> Bill: "When I started, we rode trains. The locker rooms had holes in the floor. My last two years with Washington, we flew. Everything had changed."

By November 1956, the association had signed up a majority of NFL players. They met and submitted their demands to NFL commissioner Bert Bell, who was for the most part sympathetic. When Bell couldn't persuade the owners to accept the association, the players threatened a $200,000 antitrust lawsuit. Bell responded by formally recognizing the association as the bargaining body for players in December of 1957, but he did it on his own. For the owners, it was put up or shut up time. When Art Rooney backed Bell, the owners acquiesced.

When the association elected officers the next month, the first article of business was a pension plan. Bill was appointed the association's pension consultant. It was a huge opportunity. Whoever underwrote this would make big-league money. Bill spent three months on the project. The Players Association showed it to Bell in May. It was apparent right away that the owners wanted to delay it, if they couldn't kill it.

On the day Bill and Bell watched the Greatest Game Ever Played, relations between the Players Association and the league owners were at a low. The pension plan was the main issue. Again the players threatened an antitrust suit. Again, it worked. Four months later, Bell told the press the league would accept a pension plan.

It was back to the drawing board for Bill. Once the plan was finalized, all it needed was signatures. Bill finished the job. The thing was ready to be signed. They would make an event of it. Bill and others were invited to Philadelphia to watch the Eagles play the Steelers in October. The signing would follow the game.

Bert Bell suffered a heart attack in the fourth quarter of the game. He died later that day.

Everything went into limbo. When new commissioner Pete Rozelle took the helm, his first task was to review everything. He gave the forty-seven-page Dudley pension plan to one of his assistants. The assistant took it to Carroll Rosenbloom. Rosenbloom showed it to his insurance man, Sig Hyman.

One day Bill got a phone call from the Players Association. Sig Hyman would underwrite the pension plan. There was nothing they could do about it. Somebody else had bagged Bill Dudley's elephant.

It got worse. The pension plan would only cover current and future players. Anybody who retired before 1959 was out of the plan. There wasn't enough money. Somebody had to go. The very men who created the Players Association, not to mention the ones who came before them and built the league, were cut out. A letter by Players Association attorney Creighton Miller followed: "We are now vigorously beginning to work on the possibility of raising sufficient funds to establish a retroactive part of this pension. With enough money we will be able to do anything."

We can't know what future Bert Bell envisioned through his tears that day in 1958, but he probably couldn't fully grasp what the NFL, or television, or stadiums would become. How about a Super Bowl? Other than understanding the future looked bright, who in that day could? Bill could.

The first professional football game was shown (on television) in '50 or '51—it was just beginning to be on the monetary scene about that time. I told Bert I would love to have the opportunity to own a football team. I said, "I think it's going to grow." He said "Aw, Bill, you don't want to do that." But, I did think it was going to grow—'course, we didn't know anything about television. Then it got out of sight.

The league position didn't ring true—"vigorously beginning to work on the possibility." You can work on a possibility for a long time, vigorously or otherwise, and never know when you're through. It didn't ring true because it wasn't true. It would be twenty-eight years before the plan was changed to include the "pre-59ers." The years involved more discord and controversy than vigorous work, even after there was more than enough money in the NFL to do "anything." Bill Dudley was in the middle of all of them.

By 1962, two of the most watched television broadcasts in America were NFL football games.

The year 1958 was important in another way. Bill announced his retirement from the University of Virginia spring Alumni vs. Varsity exhibition game. He'd played the game every year since leaving the school. If nothing else, the game was a good motivator to stay in shape. Now, at age thirty-seven, it was time to let it go.

He watched the first half of the 1958 game from the sidelines. He was in street clothes. After the half, he reappeared in uniform to take the kickoff. He ran it back about 40 yards in the patented Dudley dodge and scamper style.

He unretired and continued to play in the game until his fifties, keeping himself in playing shape for one game a year. It was a great run. The alumni chalked up wins year after year until school officials quietly suggested they tone it down. They were making the team look bad during spring recruiting.

Bill finally hung up his cleats after gaining 102 yards in a game. He didn't want to go out on a bad one.

CHAPTER TWENTY-THREE
The Class of 1966

As of this writing, 29,000 men have played in the National Football League. There are 295 names in the NFL Hall of Fame. Players openly long for the distinction of becoming part of that 1 percent. As fall nears winter when new inductees are announced on Super Bowl weekend, opinions about who should or shouldn't be in the Hall fill the air at America's bars, barbershops, and water coolers. Who will and who won't get in is fodder for the sports talkosphere in the weeks running up to the Super Bowl. When each new class is announced, the same talkosphere gives us a day of I-told-you-so and what-were-they-thinking. The induction ceremony is a national event.

It wasn't always this way. The Hall had, as they say, humble beginnings. When Dick McCann, longtime general manager of the Washington Redskins, wanted to start a pro football hall of fame in the early 1960s, it was a tough sell—great idea, too ambitious. The hall would be in Canton, Ohio. It was the natural home. The NFL was founded there. Jim Thorpe and the Canton Bulldogs were the pre-NFL football powerhouse and the league champion in its first two years. McCann challenged the doubters, raised the money anyway, and, by 1963, the doors opened.

They were brand new doors leading to a smallish, two-building complex constructed to house the Hall. The Hall of Fame grew with the NFL. The interior space they opened in 1963 has quadrupled in size.

In 1966, Bill got a phone call from McCann. It wasn't unexpected. They had become social friends during Bill's Redskin years. What

McCann had to say, though, wasn't expected. Bill had been elected to the NFL Hall of Fame. The ceremony would be in September followed by a preseason game in Cleveland.

> *McCann tells me I'm going to get a telegram. I'm inducted into the Hall of Fame class of 1966. I didn't know I was on the ballot. I didn't know I was being considered. I knew Dick from the Redskins. He had a hell of a time lining up people in Canton and raising money.*
>
> *I wanted Art Rooney to introduce me, but Dick wanted a current member of the Hall of Fame to do it. I felt pressure. If I had it to do over again, I would have insisted on Mr. Rooney, but I was new. I was lucky to be there. I felt honored and I wanted to do what they wanted me to do. Dick wanted Bob Waterfield to do it. I knew Bob in Detroit. He and Libba and Jane (Russell) and I would go out. Bob was in a picture I did in Hollywood.*
>
> *The thing wasn't the production it is now. I didn't write an acceptance speech. I talked about my mom and dad, my coaches, my teammates—the people who got me there. I just winged it.*

A crowd of 1,500 watched from temporary bleachers as Bill entered the Hall of Fame's fourth class along with Joe Guyon, Arnie Herber, George McAfee, and Clyde "Bulldog" Turner. Walt Kiesling, Hugh "Shorty" Ray, and Steve Owen were enshrined posthumously. For youngest daughter, Becca, the moment was more about fashion than football:

> *Jarrett, Jim and I were all there. We each had gone shopping with Mama to buy an outfit for the event. Jim had a new blazer and grey flannel pants. Jarrett had a skirt and jacket. I was 12, longing to be a teenager. Mama found an outfit in the juniors section of a local department store. I thought I looked very grown up.*

Over the years, Bill's relationship with the Hall of Fame grew. Joe Horrigan, currently Executive Vice President of Museums and Selection Process, was at the Hall of Fame for most of Bill's tenure. "He was one of the most loyal Famers, even before it was chic to be so. We could always call on him. He would always be there. He came back every Hall of Fame weekend. He was one of a handful of goodwill ambassadors in the early years. He gave the Hall credibility. A tiny little place in the Midwest, it needed something to get it going.

"He was the most unassuming person I ever knew. Unless you twisted his arm, Bill never talked about himself."

Enshrinees are selected by sportswriters. In 1977, the Hall realized that modern sportswriters lacked the living memory it would take to judge many past NFL stars. Players are eligible for the Hall five years after retirement. After twenty-five years of eligibility, players move to the seniors list. The Hall created the Seniors Committee to nominate overlooked players from the list. They tapped Bill as a member.

There is no formula for getting into the Hall of Fame. Luck plays a role. What the selection committee knows plays a role. Everything plays a role. Bill often spoke of the mystique of making the 1 percent.

> *It could be your position or your era or if you were a winner or a loser. Cherundolo was a damn good center, but he played in the same era with (Hall of Famers) Bulldog Turner and Mel Hein. Of course, I'm prejudiced about Cherundolo. If you are on a championship team, the chances of getting into the Hall are good if you have any ability at all. Ace Parker was never on a winner. It took him years to get in the Hall of Fame.*

Bill observed that many enshrinees don't thoroughly understand the Hall of Fame until they are inducted.

> *The Hall is to be enjoyed. It isn't a shrine. It's a living thing made up of mortals. The Hall will do things for you, but it doesn't owe you a living. Some players come into the Hall thinking they'll be paid to be members. They come in feeling they are owed something.*

In his view, the Hall is a blessing that becomes a responsibility. The Hall of Fame doesn't represent you. It's the other way around.

Other enshrinees shared this view. The sentiment gave birth to the Ray Nitschke Address. Nitschke, a fourteen-year All-Pro middle linebacker for the Green Bay Packers, was inducted into the Hall in 1978. His address became a tradition that began at a luncheon the day before an induction. Nobody remembers exactly what year. Joe Horrigan watched the tradition evolve:

> *The luncheon was for returning Hall of Famers and some guests. Somebody asked a player to say a few words. When he finished, he pointed out another player and told him to say a few words. It went around the room. Nitschke went last. Nitschke was never short of words. He was so passionate about being in the Hall and the responsibility of being an enshrinee in a unique fraternity.*
>
> *It became a lecture for the incoming class. The new enshrinees weren't allowed to speak at the podium. They had to listen. Every year people looked forward to coming back for it.*
>
> *Bill would talk about how it was when they did what they did. Deacon Jones would tell them, "Now you are in a class you can't be cut from, traded and can't quit."*
>
> *It got to the point, with the legend and lore of what was said, that it became more and more known about how emotional the room was. Owners started coming. It got to be an event. It was losing direction. Ten years ago, one of the players said it was time to clear the room of all but Hall of Famers. It's been a closed event since.*

Following Nitschke's death in 1998, Bill usually became the final speaker, but it was a tough act to follow.

> *Ray was a friend. Whenever we met, he'd say, "You don't look too tough to me." He was very vocal. He loved the Hall of Fame and he loved to talk about it. About how lucky he was to be there, how lucky everyone was to be there.*
>
> *The Hall of Fame is a wonderful honor. It is hard to put into words just how you feel when you get such an honor, but how many people did it take to get me there?*

It is a very good thing I played when I did. Now in the day of specialization, I don't know if I could do any one thing well enough to stick.

Bill's Quadruple Crown Plaque is in the Hall. And, for the record, here are the eleven ways to score in a football game:

1. Rush for a score.

2. Kick for a score.

3. Pass for a score.

4. Receive a pass for a score.

5. Return a kickoff for a score.

6. Return a punt for a score.

7. Return an interception for a score.

8. Recover a fumble for a score.

9. Lateral for a score.

10. Receive a lateral for a score.

11. Tackle for a safety.

CHAPTER TWENTY-FOUR
Football's Last Call

JUST AS IN BLUEFIELD, THE DUDLEY FAMILY BUSINESS WAS BEING BUSY. Except for scouting trips, Bill was home in fall now. His last full football season was as a backfield coach for the Steelers in 1956.

Bill and Libba Dudley now had three children, twelve and under, and along with them the PTAs and sports leagues and dance recitals, plus the bruised knees, braces, and adolescent stirrings.

They were the go-to couple for civic organizations. Over the next decade and beyond, Libba would work with the Women's Club of Lynchburg, the Poetry Society of Virginia, the Lynchburg Fine Arts Center, the Association for the Preservation of Virginia Antiquities, and the Virginia Museum of Fine Arts.

She was on the boards of the Junior League, the Lynchburg Child Care Center, the Lynchburg Guidance Center, the National Council of Catholic Women, the Lynchburg Historical Society, the Virginia Center of Creative Arts, the Lynchburg Volunteer Bureau, and the Holy Cross Church Religious Education Board.

In 1966, she served on the Virginia Cultural Development Study Commission. In 1968 she served on the Virginia Commission of the Arts and Humanities.

Statewide, Bill would be chairman of the board of the Bank of Central Virginia and on the board of directors of First Community Bank. He served on the University of Virginia Board of Visitors and the State Board of Corrections. He was chairman of the State Athletic Commission and was appointed to the Governor's Committee for Youth and the Metropolitan Transportation Study Commission. He was a director of the Auto Club of Virginia.

Locally, he was a board member of the Lynchburg Chamber of Commerce, the YMCA, the Heart Association, the Cancer Society, the Lynchburg Scholastic League, and Seven Hills School. He was a Red Cross campaign chairman.

Parents who were thrilled to learn their son's Little League coach would be none other than "Bullet" Bill Dudley got a dose of reality at game time. Bill just couldn't grasp the idea that every player gets in the game. You can't win that way.

Like most American families in the early 1960s, the Dudleys were a one-car household. In their case, one car wasn't enough. If Bill wasn't on the road, Libba got the car. If Bill was leaving town, Libba would sometimes drop him off on the highway so he could hitchhike to a nearby town or an airport.

Bill's business success and his dual careers put the Dudleys in a position to splurge even more. They didn't. They had the money for any car they wanted. The average new car in the early 1960s cost $2,600. Bill and Libba finally bought a used one.

There were only two big items in the Dudley family budget that were always fully expensed—education and country clubs.

Libba's parents were college educated and assumed a college degree in the future for their children and grandchildren. Bill's parents had elementary and high school educations. They didn't assume anything, but they considered a diploma indispensable and were willing to undergo austerity to pay for it. This rubbed off on Libba and Bill.

But Grosse Pointe rubbed off, too. Bill liked country clubs. He was a man who mixed comfortably in any company, but the jacket and tie, golf and card game, cocktails, dinner, and dancing world of country clubs suited him. Libba, of course, was a natural when she was in that setting. The world wouldn't be quite right if she wasn't. Still, it wasn't the kind of thing Jewell Dudley's boy was supposed to do. You could almost hear the sound of her palm purse clicking shut. Bill's son, Jim, heard the sound and it was louder than a click: "You didn't want to be around Daddy when he was paying the bills. He'd have his sleeves rolled up and he'd be bent over. He'd see the hamburger charges from the country club and he'd blow up. When he was scolding, it was always the same thing. How many times did I hear it? 'He didn't come from money.' 'Money didn't grow on trees.'"

He was a loving father who made time for the children. When he was home, he was home. There were games and tickling and roughhousing in the den. He made buckwheat pancakes on Sunday mornings. He made milkshakes with eggs in them. He cooked hamburgers in the fireplace. He had a gentle bedside manner when illness struck.

Becca recalled that he was the unofficial neighborhood coach. "On weekends, when we played touch football or some game with the neighborhood kids, Daddy would often come out tossing the football or giving pointers as to how to hold a football, how to throw it, and how to run with it. I don't think any of us kids really knew just how cool it was to have Bullet Bill play football with us. He was just Daddy or Mr. Dudley."

There was discipline, but never out of anger. He was a good listener, even if he rarely changed his mind. As his children reached their teen years in the turbulent 1960s, listening was a trait that worked for him, as Becca remembered:

> *He was very black and white. However, he often tried to understand the other side. Once when driving to the beach—it was sometime early 70s—Daddy picked up a guy hitchhiking who had long hair. Daddy often picked up hitchhikers as he himself thumbed earlier in life. Anyway, he had picked up this particular guy because he wanted to know* why the long hair? *He talked with the guy about it until he dropped him off near Suffolk. Daddy just couldn't see it—couldn't understand why a man would want to look like that. An interesting conversation, but still left Daddy bewildered.*

Johnny Cates was a page in the Virginia General Assembly when Bill served in the Virginia Legislature in the 1960s. Cates worked in the House and Senate Post Office. "He always took the time to talk with me and other young people. He wanted to know what you were thinking. He made you feel like you were the most important person in the room. He might disagree but he didn't poke you in the eye with it. He looked tough, but he was a Teddy Bear to me."

There was also encouragement; he became a sort of modified form of Beefy. He was there to tell his kids to tackle the risk. It could be a sled, a bike, an ocean wave, or an intimidating project. The message was always the same: Don't be afraid to try.

It wasn't always easy to be the son of a famous athlete. Bill's ability to pull peak performance, and then some, out of himself was and is exceptional and rare. He expected it from his children just as he demanded it from teammates during his playing days.

"He was never one to praise," said his son, Jim. "It didn't come often. He also never praised himself or felt he wasn't given his due. He was always the first to say there was room for improvement in our performance, sports or otherwise. It's just doing a job."

It wasn't always a cakewalk being a Dudley daughter, either. Lynchburg may have grown accustomed to their celebrity citizen, but teenage boys trembled before him.

There was the Dudley bluntness. If you came to the dinner table armed with an opinion, you'd better be able to defend it . . . and you might consider carrying a shield.

And there was the Dudley temper. Sometimes it was funny. Some of Bill's friends egged him on. They enjoyed the show when Bill lost it, especially on the golf course. On the links, Vesuvius could rumble, but Dudley erupted. His friends got their money's worth one night at a cookout when Bill was frustrated by a new grill he was using for the first time. When he banged the grill top in frustration, it sent the steaks flying into the maw of a large, delighted dog. It was time to hide the women and children.

Sometimes it wasn't funny. There was on occasion the old Bluefield Dudley pattern of shattering outbursts followed by tears and reconciliation. No outburst, though, was ever directed at Libba. She was the mollifying force.

On fall Saturdays, Bill and Libba and family could be found in their seats in UVA's Scott Stadium—at the 50 yard line just below the press box—where he filled the role of Virginia's Most Impatient Fan. He was ever a hard man to satisfy. He rarely made it through the third quarter. Bill would tell you he usually knew where a game was going by halftime. Once that was settled, it was, well, settled. "If you win, you win. If you lose, you lose. The score doesn't make a damn bit of difference."

There was a third big splurge—summers at Virginia Beach. The family rented a house each summer, Bill came down on weekends, working his way from Lynchburg making client calls.

Except for one summer when Libba and her friend Margaret Ann Schoew decided it would be clever to pay for their vacation by operating the summer house like a bed-and-breakfast—this leading to the equivalent of a prolonged episode of *I Love Lucy*—the beach seasons were gently uneventful and the stuff of nostalgia.

There was a routine in the Lynchburg home. It was the desire to be ordinary lived out. And there was always Libba.

"He put her on a pedestal and kept her there and he did all he could to freshen the pedestal and adorn it and add to it," said Jim. "It was his duty and his pleasure and his blessing. He met her and said, 'I'm going to marry her.'

"He believed God made the marriage happen and he did his utmost as long as he lived to live up to that—to continue acknowledging the blessing."

Bill doted on Libba. He left her tender notes for no reason. If she had a wish he could grant, it was granted. He never walked in front of her. If they were together, she was on his arm. He took her for long vacations in Florida every winter, just the two of them. As a boy, son Jim once posed a hypothetical question to his father. What would he do if he had to choose between saving all his family and his wife?

"Before I even finished the scenario, he answered, 'Your Momma.'"

In 1966, Bill came home from the Super Bowl with a brand new Lincoln Continental Smith Ferebee had given him—bronze and beige two-tone color, suicide doors, leather, the works. It was a fantasy car for ten-year-old Jim Dudley. The fantasy didn't last long. "Daddy said, 'I'm not that successful. I don't want to look that successful.' He replaced it with a pea-green Olds Cutlass. No air or power steering. Roll up windows."

It was too much car for Bluefield's Bill Dudley, but it would have looked swell at a country club.

Football was always calling—Bill still didn't have his championship—but a football life couldn't square with a Lynchburg life. Bill finally forced himself into a final choice.

Harry Wismer was a businessman and successful broadcaster who owned a quarter of the Redskin franchise when Bill played there. He was also a producer of the *Triple Threat* movie. Wismer got a charter franchise in the American Football League and started the New York Titans in 1960. The Titans didn't bring in the fans and by 1963, Wismer found himself with a debt burden.

Well, Harry was a good friend of Mr. Marshall's and he bought the New York Titans all by himself. I said, "Harry, if you ever think about selling the ball club, would you give me a call?" He said, "Bill, I'll do it." Along in the 60s, I had just made the transfer from Home Life to The Equitable, making a good living and raising a family. And Wismer called me up when I'm in California at a meeting in San Diego. He says, "Bill, you told me, if I was to ever sell the ball club, to give you a ring."

I said, "How much do you want for it?" He said, "I want $200 or $250,000 free and clear for me." I said, "Well, how much do you owe?" He said, "Probably between $300–$400,000." Harry wanted an answer by Friday and this was Tuesday.

Now, we're talking about a franchise in New York—the Jets, but they were the Titans then. I'd have to have raised at least $530,000. So, I got on the phone and started calling people I knew. I called a boy named Lawrence Lewis in Richmond. I told Lawrence, "Football is big money—it's going, period." I told him the coaches, players are incidentals. Number one, I could be the coach, general manager and we would save lots of money. He said, "Hell, I'd have to fire ya' the *first year!" I said, "Yeah, maybe, but at least we would have something to work with."*

Now, if I had been in Lynchburg, I would have told Harry that I would meet him in New York on the next train. I would have raised the money because I had contacts with the banks there. So, I told him, "I want it, but can't do anything about it for a couple of days." He said, "I'm sorry I can't give you more time, but that's the way it is." I have no doubt in my mind that if I had been able to go up to New York right away, I think Harry would have worked with me and I would have owned the team. It would take at least three weeks to raise the money.

But perhaps, it was fate, as you call it. Today, the club is worth millions—I didn't know it would be worth that much then, but I knew it would be worth something and I knew it would work. I know I could coach and win the day. I believe that.

But it just didn't fit. Number one, to win, you gotta move, and I didn't want to move my family. Number two, a successful coach is busier than a one-armed paper hanger. I batted it back and forth. I had three children and ten years in business. Did I want to junk all that and try to raise the money. I talked it over with Libba. It was over her head. She said, "Anything you want to do."

I didn't want it bad enough.

The desire to be ordinary and the longing for a championship met for the final time. Ordinary won, as it had before. Football, at least the kind played between the lines, never called again.

Sonny Werblin bought the Titan franchise for one million dollars. He changed the team name to the Jets and risked huge money when he signed a guy named Joe Namath in a bidding war with the NFL.

CHAPTER TWENTY-FIVE

Nobody Was Going to Tell Him What to Think

IN 1966 VIRGINIA, IF YOU WERE FOR LIMITED GOVERNMENT, LOW TAXES, and fiscal responsibility, you were a Democrat. This was about to change. The Byrd Machine was dying.

For the previous four decades, the Byrd Organization had picked favorites—from governors to dog-catchers—and put them in place through its county courthouse network. It was controlled by Harry F. Byrd Sr., a former Virginia governor and US senator.

All political machines run out of steam sooner or later. The Byrd Organization hastened its own end when it came down on the wrong side of public school integration and history in the 1950s. After the *Brown vs. Board of Education* Supreme Court ruling declared separate public schools for black and white students to be unconstitutional in 1954, the state engaged in a colossally futile policy termed Massive Resistance.

It wasn't much of a policy—any public school that attempted to integrate was cut off from state funding and was closed. Massive Resistance didn't last long in political terms—it was all over in three years—but it was the beginning of the end for the Byrd boys. And three years *is* a long time in the education of a child.

In 1966, Massive Resistance was long gone as an issue. The Byrd Machine was still strong enough to elect Harry F. Byrd Jr., into his father's Senate seat. Mills Godwin, a Byrd Democrat, was elected Virginia's governor. It was the machine's last turn of the cog. The Democratic Party in Virginia was still, though, the party of limited government.

Bill didn't just wake up one day and want to be in the legislature.

I never considered politics before I was approached. When (State Legislator) Tommy Glass retired, I was asked if I would consider running by the Chairman of the Democratic Party in Lynchburg for the seat that took in Lynchburg and Amherst County. Glass was a Democrat. His father was Carter Glass, a U.S. Senator. I talked it over with Libba and then I talked it over with brother Jim.

Jim showed Bill the results of a personality evaluation Bill had taken in 1951 when he applied with Home Life Insurance. Under aptitude, it said "politics."

It wasn't Bill's first foray into politics. That occurred in 1960 when Bill Battle, son of a former Virginia governor and later an unsuccessful candidate for the office, asked Bill to campaign for John Kennedy in the presidential election. Battle was an old Kennedy friend. In World War II, he was in Kennedy's naval squadron, which was famously marooned on an island and rescued.

I was all set to oppose Jack Kennedy when he was running for President because I was concerned about the right to work law. Bill Battle talked with me and said, "You can rest assured that Jack Kennedy will not disturb the right to work law." I took his word for it and went on and supported Kennedy and he never did.

Right to work laws break a union's hold on a worksite. In a right to work state, a citizen who wants to work at a union-controlled concern isn't required to join the union.

Bill supported Kennedy, but he didn't campaign for him. Battle wanted Bill to work in West Virginia, a key state in the election. Bill met Kennedy on the road there and watched as Kennedy spoke before a labor group. Most people who walked away from the speech thought Kennedy opposed right to work laws. It sounded like he did. Bill knew he didn't. Kennedy was insincere. This just wasn't the Dudley way. He declined. "I wasn't interested. I had a living to make."

Six years later, Bill was interested. Running for a seat in the legislature seemed possible.

In just about anything you want to do, it helps to be a football hero. In politics, there are few better things to be. Bill had been a Virginia celebrity for thirty years. He knew people. He knew Virginia's power brokers. His campaign came together quickly.

Bill built his first campaign on four issues. The first two were new. He would work for a statewide community college system that included a school in Lynchburg, and he would work for raising the driving age from fourteen to sixteen years old.

The second two were longtime Byrd Democrat issues that Bill supported—highway improvement and limited government spending. He won. He went to Richmond and was placed on two major committees, finance and education. He was on the Labor and Corporate Banking Committee. Now, he was a rookie again.

Oh, I felt like a real rookie. I didn't know which end was up. I did things you weren't supposed to do. I didn't know any better. This is a true story: the speaker was in the restroom and I saw him there and I had a bill coming up and I said, "Mr. Speaker, this bill doesn't have much of a chance, does it?" He kind of grinned and shook his head. So I get up on the floor to speak and say, "The Speaker and I were discussing this in the restroom not too long ago, and I know this bill doesn't have much of a chance, but . . ." You should have seen his face.

Governor Mills Godwin also wanted to develop a community college system. Bill wanted to finance the capital spending for the system by addressing another political issue. He would change Virginia's alcohol laws to permit liquor by the drink—a proposition that had popular support—and then tax the liquor.

He'd consulted Toots Shor and bar owners he knew in Pittsburgh and Washington on the financial profile of a drink. In that era a wholesale fifth of liquor averaged four dollars. There are twenty drinks in a bottle and bars were selling drinks for about ninety cents. Bill's legislation would add $1.20 to the cost of the fifth. It works out to about five cents a drink. With that setup, the bar should profit just under thirteen dollars per fifth. It was a three-way winner. It was a good source of revenue for the bar, there was room in the cost for the tax, and every person who ordered a drink knew where their nickel was going.

He estimated revenue to the state at ten million dollars. In Bill's mind, it wasn't a tax increase. It was more like a fee you paid for something you wanted. And it went to a good cause and it wasn't punitive. He noted that beer was already taxed more than soft drinks.

I had a bill that put the tax on whiskey. Mills called me into his office and says, "Bill, you know I pledged no new taxes." And I said, "This is no new tax, Sir." He said, "Ohhhh, yes it is." I said, "We need the money. I don't know where else to get it without hurting people. It's the best place I know to get it without drawing a lot of criticism."

I had gathered support in the House and Senate. Three senators opposed it. I told Mills I had talked with Sen. (Peck) Grey and two or three other senators and I got their support. And Mills says, "Oh?" I say, "Yes, Sir." Mills says, "Excuse me a minute."

When he came back, we talked a few more minutes and there's a knock on the door and in comes Senator Grey. He and Mills had been close for several years, but I didn't know that. And Grey says, "Governor, Bill, how are you?" And I say, "Fine, Sir," and Mills says he'll see me later, but then says, "Oh, by the way, Peck, Bill tells me that you're for this bill he's got with a tax on whiskey." Senator Grey looks at him and says, "Governor, I don't see anything wrong with it."

I walked on out the door. Inside I could almost bet money that Mills couldn't quite believe me and perhaps called Peck up to call my bluff. Just checking me out, you see. I found out that those things go on in politics and I think Mills found out I'm just not that way.

And Bill wasn't that way. The moment began a long and fruitful relationship with Godwin. Nobody needed translations to determine Bill's position on any issue. Words like "direct" and "unvarnished" began to emerge in press accounts of the junior legislator.

The *Lynchburg News and Advance*: "Probably the greatest difference between Dudley and the average member of the general assembly is his bluntness and his seeming indifference to publicity."

Bill: "I'm not a horse trader. If you like what I've got, fine. If you don't, fine."

Few legislative items in that session generated more hate mail than the bill to raise the driving age. When Bill introduced it, the legislation was a recognition that the past had been trumped by the future. Driving had changed. There were more cars on the road. Detroit produced just shy of nine million cars in 1966, almost three million more than a decade earlier. The cars had changed. Detroit was entering its muscle car era—exceedingly overpowered and, if not as clumsy as their ancestors, wider and longer vehicles. The roads were bigger and speeds were faster. Interstate 81 opened in the western part of Virginia in 1966. Interstate 95 in the eastern part was already open. In the era of muscle cars, the driving age of fourteen was a throwback to Model As and dirt roads. A fourteen-year-old at the helm of a 396 Super Sport Chevelle was, and is, a frightening prospect. It became Bill's signature legislation.

My first term there, I increased the driving age to 16 which was very unpopular with a lot of the farmers and those with children. But I talked with all the people who supported it. I remember when I went to Richmond and talked with a delegate from southside Virginia—Pope I think was his name—and he was very much opposed to increasing the age from 14 to 16. I went to see him and said, "Sir, I'm Bill Dudley and have this bill to increase the driver age to 16 and I understand that you're opposed to it." And he was an old timey legislator. He puts his glasses back on his head and says, "Well, Mr. Dudley ..." and went on to launching into his opposition. He says, "Bill, it's been killed in the house before in the past." Anyway, I said, "Sir, I got this bill and I can understand if you oppose it, but it's one that I'm for."

People would buttonhole Bill on the street—mothers who looked forward to lesser driving time, farmers who needed their kids working on the road. Bill stuck with it and won. To him, it was their inconvenience versus their own children's lives. "I had the Senate votes—I had two or three of them who were gonna support it. It passed the house and the senate, and I think we may have saved a few lives by increasing the age to 16."

By the time campaign season rolled around two years later, Bill could report he'd achieved all four of his goals. The new community college system would include one in Lynchburg. The driving age was changed. Roads were being built, and spending was under control. He won a second term handily, beating two opponents.

Delegate Pope, by the way, spoke against the driving age bill on the floor of the House and then went on to become Bill's political ally.

The Virginia legislature meets for sixty days in January and February of every other year. In odd years, it meets for thirty days. It is a system designed to give lawmakers enough time to do the business of the Commonwealth but not enough time to get into mischief.

Bill stayed in a Richmond hotel and came home on weekends in his first term. By the second term, he had found an apartment. Libba would join him. He liked being in the legislature, but for one or two months of every year, Bill wasn't writing any business.

During the legislative session, Peggy Moody worked weekends so Bill could keep up with the mail, service clients, and line up prospective clients to meet after the session ended. There was no room on the calendar for downtime. "I started the year down two months in business. The pay for a legislator was about $300 a month. I just had to work harder."

Bill and Libba were a glamour couple in Richmond, the state capital. During the legislative session, it was a rare day when one or both of them didn't appear in a published photo. There was some kind of soiree every night—the lobbyists and interest groups and media had only sixty nights to work with—and it was gowns and black tie or cocktail dresses and jackets. The Libba Dudley charm that won over Grosse Pointe soon owned Richmond.

Bill ran unopposed for his third and fourth terms. He was, as we would say today, on a roll. Higher office beckoned. He was being told he could beat Republican congressman Dick Poff.

It was pretty much at the end of the Byrd Machine. A friend of mine said I should go up and talk with Sen. Byrd. If he puts the finger on you to run, you run. If no, you don't run. I got an appointment with him. He harrumphs. "Mr. Dudley, I understand you're thinking about running. Let's look at Poff's record. He and I think an awful lot alike."

He reached into a file and pulled out Poff's record. He said, "I can't complain against the way he's voting. Can you?" I said, "Well, Sir, I was told to come here to see if I could seek your support. If I didn't think I could do a better job, I wouldn't be here." He said, "Well, he's doing a pretty good job." I said, "I think I get the picture and I won't take up any more of your time." He didn't say a word and I left.

I had to have his support because he (Byrd) had the district in his pocket. Sen. Byrd never came out, to my knowledge, saying he supported anybody. But there was an undercurrent, regardless of party. He may not say he's for you, but he didn't say he was against you, and that's all it took.

Bill liked the committee system. He found it to be the most interesting part of lawmaking. To him, committee rooms seemed like courtrooms where good versus bad were put on trial. As a member of the Finance Committee and the Education Committee, he was confronted with tax issues in every legislative session. Education and taxes go hand in hand. In the Dudley mind, it was the public duty to spend every possible dime on education.

Tax increases aren't conservative or liberal. They are either necessary or not. Taxes are a fact of life. I ran on a tax increase and won. If you let people know what the money is going for, you'll have a chance. If you say, "It goes for education." No. People want to know what part of education—buildings, meals for students, teacher salaries, higher or lower ed. If you are specific and let the public know, you can get the tax passed.

He was a fiscal conservative, but he understood taxes pay for the society you want—you should be happy that life is good enough you can afford to pay them. With his personal finances, he was Jewell Dudley's son. Every penny of expense had to be justified—and it was pennies. When the price of stamps went up, woe to the poor postal employee who worked the counter that day when Bill Dudley strode in.

He was known for showing up at committee meetings with a pencil and a skeptical attitude. When a bill that was said to impose a 2 percent titling tax on new cars came before the Finance Committee, Bill described with pencil and paper how it was in reality twice that. "You have to be careful with these things and be sure you don't pass a bill which will encourage both customers and dealers to do anything within legal bounds to circumvent the tax."

By the election year of 1974, though, Bill's idea of a necessary tax and his approach to spending the public's money had drifted far from his own political party's notions.

I wasn't much of a party guy. In Lynchburg I was criticized for being too state oriented. "What are you doing for the city?" I did what I thought was right. I believe that when you're elected a representative you should take the issues in hand, listen to the pros and cons, then stand up and do what you think is best for the people. I'm there to do the best job I can, and if the voters don't like the way I do it they can throw me out.

Bill's campaign speeches began to again and again emphasize "responsible, conservative Democrats." More and more he warned of government encroachments on the rights of people—that only sound state and local government could stem federal government growth. He ended one speech by saying he didn't believe in a "totalitarian type of government."

The Virginia Democrats were now a mirror of the national Democratic Party, which was growing ever more statist and liberal. The growth of government that started in the Johnson administration led to mushrooming population in the Northern Virginia counties surrounding the District of Columbia. These were now Democratic voters.

The Byrd Machine was gone—broken in 1969 by the election of a Republican governor—and with it, fiscal conservatism. Neither the dominant moderate Republicans nor the rising liberal Democrats of that era were interested in Byrd-era constrained spending. It was time for new coalitions.

Before the 1973 elections, Mills Godwin switched parties and became a Republican. Godwin, who had supported Massive Resistance in the 50s, radically changed his position and alienated segregationists by supporting liberal Democrat Lyndon Johnson in the 1964 presidential campaign. He supported Johnson's Civil Rights Act. After Godwin became a "Democrat for Nixon" during the 1972 presidential election, he was denied access to the Democratic Convention.

Bill, too, switched parties.

I liked Godwin. I could talk to him. He knew Libba real well and he put her on some commissions. I was a very strong supporter of Mills and I think he was the best governor we had. At the time Godwin shifted parties, he called me up and said, "Bill, you didn't have to switch because I did." I said "Mills, I know that, but I can't support my own running mate and I can't support the Presidential nominee, McGovern." I can't tell a lie very easily—I'm not a double talker. And people who know me, know if I say something, that's it.

I couldn't get along with the Democrat from Amherst (County) who was my running mate. We didn't think alike. I couldn't honestly tell people to vote for him. That's wrong. You ought to be able to support the person you are running with. In the party, you had to sign a pledge that said you support all Democratic candidates and I wasn't gonna do that.

Bill would say then what Ronald Reagan was to say later: He didn't leave the Democratic Party. The Democratic Party left him.

I don't regret changing parties. The whole philosophy of the Democrats changed. I enjoyed politics. I'm naïve enough to say that if I had stayed in and stayed a Democrat I could've run for governor. Whether or not I'd have gotten elected, I don't know. But I think even if I could have tried to put the Democratic party back on a conservative track—it would not have gotten there, but I think the effort would have been enough to swing some conservative votes. Virginia is conservative.

It was a bad time to switch parties. Republicans in Virginia weren't accustomed to winning local elections—in many localities, they still aren't—and were ham-handed about election strategy. In 1973 they ran Bill and his best friend, Bobby Watts, as the ticket to represent Lynchburg and Amherst County.

I never would have run if I had known my close friend was gonna be running with me, which I didn't know at the time I accepted the nomination of the Republican party. We lived about 200 yards apart. I told Libba when I came home, there's no way we can win. We'll make the people of Amherst mad. Bobby's my best friend and if I had known he wanted to run, I'd have never committed myself.

And we lost. I felt the head of the party was pretty stupid. Either one of us alone could have won. We had the votes for the primary, but not for the general election. I had not been a Republican long enough to stop it and I'm not one to make waves. At least I don't think so—a lot of people think I make a lot of waves.

Of course 1973 was also a bad year to have an "R" by your name. Richard Nixon and Watergate were political poison. Bill lost. Godwin won. Godwin later made Watts Virginia's treasury secretary. For Bill, it was the end of politics.

Bill viewed each of his four terms as a two-year contract negotiated with the people of Lynchburg. He was proud of his four terms. He was proud to be in the state legislature. The Richmond Capitol Building is a historic place—it is the oldest democratic body in the world. Bill was ever aware of the people who trod there before.

Even so, he was ambivalent about politics. Even when he was considering a congressional run, he was unsure. Political powerbrokers urged him to run for governor.

If I'd played my cards right, I could have run for higher office, even the governorship, but I was a poor politician. The longer you're in there, the more you have to play the game. I don't play it well. I wasn't sure. Politics didn't offer any security that I had in my insurance business—I had a good job. If I had gone into the House of Congress, I'd have to give that up.

Bill left politics the same way he went in. Nobody was going to tell him what to think.

This fella and I were talking one day in Richmond. He said, "Bill, you know, you're a damn good legislator but a piss poor politician." I said, "I consider that a compliment." He says, "I meant it as one."

Perhaps it was best. A month after the election, Bill landed in Lynchburg's Virginia Baptist Hospital with a bleeding ulcer. He needed surgery. Bill loathed hospitals. They caged him up. In the spare confines of his hospital room, he smoldered—it was all nonsense, he shouldn't be there, he had things to do. He lashed out at people.

Bill was always intense, but this was out of character. Peggy Moody came by and watched him rip a phone from the wall and throw it. This time she did think it was supposed to hit her.

One night there was a knock on the Dudley door. Libba opened it. There was Bill in his hospital gown and slippers. He'd ripped out his IVs and walked the two miles home in a snowstorm—the kind of storm that closes down a southern city.

Libba called brother Jim in Atlanta. Jim was there in six hours—a feat in a snowstorm—and he was worried. Bill had been pushing too hard for too long. He'd tried to balance his legislative duties with his business. He had expenses—a daughter in college and a son in private school. He was impatient, competitive, and driven to begin with. Now, there was too much. Bill couldn't even grasp the idea that it is possible to ask too much of yourself.

Jim understood that Bill was three years older than his father Sheb had been when Sheb had a nervous breakdown. It was time, Jim counseled, to step away and take a breath. With the exceptions of his father and Art Rooney, the only person Bill could be counted on to listen to was brother Jim. Bill heeded his brother. He slowed down. Not much, but enough.

CHAPTER TWENTY-SIX

The NFL Alumni and an Answered Prayer

THE NFL ALUMNI ASSOCIATION GREW OUT OF A GESTURE BY THREE former players, all of whom had difficult names to spell.

In 1966, Hall of Famer Alex Wojciechowicz, Frank Szymanski of the Lions, and James Castiglia of the Eagles were all acquainted with a former teammate who was down on his luck. They asked for donations to give their teammate a hand. It worked. People noticed. There were other players out there who needed help—pre-59ers who were shut out of the pension plan.

A year later, the NFLAA was formed around thirty charter members who were a Who's Who of early professional football. Wojciechowicz was elected president. They raised money for hard luck ex-pros and sent the word out they were ready to help. After Wojciechowicz died, former Detroit Lion Leon Hart took over.

The association was all-volunteer and the fundraising and spending structure reflected that. Letters would come in from old players, slowly at first, and a committee would determine the need and checks would follow. The association raised money where it could. If a local chapter knew a player in need, it would do a fundraiser. It was a Band-Aid approach, but it was all they had. Then the flow of letters increased.

The NFLAA responded by becoming the organized arm of the pre-59ers and establishing a formal Dire Need Fund to raise and issue money for the ex-pros. The NFLAA had two tasks beyond the Dire Need Fund. They pressured the league for inclusion of the pre-59ers in the pension plan, and they threw a swell party every year around Super Bowl time.

In 1977, Hart wanted to step down. The NFLAA wanted Bill to take over. It didn't look promising to him. "All we did at the time was have a meeting and a big dinner every year. We needed to either move forward or die. We needed somebody to run it. Somebody with time and organization. I wasn't going to be president of a dying thing."

There were open issues and some infighting. The NFLAA had entered into several lawsuits against the league—all linked in some way to the pre-59er pension issue. Meanwhile, the NFL Players Association was now a union and behaving like one. Some NFLAA members wanted the alumni to join the union. Others did not.

They were driving away future members. From the outside, the NFL Alumni Association looked like so many grumpy old boys who raised a little money and griped about pensions. Younger NFL retirees stayed away. A few dedicated members at the helm kept the donations coming and the organization afloat.

The NFLAA needed restructuring. That's when Bill heard about Vic Maitland through a mutual acquaintance. Maitland and his son, Jack, had joined the alumni group. Maitland played for the Giants and Steelers in the 1940s. Jack played for the Patriots and Colts, capturing a Super Bowl ring in the 1970s. Vic and Jack ran a marketing and communications, public relations, and ad agency. They had national clients and knew market research. Bill set up a meeting for the NFLAA convention in 1977.

Bill: "We needed a marketing consultant firm to analyze the NFLAA, but we either couldn't afford them or they didn't understand football. Vic was planning to turn the agency over to his two sons. They agreed to do a study for us. No charge."

Maitland: "The players wanted to sue the owners and the league and they wanted the public on their side. Would I get publicity for the lawsuits? I said, 'You're crazy. You don't sue your mother and then ask her to make you lunch. It makes no sense. It's doomed to failure.' They said, 'What should we do? We want money for the pre-59ers.' I told them I didn't know. We'll do the research as a favor and we'll see what comes out of it."

When Maitland unveiled the study at a meeting in Canton, it was a complete restructuring of the organization and it reset its purpose. The NFLAA, he told them, needed a better image and more members, and the members needed a reason to join beyond the Dire Need Fund and the pension issue.

He would structure the association as a 501(c)(3) charity. Along with the Dire Need Fund, the NFLAA would sponsor and raise money for youth services, especially those related to athletics, in chapter cities. He called it "Caring for Kids."

He organized the association like a corporation with elected officers. There was a governing body that included a president, five vice presidents, and an executive director.

There would be placement services and career counseling for members, group medical insurance, legal and financial assistance, management for endorsements and appearances, travel discounts, and death benefits.

Members would wear the brand. They would get a card, a blazer patch, and a necktie. There would be newsletters. The NFLAA would set up their own awards and awards programs.

They would raise money through memberships and through golf tournaments. They would partner with the Hall of Fame and Pop Warner Football for events and programs. Not only would they drop all lawsuits, the NFLAA would stand on its own and no longer be dependent on the NFL for funding.

Do the plan, he told them, and the pre-59ers would get their pension money in ten years, guaranteed.

"There were 30 or 40 players in the meeting," Maitland said. "After I guaranteed the pre-59er parity, there was a ha ha and a hee hee. Nobody thought you could just walk in there and get it. I got mad and walked out. After a while, Bill brought me back in. When we came back in, he said, 'We have voted unanimously to give you the opportunity to head our group.'"

Bill told him, "Working for the NFLAA would be a hell of a lot more satisfying and a hell of a lot more fun than worrying about the problems of an oil company or grocery store chain, wouldn't it?"

Maitland came into the meeting with a plan. He left with a job. He was the executive director of the NFLAA. He took the job with no pay. The meeting, with its flash of hostility, would define the Maitland/NFLAA working relationship for the next fourteen years. Maitland viewed the football player mentality as an odd combination. On one hand, they were too cocky. On the other hand, they were too cautious. Maitland was an ex-pro, too, but he felt he wasn't in the league long enough to get that way.

For his part, Maitland was impatient and rebarbative. Working with retired football players was more fun than working with grocery store chains, but at least big business CEOs were decisive and moved fast. It put Bill into role reversal—playing diplomat for a blunt man who might let anything slip.

"They were a bunch of cocky bastards," Maitland said. "Any proposal got a fullashit answer. They said it about Caring for Kids. They said it about the golf tournaments. They said it about parity for the 59ers in ten years. They were all worried about attaching their names to something that might not work."

But to Bill, Maitland "was the answer to our prayers."

There was one more item on Maitland's to-do list for the NFLAA, and it was a big one. They would build a hospital dedicated to sports medicine. The hospital would be at the center of a retirement village for injured athletes.

CHAPTER TWENTY-SEVEN

The NFLAA and a Broken Dream

At the turn of the twentieth century, football had been around about thirty years. Calls for banning the sport had never been higher.

In 1905 President Theodore Roosevelt was under pressure to ban the sport. The mortality rate was too high at every level, from the schoolyards to the pros. But Roosevelt liked the game. He thought it built character in young men. The word went out: What can be done to save the game?

The short-term answer was to outlaw obviously dangerous tactics like the flying wedge, a formation that looked like it sounds. Players went to the extreme of having suitcase handles sewn into the seats of their pants. On a kickoff, the team would form a V in front of the receiver, grab handles, and thunder upfield. If you were coming the other way and got to the receiver before the V formed, fine. If you didn't, you could get killed.

The long-term answer was to spread the area of attack. It gave football new offensive formations and it gave us the forward pass in 1906. The link between better rules and a better game was established.

The game returned to the headlines in 1931, a bad year for football, in which there were thirty-one fatalities. Again there were rules changes. The NCAA adopted the dead ball rule. Piling on became a penalty. The first football fatality survey was compiled. It became a yearly report issued by the five-man Committee on Injuries and Fatalities of the American Football Coaches Association. Every year the conclusions were the same: Better blocking and tackling fundamentals and better equipment equal fewer injuries and fatalities.

By the time Bill returned to the Steelers for his 1946 season, the committee had some data. If you had the ball, you were in the most danger. Halfbacks and ends accounted for the most injuries. A third of injuries were caused by tackling. Fatalities were all the result of head and spinal injuries. Playing defense, though, was gradually becoming more dangerous than playing offense.

The 1946 season supported the connection between equipment and safety. Fatalities spiked. Wartime restrictions meant equipment, especially on the sandlot and high school level, was either old or unavailable. Still, the committee concluded that football was safer than driving a car or hunting.

Bill was knocked out twice in games, once in college and once in the pros. His shoulder was dislocated so many times he could yank it back in place during games until he designed a shoulder pad that prevented dislocations.

He suffered from shoulder and neck pain for the rest of his life after football. By the 1980s, his knees were shot to the point that one leg became shorter than the other, which also caused him to have back pain. When he had the knees replaced, it straightened his legs and he became two inches taller. He had to buy all new pants.

With the exception of the introduction of plastic helmets in 1940, the uniforms and equipment Bill used in 1953 were little different than what he wore at Graham High School.

When they first came out with plastic hats, I couldn't get one that fit. My hat size is 6¾. In Detroit, the first hats had rivets on the side. You could feel them when one helmet got knocked against another, like on pass plays. That year one guy got knocked out. You could see the imprint of the rivet on the side of his head. I told the guy from Riddell they should put sponge rubber in so the helmet will mold to the head. I wish I patented it. That's what they had the next season.

Bill never wore a face guard. He joked about his multi-broken nose.

My nose was never broken. Just badly bent. I had it ripped once. You could take the top of my nose and touch it to my forehead. After the ball game the doctor was sewing it up. He said, "You gotta date this weekend? You're not gonna be any good."

The injuries left him with a lifelong sinus problem and a signature throat-clearing rumble.

The helmet, and its use as a weapon, became a lifelong passion for Bill. He opposed "raking," a maneuver in which a lineman brought his face mask up under the chin of his opponent. He especially opposed spearing. "I'd like to see a rule put in where any boy who uses head gear as an instrument of injury should be banned from the game. I think it's wrong. If a defensive back tried to do that to me, I'd take out the sonofabitch if I could get up."

In 1991 Bill sent a letter to then-commissioner of the NFL Paul Tagliabue.

I have been thinking for the past two or three years that something is wrong when a defensive football player, particularly a back, can take a shot at a pass receiver or ball carrier's head with head gear or shoulders and not get penalized. Whereas even a hand, not a slap, to the face mask or head, can draw a penalty on the defensive line.

It appears to me that there is an interpretation of the rule that it is open season on pass receivers, whether crossing the middle or down the sideline. There is no doubt in my mind that when any player aims for the upper body—neck, face, head—he is intending to hurt the individual.

He followed in 1992 with another letter to Tagliabue.

The neck, head injuries we are experiencing in the NFL today would not only be cut down but almost eliminated if you went back to leather helmets and shoulder pads, or some other material that would give on contact, and removed face masks.

True, removal of face masks will call for possibly more facial cuts and busted noses, but you will not have the type of reckless hitting using the helmet and face mask as a weapon rather than a form of protection.

Leather helmets. He meant it.

When Bill saw Vic Maitland's proposal for a sports hospital and retirement village, he went all in. He didn't need convincing. He knew what years of contact had done to his own body. He knew what it had done to other players, especially the NFL alumni who petitioned for Dire Need funds.

It was big—The NFL Alumni Village and Center for Athletic Medicine. There was nothing like it. The plan included a hospital that would also be a clearinghouse for information to distribute to teams, coaches, and team physicians at every level of football, including little leagues. There would be regular seminars for pros.

The medical center would also be a practicing clinic for consultation, diagnosis, and treatment of athletic medical problems. The 125-bed hospital would be managed by specialists in sports medicine.

The medical center would anchor the village—houses and 600 apartments, a forty-room hotel, a visitor center, a health club, golf course, theater, shopping, and a shuttle service.

The major attraction would be a museum of American sports—an octagonal building with each of the eight arms devoted to a sport—football, baseball, basketball, boxing, hockey, track and field, golf and tennis, and swimming. The vision was for it to be a miniature Smithsonian celebrating the sport. The major attraction would be a 360-degree theater that put the viewer inside a football game or boxing match. If Disney could do it, so could they.

The hospital would cost ten million in 1977 dollars. It would be self-supporting with normal hospital fees. Athletes who could afford it would pay rent. Athletes who couldn't afford it would be subsidized. The village would be a tourist attraction. You could walk the streets with Red Grange or Bronko Nagurski. Maitland already had the land. A donor offered 1,000 acres in Florida. Maitland had big donors lined up.

Not everybody lined up. It scared the daylights out of Pete Rozelle. He told Bill and Maitland as much, except he didn't say daylights. The owners were concerned. It was too big. They supported the NFLAA, but wanted it known they weren't a party to the large-scale projects.

"Rozelle fought it tooth and nail," Maitland said. "He told me I was crazy. The League finally blew up the village. They insisted I cease. They sent a guy down to Florida to warn me. They were lawyered up. Rozelle thought I was trying to make a financial killing with the village."

A year after it was announced, the plug was pulled on the hospital and village, leaving a 1,000-acre "what if?" behind. It was a blow, but otherwise, the Dudley/Maitland years were a great run.

Top: In the Oval Office with Richard Nixon. Middle: (left) with President George Bush in 1992, (right) with Virginia governor Mills Godwin and President Gerald Ford. Bottom: (left to right) President Ronald Reagan, Vic Maitland, Bill Harder, Bill Dudley, Jack Kemp

CHAPTER TWENTY-EIGHT
The NFLAA and Unworthy Opponents

Two years after the Maitland meeting in Canton, the rebranded NFLAA was the largest nonprofit organization of its kind in the world. Membership increased from 160 to 7,600—and now included non-players—even though fees and dues increased fourfold.

The golf tournaments were a success and now funded the association. There was a tournament in every NFL franchise city. Golfers loved the fivesome format—four players and one NFLAA member in each group. The winning fivesome from each city competed in the Super Bowl of Golf at Hilton Head. The winners got a ring.

Fundraising was a success. Maitland understood the best resource the alumni had was their own membership. He armed the members with fundraising kits, slide shows, and brochures and sent them out in branded jackets and ties. The brochures were especially good. They had an emotional pull.

The rallying cry was "No More Jim Thorpes." Thorpe—the World's Greatest Athlete—ended his life broke, digging ditches to get by. By 1983, the NFLAA was out of debt.

Maitland thought big. He was a friend of Bob Hope. Maitland came up with an idea for a national television affair. "Hope for a Drug Free America" would trade on Hope and Nancy Reagan's anti-drug campaign and the NFLAA's focus on kids. It became a one-hour show on Super Bowl weekend in San Diego. Sports figures like Grange and Nagurski crossed the stage with a who's who of Hollywood celebrities. To this day,

Libba Dudley will be glad to tell you how handsome Charlton Heston was when he took his seat next to hers at the table, or how skinny Frank Sinatra looked in person, or how miffed Bill became when Sammy Davis Jr. swore in front of her.

Maitland thought bigger. He wanted to do a telethon. He asked President Gerald Ford to ask the Pope to make an appearance. Ford asked. The Pope declined, but he did send a letter.

He could also think small. When Bill's son, Jim, observed that Bill's doubleknit sport coat looked like a cheap knockoff of a blue blazer, Bill told him Maitland didn't care. It looked like the real thing on television.

But there was one underlying issue that remained unresolved—the pre-59ers' pensions.

The behavior of the league and the players toward the old-timers was shameful. There is no other way to put it—it was a quarter-century of greed and indifference. In 1986, the alumni's Dire Need Fund was sending players $1,000 per month—hardly more than the pre-59ers wanted from the league.

To sift through a box of old letters to the Dire Need Fund is heartbreaking. They are all handwritten. They are from once proud and accomplished men who are reduced to pleading. None claim victimhood. Hard times came on these men in different ways, but none blamed football.

In 1972, the NFL Players Association lowered their own pension age from sixty-five to fifty-five and the players wanted it lowered even more. That same year, the pre-59ers asked for 20 percent of what the current players were getting. The Players Association said no.

In 1974, the NFL Players Association picketed the Hall of Fame exhibition game. Never before had striking players protested at a game in any pro sport. That, said the old-timers, stinks. The NFL Alumni picketed the pickets.

Paid attendance at NFL games doubled in the first ten years after 1959. The league was a billion dollar industry. The average player salary grew from $6,000 in 1959 to $230,000 after player strikes in 1974 and 1982. In 1986, they were ready to strike again.

Adjusted for inflation, the average player salary in 1986 was worth about double what Bill's record-breaking, one-of-a-kind salary was worth in 1947. The league had money and lots of it.

The NFL Players Association was now openly hostile to the old-timers. Union attorney Ed Garvey made himself dartboard material when he told the old-timers there was only one pie and the union was looking for the biggest part of it. The NFLAA, he said, could go take their best shot at what was left.

Dante Lavelli: "They treat you like a leper. What do we need with you, they ask."

The union used parliamentary ploys to disenfranchise the pre-59ers. Union leaders patronized the old players in the media—and it was, now, The Media. The press boys of old were long gone—and with them the living memories of the formative years of the NFL. The fedora-topped, smoke-wreathed, word-spitting newsroom boys who never darkened the door of a college classroom were replaced by a smoother, less plain spoken, homogenized Media.

By 1986, few members in the Players Association even knew of the pre-59er role in creating their own union. The press had stopped reporting it years ago. It was a tired old story. Living in an information vacuum, the players considered money for the pre-59ers a handout.

The old-timers pressed their case before closed ears. They had risked their jobs to start the Players Association. Now, charter members weren't getting a nickel.

Meanwhile, teams and stadiums were using their names and likenesses for promotions and marketing and advertising. They were on toys and posters and flags. They were in thousands of publications and network television specials and commercials.

When the NFL was competing for players with the AFL in the early 60s, the old-timers were asked to babysit wavering players. What did they have to sell? The pension plan they weren't a part of.

And, the pre-59ers asked, what about the trail-blazers? Did O. J. Simpson owe a debt of gratitude to Marion Motley, the fullback who paved the way for black players in the NFL?

Why wouldn't anyone listen?

In 1988 *USA Today* published the result of a survey of NFL players. Among the findings:

- 42 percent of players made three or more career changes, including the switch from football.

- 62 percent had some emotional problem in their first six months out of football.

- 62 percent said they had "permanent injuries."

The most telling finding, though, was the attitude of players when broken down by era. Those who retired after 1970 were more likely to have problems than those who retired before 1970.

Post-1970 players viewed football as a twelve-month-a-year job and a career. Pre-1970 players viewed it as a temporary job. The Bert Bell lecture was brought to life.

Bill: "Football is an opportunity to do what you love doing and get paid for it. Nowadays you get paid damn well. You can play for 8–10 years and wait until retirement at 55 and have a nice pension waiting. An ordinary man can't say that. He has to work his tail off his whole life. God gave you the ability to play pro ball. You're lucky. It's an extra blessing granted to you. Others would want that blessing."

The modern players, of course, didn't see it that way. That pension they waited for, or Ed Garvey's pie, would be smaller if the old-timers were included. That was that. It was just money.

The long dispute ended quietly. In May 1987, in the aftermath of a failed player strike, the 750 remaining pre-59ers were sent letters. They would get sixty dollars per month for each year they played in the NFL. It was the same amount in the original Bert Bell plan, which was three bargaining agreements old. Of those 750 men, about 200 were thought to be eligible for Dire Need.

For Bill, his long crusade was about those 200 men. He didn't need the money. It was also a moral issue. Professional football can and did take more out of men than it returned in those early years.

The money was little more than a rounding error for the league. How many men lived in reduced circumstances for more than two decades while the league delayed? Who knows how much money the NFL saved by just sitting on the issue all those years while old players died?

Bill with Hall of Fame players Bronco Nagurski (above on left), and Otto Graham (below on right)

CHAPTER TWENTY-NINE

The Gold Jacket

Bill Dudley was always a sport coat guy. He got the habit at UVA and it became his permanent look after Grosse Pointe. He liked wearing them. If you traveled with him or socialized with him in public, he expected you to wear one, too.

In spring of 1978, as he did every spring, Bill watched the Masters Tournament on television. He'd played Augusta twice and was a fan. As he watched Tom Watson slip the green jacket onto Gary Player, Bill had one of those ideas that really do seem like a lightbulb going off. What if the NFL Hall of Fame awarded a jacket to inductees and what if the NFLAA donated the jackets? He picked up the phone and got Vic Maitland.

Maitland put together a proposal, went to Canton, and pitched it to the Hall of Fame board. The Hall was between directors and wouldn't have one for another year, so the board governed it. The board, behaving like a board, couldn't come to a decision and turned away the idea.

Maitland, behaving like Maitland, said, "Fine," and proceeded to have the jackets made anyway. He went to Haggar Clothing in Dallas. The jacket would be gold and it had to do a lot more than just look good on television.

The jacket would be lightweight wool with a tight weave so it could be both strong and light. Today, the jacket has a custom lining and buttons with the Hall of Fame logo. Today, the outside breast label has a stitched Hall of Fame logo. The inside breast label bears the inductee's name and enshrinement number. In 1978, the breast pocket bore the NFL Alumni logo.

Maitland: "I went to Haggar. Went to their head people. I said, 'Some of these guys are slobs. Wouldn't it be better if we put a good looking sport coat on them?' I told them the truth. That the Hall wasn't enthusiastic.

"Haggar loved it. They said they'd do it for the publicity and they'd make jackets for that year's class. I said, 'I'll get the coat sizes. I won't let anybody know we have them. I'll get them in there.'"

At the private dinner reception on the night before the induction ceremony, Maitland showed up with the jackets. He didn't try to hide them. They were too big to hide, anyway. Earl Shriver, who headed up the affair in Canton, resisted.

"He put us way off in a corner," Maitland remembered. "We had dinner and watched the speeches. After the speeches I went to the mic like I was supposed to be there. I said, 'I gotta little present for you.'"

Lance Alworth, Weeb Eubank, Tuffy Leemans, Ray Nitschke, and Larry Wilson all wore their jackets to the ceremony the next day. And the other Hall of Fame members wondered where theirs were.

In fact, the Hall of Fame never disliked the idea of a jacket. They were reluctant to have anything bearing the logo of another entity awarded to enshrinees. It was all resolved quickly. The jacket would stay—with a Hall of Fame logo—and the NFLAA would present it. The Hall of Fame's long relationship with Bill was the key.

"Bill became the face of the alumni," Joe Horrigan said. "He built it into a credible organization. The Hall of Fame aligned with the NFLAA because of Bill. Because he was behind it, it was accepted. We got together almost exclusively because of him. As long as he was involved, we could grow with them."

Other than the Hall of Fame bust, the gold jacket is the most visible symbol of membership. Today the jacket has taken on special meaning. After the phone call announcing their induction, the measuring and fitting for the coat is the inductee's first moment of contact with the Hall of Fame. Some bring their families to watch.

When the jacket is slipped onto their shoulders in Canton, it is the first tangible moment in the induction. The jackets are worn for life and replaced when needed. Some Hall of Fame enshrinees have been buried in their jackets.

Haggar still makes the jacket. The color, which was recently changed a bit to look better on high definition television, is a secret kept under lock and key.

Until his death, Bill Dudley came to Canton each year and slipped the jackets on the enshrinees.

Maitland left the NFLAA in 1986. Bill retired as president in 1991. Much of what was started in their ten-year run remains intact today. In 2007, the Dire Need Fund was merged into the NFL Player Care Foundation, which greatly broadened its resources and responsibilities to include health care, especially for athletic injuries. Bill and Maitland never got their hospital, but players who needed care were now getting it. They were a good team.

Bill: "Maitland was a doer. I had entrée to the League. He got things done. I trusted him."

Maitland: "Bill never pulled against me. He supported 90 percent of the things I did. But he did keep warning me, 'The League won't like this. The League won't like that.'"

Randy Minniear, a running back with the Giants and Cleveland, has been on the board of the NFL Alumni since 1977. "Bill fought like mad for the pensions and for the Dire Need Fund. He would say, 'We have to try and take care of these guys.' A lot more players need help than you'd think. I can't tell you how many nights we'd talk about it over dinners. Only a football player would knock his head against a closed door that long. Even when he retired as president he was still always a force."

CHAPTER THIRTY

Anybody Else Would Have Been Ruined

THE INSURANCE BOYS IN LYNCHBURG HAD A MORNING COFFEE KLATCH. They met in a drugstore near The Equitable offices. Bill Dudley was a regular. Another was a bright young man named Steve Phelps. It was 1970.

Phelps was twenty-six and a data analyst for Blue Cross. He was affable and had a natural way with people. He fit in with the veteran agents. One morning he arrived with news: He was out of work and he had a story. He'd asked for a raise that morning. When the boss told him if he didn't like his salary he could go drive a truck, Phelps quit on the spot. His former employer owed him $300. Could anybody help him get his money? This was on a Friday. Bill called Phelps to his office the next week. The money was there.

Phelps had a strong resume. He attended VMI on a scholarship and played football and basketball. He was recognized as the "Most Well Rounded Senior" at VMI in 1966. He coached championship high school football and basketball teams. He had been an officer in the US Army. He was a local boy.

Bill was known among the agents as a mentor. He made time for young agents and tried to teach them the lessons Jim Dudley had instilled in him. Phelps would be his protégé. Bill persuaded Phelps to study for a license with The Equitable.

Soon they were a team. They needed each other. Even with his business clients, Bill was a kitchen table salesman. Phelps had the spreadsheets and slide shows and the swagger for bigger productions. Bill had the contacts and the Dudley stamp of approval that Phelps needed. They formed the Dudley Phelps Insurance Agency, a property and casualty firm, but it turned out to be a management headache. It was brief. They closed the agency and returned to The Equitable offices.

They worked together for twenty-five years. Through Bill, Phelps gained entrée to a world far beyond central Virginia, including the Rooney family and the NFL. Phelps was successful. He knew how to strut. If he was in the room, everybody knew who he was. He made himself the center of conversation—first, though, he had to take it over. He always had a new story. If he was at the table he picked up the tab and never kept it a secret. Most people either liked him or disliked him instantly. There was no in between.

His clients loved him. They could call with the least little problem and he would take care of it.

It looked like a storybook life. He and his wife Joan remodeled a spacious farmhouse in nearby Rustburg. They threw parties. Big ones. By the time Phelps turned fifty, his son and his daughter had both launched promising careers. He seemed at the top of his game.

The signs of trouble were all there, at least in hindsight. Phelps was a big producer, but he wasn't *that* successful. He spent a lot of money on expensive things—cars, travel, home improvements—but he would call on Wednesday before the checks came in from New York. He wanted the secretaries to make sure his checks were deposited before two o'clock, which was, at the time, the close of business for banks. He was playing it close.

He was often open about gaming the system. He taught agents who would listen how to work the gray areas. Agents would sometimes walk out on him during these sessions.

Auditors and managers at the agency were trained to look for red flags. By 1985, though, Phelps was a district manager. He knew the flags.

Then, it started. Other agents got wind that Phelps was talking to their clients. A check with headquarters, though, showed he wasn't poaching. Phelps was talking about something else. What was it? At one meeting in Philadelphia, Bill and Phelps were making a pitch to a wealthy client. When Phelps left the room for a moment, the client turned to Bill and pointed a finger. The message: If Bill ever brought Phelps back into his office, they would never do business again. There was Phelps himself. You could see it. Phelps was working too hard, yet stuck in place.

He was running a Ponzi scheme. They all work pretty much the same way. If you are running the scheme, you approach a client and guarantee a consistent high rate of return on an investment. This works fine until the market shifts—and the market always shifts. If you've guaranteed 12 percent and the market is returning 9 percent, you have to make up the money somehow. You make it up with other people's money.

In the early 1990s Phelps became manic. As the prosecutor would later phrase it, he had overreached his ability to keep all the balls in the air. He had funded his scheme by misrepresenting annuities and life insurance policies to clients. It was later estimated he took about $1.3 million. Now, he'd run out of other people's money. He turned to bank loans. He forged documents and lied on loan applications. That was another $1.1 million. Central Virginia had never seen such a swindle.

One day in May 1995, The Equitable office got a call from Pittsburgh. It was an accountant for the Rooney family. Phelps had just sold Dan Rooney a $200,000 life insurance policy. He asked that the check be made out to the Dudley Phelps Insurance Agency. This had never happened before. All money went through The Equitable. What was up? The accountant was met with a moment of silence. Then he was told that the Dudley Phelps Insurance Agency had been closed for more than twenty years.

All Ponzi schemes fail. It's just a matter of when. It usually dawns on the people left to pick up the pieces that they had been looking the other way all along. So it was with the Phelps case. People found themselves to be surprised, but not that surprised.

For the victims, it was a matter of reality in hindsight. There is no such thing as a guaranteed investment and there never will be.

Phelps kept two sets of books—the real set at home and the fake set at work. When investigators opened the real books, they were stunned. They thought they would be looking for a needle in a haystack. The first policy they examined was obviously faked.

In the Phelps case, though, the victims had another reality to accept. He had preyed on friends and family. It was sad.

In January 1996, Phelps was charged with one count of mail fraud and five counts of making false statements to federally insured banks. He pled guilty to all. He was sentenced to two and a half years in prison and ordered to pay $1.3 million in restitution.

His wife Joan watched as their house and property were taken. She was left with nothing.

The Equitable negotiated settlement with eighty clients. The Rooneys sued for four million dollars. They didn't charge Phelps with taking money. The suit alleged the terms and conditions of insurance policies were misrepresented and didn't perform as promised. The Equitable settled.

Two years after Phelps went to jail, the central Virginia Equitable office was one-fourth the size it had been before he was caught. It would take years to rebuild.

It devastated Bill. He had treated Phelps like a son. Now, the Dudley name was sullied. He'd been deposed during the trial. A month before Bill died, Peggy Moody visited him. She found him agitated. Bill had just gotten off the phone with Phelps, who wanted Bill to know he'd put his life back together. "I can never forgive him," Bill said.

Every person interviewed for this book said at some point in the conversation that anybody but Bill Dudley would have been ruined by the Phelps affair. It was a paradox. The only scandal in his professional life proved to illustrate his integrity. Bill was harmed notwithstanding. Doors were not closed on Bill because of the Phelps case, but, as one person put it, some doors were never opened.

CHAPTER THIRTY-ONE
Modernity and History

BILL WENT TO THE OFFICE EVERY WORKING DAY UNTIL HE WAS EIGHTY-three. The work had dwindled, but there was mail and plenty of it.

They came from fans of every kind—a child here, an old-timer there—and from all over the world. Bill answered every letter. A woman wrote wanting to know about reading material for her sons. What did an extraordinary man like Bill Dudley read? He told her James Bond novels and the Bible.

Other letters were requests for assistance. Parents wrote. Could Bill Dudley get their child into the University of Virginia? His answer was no, but he would be happy to write a reference letter if the youth would come and talk with him.

Over the years, requests for autographs were constant. He averaged one request per day. Bill had no clue why anybody wanted one, but he obliged, usually requesting a donation to his scholarship foundation in return.

The Bill Dudley Scholarship Foundation was established in 1993 and continues today. It awards a college scholarship to a Richmond-area high school senior football player. It was Bill's way of honoring the Richmond businessmen who funded his own scholarship in 1938.

Every December, Bill was the speaker at the Dudley Award Banquet, also in Richmond. The award has been presented annually by the *Richmond Times-Dispatch* and the Richmond Downtown Club since 1990. Sometimes called "Virginia's Heisman," it is given to the top college football player in the state. It is the only award of its kind in the country.

He followed college and pro football closely. He found a lot to like in the modern game, and some things he didn't like—pay for one. He thought high salaries changed the game in a subtle way.

I actually think salaries have gotten too big. It boils down to show business. I think there are certain ballplayers that after they get a certain amount of money, start to worry about getting hurt. As a result, near the end of the season and if they have a contract coming up, maybe some of them might not play as hard. I've seen that happen.

To me, it would make sense if they would work out a scale from a team standpoint. Everyone works on the team, you say? Alright. Everybody who starts is going to get an equal share. And from thereafter, things are going to be graded and all the players won't get the same amount of money. At the end of the year, whatever the team makes, the owner pays the coaches and the owner's money is taken out, then the rest is split up among the players. The owner takes out his chunk but needs to have some left for emergencies and some for the next man to take over.

The behavior of some modern players disturbed him, especially in the end zone after scoring. Players were doing things that would have gotten him booed by Pittsburgh fans and pummeled by his own teammates. He thought what we now call "end zone celebrations" were, in a word, unmanly.

I got a telephone call from a writer who asked, "Bill, what do you think of (University of Virginia and Pittsburgh Steeler end Heath) Miller. I said, "He's a damn fine football player and not only that, a fine fella." He said, "You know what they're trying to do with him in Pittsburgh? They're trying to teach him how to react after he catches for a touchdown. You know what he does?" I said, "Yeah, he turns around and gives it to the referee." He said, "Yeah, that's right. And they want him to change. What do you think?" I said, "I think it's a class act." All of a sudden, there was a silence on the other end of the telephone and I said, "Thanks for calling."

I've watched this game for a long time. It's a team sport—a chain reaction—and it takes more than one person to get the job done. As a result anyone who calls attention to themselves is an ass.

So many people help you get there, that I think it's disrespectful to them to go in the end zone and show off.

Bill gave interviews. Most of his career was well documented, but now and again he released a surprise. In a 2005 interview, Bill revealed he always wanted to be . . . a ski jumper. "I always wanted to ski jump. When I was a kid, I would go to the movies and see it on the sports newsreels. Bluefield gets a lot of snow, but I was too bow-legged to snowplow. I'd come down the hill and just slide like I was going into second base. Ski jumping. I would have loved that like it was going out of style."

He liked it that his grandchildren sought his advice. He liked being part of their lives. He liked being current. His trophies, ribbons, plaques, and busts were eventually shifted to the garage. Libba called it The Shrine. "All those awards, and his hat size never changed," Libba said.

Bill: "If all you give people to talk about is your past, you won't be doing anything for anybody in the future."

And Bill also wrote letters. Bill knew four NFL commissioners—Bert Bell, Pete Rozelle, Paul Tagliabue, and Roger Goodell. He sent each one of them the same letter. He wanted to change the NFL's goalposts.

The idea was to center a little goalpost inside the regular goalpost and award points for accurate kicking. There were different designs. The little bar would be higher and the width of the posts narrower—in some designs as short as three feet and as wide as six feet in others.

The inner goal would be attached to the standard goal and would be a few feet behind the standard uprights, so if a ball hit the little goal, the kick remained good. If a field goal went between the uprights it would be the usual 3 points. If it went through the inner goal it would be 4 points.

On extra points it would be one for a standard kick and two for passing through the inner goal.

Nobody bit. It might have been because the design wasn't Bill's. It was sent to him by a friend who'd patented the design and named it the Skil-O-Matic. It could be the league didn't want to pay a royalty on every kick.

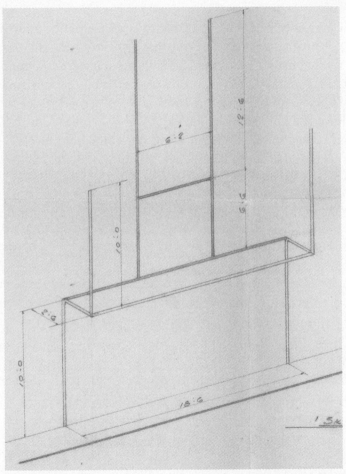

The Skil-O-Matic goalpost within a goalpost. Bill tried to get three NFL commissioners to accept it.

CHAPTER THIRTY-TWO

The Last Super Bowl

Bill's last Super Bowl was in Jacksonville, Florida, in February 2005. Lots of football business happens on Super Bowl weekend. It's a gathering. The owners meet. The NFL Alumni meet there and deliver their Player of the Year award. The Hall of Fame announces new inductees. Hall of Fame enshrinees gather for a fundraising golf tournament and a signing event.

The Hall of Famers were housed at a resort on Amelia Island, a short drive from Jacksonville and the site of the golf tournament. One Hall of Famer would play in a foursome with three people who paid handsomely for the privilege.

Long before tee-time, the Famers began to gather near the pro shop. It was the one time in the weekend they would all be in the same place. Old veterans mingled with newer enshrinees. It's a hail-fellow-well-met morning. If you ever want to grasp the feeling of the football fraternity, you need to be there at a moment like this.

Bill was the acknowledged patriarch. Amid the handshakes and backslaps, a veteran Famer would sidle up to Bill. The conversation would begin, "Have you heard about . . ." and fade to whispers as the veteran filled Bill in on the plight of an ex-pro out there who'd fallen on hard times. Bill would pull a little notebook from his pocket and take down some notes. They would nod at each other and the conversation would swell to full-voice.

There was a signing event that night sponsored by the Hall of Fame. The Famers were loaded on a bus at Amelia Island.

You could almost draw a line down the mid-section of the bus and see the 1988 *USA Today* survey lived out. The old-school players sat with their wives in the front of the bus, each in his Hall of Fame jacket. The newer players were in the back, single and jacketless. A couple fit Maitland's definition of a slob.

As the bus pulled off the island, an old-school famer couldn't take it anymore. He got up and delivered a Ray Nitschke–style address to the boys in the back. It was done with a smile, more or less, but the message was clear—they belonged to something meaningful and they should look and act it. The little speech was interrupted with bursts of applause and asides of "Ain't that right, Bill."

At the signing, the old-school Famers embraced the crowd and chatted up the fans. The fans had paid to get a signing ball—a football that is white on one side—and admission to the room. It was a party. The old-school players' wives grabbed signing balls and went about the room gathering signatures just like the paying customers. The newer enshrinees were less enthusiastic. Some got into the moment. Some just got through it. Others wished they weren't there and didn't hide it. Merlin Olsen and Roger Staubach were exceptionally rude.

The next night was the NFL Alumni Player of the Year Award, a black-tie dinner and ceremony. Again, it was back on the bus. No jacket problem this time. The younger enshrinees weren't there.

On Super Bowl weekends, every limousine and bus from three states is enlisted at the venue. It creates a driver deficit. The Famers' bus took forty-five minutes to get off the island. The driver didn't know the area and landed the bus—and it was a big one—in a tree-lined circular cul-de-sac in a residential neighborhood. The bus was halfway around the circle. The left side abutted a tree. The front nosed up to a mailbox. The rear had inches of clearance from a parked car.

It was going to require more than a three-point turn. About thirty tuxedoed Hall of Famers piled out to assess things. It was like being on a team again. One Famer persuaded a bug-eyed neighbor to move her car. The rest worked all four corners of the bus as it inched point to point until it was free.

They piled back in and escaped the neighborhood. The bus stopped at a gas station and they got a map.

The dinner and awards ceremony went off smoothly. Bobby Mitchell spoke eloquently about what it means to be a football player, clips were shown, and the NFL Alumni Player of the Year awards were delivered.

The new class of Hall of Fame enshrinees was announced before the event. In the men's room during a pause in the goings-on, some of the Famers groused about the choices. It wasn't personal. Nobody thought Benny Friedman, Dan Marino, Fritz Pollard, and Steve Young didn't belong in the Hall. It was just that three of them were quarterbacks. Quarterbacks. They said the word and shook their heads. If induction in the Hall was based on name recognition, it would be nothing but quarterbacks.

As a group, the old-school players shared more than their football careers. They shared an ineffable carriage and comportment. Lifetimes of sitting on the dais and standing at the podium at events big and small, of lending their names and sheltering them, of being noticed and being secure within themselves when they were noticed—of standing for something—gave them a composed and independent bearing.

On the ride home, it was hard not to conclude that the old-timers, the ones who weren't financially enriched by the game, who understood Bert Bell's admonition that football is not an end in itself, were happier people.

Bill Dudley loved the men who played professional football and he spent much of his life concerned with their well-being. It's a small fraternity, but it isn't exclusive—if you can play your way in, you're in.

What I cherish most are the people I got to meet. There's something about the game of football that attracts characters. They are such delightful, down to earth people. Pros are not like other people.

You have to want to play pro football. Sooner or later, you are gonna get the tar knocked out of you.

In the pros, you are not supposed to make mistakes. You are paid to not make mistakes. You're paid good money. You're supposed to be better. You're supposed to make the tough catches. You're supposed to score. You have to love the game to play it professionally. We give joy to people who like to watch us kill ourselves.

I have had the privilege and pleasure of watching pro football grow up—from Forbes Field with holes in the dressing room floor, to first class hotels, plane travel, and television.

I'm one of the few people around who knew Bronko Nagurski, Red Grange, and Jim Thorpe.

I had a wonderful career. I'm genuinely surprised people remember. You know I've wondered how I took up football. I only know I've loved the game ever since I started playing. It's a great game. I wish to hell I could still play it.

Tossing a football to grandson Blair in 1990

CHAPTER THIRTY-THREE

Belief

Tom Nygaard was a very young assistant professor at the University of Virginia Hospital in the fall of 1983—there after completing a fellowship in cardiovascular disease, arriving in Charlottesville by way of Vanderbilt and Johns Hopkins—when he got a phone call one Sunday.

"A man named Bill Dudley was seeing Dr. Bob Brennan—a partner of Mr. Dudley's physician, Dr. Charles Sackett—in Lynchburg," Nygaard remembered. "Dr. Brennan and I knew each other well, having trained together at Johns Hopkins. Mr. Dudley was complaining of chest pains. There had been two events. The first occurred while he was rushing through an airport. The second accompanied minimal activity after arriving home in Lynchburg. After discussion between Dr. Brennan and me, it was arranged to have him admitted to The University of Virginia Hospital that same day."

Nygaard had a vague idea of who Bill was. He knew he was a famous football player. That was about it.

When he met Bill at the admissions office, Nygaard was struck by his humility. His first recollection of Bill was that he insisted on carrying his own suitcase through the hospital. They got Bill checked in and then into a room. It was about then that the phone started ringing. "Next thing I know, I'm getting phone calls from everybody. Here I am one of the junior faculty taking care of Bill Dudley who was not only an icon in the state, but also on the Board of Visitors of the University."

The callers posed two questions. The first was direct—did the young doctor know who his patient was? The second was implied—was the young doctor up to the task? By the time the university chancellor called, Nygaard had ready answers for both—yes and yes.

Bill had already been sent up for cardiac catheterization. They found a blockage in a major artery in the heart. He needed a balloon angioplasty; this was well before the years when coronary stents were available. These were the early years of angioplasty and there were few doctors trained in the procedure. Two days later, Nygaard and Dr. Larry Burwell inserted a balloon into the artery and opened the blockage. The procedure went well and they sent Bill home with some blood thinners the next day.

Like so many others who crossed Bill's path, Nygaard became a friend for the rest of Bill's life. When Nygaard moved to Lynchburg in 1986 to set up a cardiac catheterization lab, the friendship grew.

We had a very long relationship. Early on, we had lunch from time to time. He introduced me to people. My kids adored "Mr. Dudley."

Over the years, his office visits always lasted long enough for my nurse to worry about me getting behind with other patients, but they were as therapeutic and reassuring for me as much as Bill. This became what I think we both considered a great friendship. In later years, I made house calls on a fairly regular basis, but they were really social visits with Bill and Libba more than medical care.

It was up to me to figure out what he needed but not to over-react. His body was beat to hell in his years of football. He had taken a lot of hits to his chest, knees, shoulders, and neck—he had almost constant pain. He couldn't breathe well as his nose had been broken so many times.

Bill later needed a coronary bypass operation. About five years after the operation, his younger brother, Tom, died of sudden cardiac death. It was soon after that Bill began to have blackout spells and eventually needed a permanent pacemaker.

I made a pact with Bill that I would treat him as I would one of my family members. He was very realistic about death. He wasn't afraid of it. He knew he couldn't have a better life or family. Most of his end of life decisions were made years in advance of his passing away.

The Catholic Church is very clear that it is alright to withhold care in certain situations at end of life. Bill knew that and we talked about it on a regular basis as he grew older.

Like most people of deep faith, Bill's faith was effortless and constant. In his darkest moments, the one thing never in doubt was his belief in God. Faith was something you don't have to summon. It's already there.

He wasn't evangelic in the broad sense, but if you told him good fortune had come your way, he'd tell you who to thank and suggest you do it on your knees. Of the two prominent evangelicals of the day, Bill was friendly with Jerry Falwell, but he couldn't abide Pat Robertson.

Bill was a charter member of the Tuesday Morning Fellowship, a group of Christian laymen that was formed in the 1960s and still meets in downtown Lynchburg. Other than that, his religious practices were personal.

No meal could begin without a word of thanks. He began his days with prayer in his bedroom—sometimes gathering the family to join him—and ended them by reminding his children to say theirs. His Bible was well worn. Church attendance was mandatory, as daughter Becca remembered:

Growing up we never missed church on a Sunday—even if we were out of town somewhere, Daddy would check with the hotel concierge or look in the phone book and find a Catholic Church and times for Mass. I remember thinking when traveling on a Sunday, "Yes, we get to sleep in." But, no. Daddy would wake us and off we would be for Mass, then we continued with our travels. Now, while Daddy believed it important to go to church every Sunday, he was always the first one out of the service.

In his playing years, he rarely missed church.

Bill: "A lot of football players were churchgoers. On the road, I used to ask people to go with me. Now when I went to Pittsburgh, my roommate my first year, Chuck Cherundolo, was a staunch Catholic. I would go with him to an early Mass. He went on a regular basis."

His approach to faith, and the way he practiced it, was straight-forward. Even his switch from the Baptist Church to the Presbyterian Church and then his switch to the Catholic Church were uncomplicated, mostly because he did things his own way, anyway.

I think the thing is to believe. I think Catholics go a bit further. Pres-byterians believed in predestination. I don't know anything about that. I just started going to the Presbyterian Church because it was close to the house in Lynchburg. When I was in high school, we used to have a prayer before every game. My coach said one time, "I'm gonna ask Carl Ed to ask a prayer before the game, and now, he's Catholic. Now a lot of you boys don't know what a Catholic is and he may use some terms you don't understand and I'm not gonna try to explain it to you. But he's a member of our team and a member of Christ's team so he's gonna say a prayer." That's the first time I remember anything particularly Catholic because he said something at the end of his prayer about Holy Mary, Mother of God, and so on.

When I switched to the Catholic Church, I just thought that it would be better if Libba and I were going to the same church. I started taking my instructions—but I didn't take many instructions because I knew the priest there and said, "Now, I'm not gonna change."

Bill would also say he wanted to make sure that if heaven had sepa-rate places for different faiths, he was going to be where Libba was. He sounded wry when he said it, but it was also obvious he meant it. When Bill was confirmed as a Catholic, Art Rooney Jr. traveled to Lynchburg to attend. Art Rooney Sr. had passed away. Art Sr. was a Catholic and used to tease Bill that the Pope would someday sweep him in. "He'd say,

'We're gonna get you, Bill. We got Bert (Bell).' Bert became Catholic just before he died."

Other than church attendance, Bill's outward expression of faith took the form of gratitude. Late in life, he would express—sometimes with genuine surprise—the good fortune he had along the way. He saw the moments of serendipity and the moments of misfortune he encountered as equally divine interventions.

Bill: "I think all our prayers are answered, just not always in the way we want them. I consider myself as lucky as any man has a right to be."

Bill and Libba surrounded by their children—Jarrett (left), Jim, and Becca—on their fiftieth wedding anniversary.

CHAPTER THIRTY-FOUR
A World He Made

Bill Dudley wasn't the only NFL player to come out of little Bluefield, Virginia. Ahmad Bradshaw played football and basketball and ran track for Graham High School. He went from there to play for Marshall University. He was drafted by the New York Giants in 2007 and retired with two Super Bowl rings.

Bill Dudley would have traded every honor, every award, his Hall of Fame bust and ring and jacket for just a shot at one of those rings. In twenty-two hours of taped interviews, he said the words, "I want to win" 121 times. He said the words, "I don't like to lose" more than fifty times.

He never made peace with his decision to leave Pittsburgh—his best chance for a championship as a player—even though he knew it was the right decision. He never made peace with his decision to forgo coaching—his best chance for a championship of any kind—even though he knew it, too, was the right decision.

Tragedies are written about men who must choose between things they love. Bill's life was anything but. He was not a man of regrets. When he looked into the rear view mirror, you might say he saw wishes instead. There's a difference. Wishes aren't burdens.

He wished he could have played his entire pro career in Pittsburgh. He wished he could have had a championship. Ask him about coaching football and he'd lean toward you and you'd hear him say, "I could have won." He didn't so much speak the word as breathe it. If you were close enough, he'd grip your knee until it hurt.

He wished he'd been more measured. As he aged, it bothered him that his blunt manner offended people, that people feared him. It wasn't what he intended.

And there were the ones that got away. It would have been marvelous if he'd played that one more year with the Steelers or closed the NFL pension deal or procured that NFL franchise. Or would it? What would have been the price of success? What would he have given up for it?

Again and again, his desire to be ordinary trumped his aspiration—in football and later in politics. Again and again, he gauged success on a larger stage and found it wanting. He lived in a world he made and he lived it like he played football games.

"I couldn't relax until the thing was over. Win, lose, or draw, I never left anything on the field. I tried."

Six weeks before a massive stroke took his life, Bill's family gathered for a birthday celebration at his home in Lynchburg. He was newly eighty-eight. To the casual observer, he was exceptionally vibrant for his age. To his children and those who knew him, he'd slowed. They could tell he didn't like it. Being busy was the Dudley family business. Nobody said anything about doing it slowly.

It was Christmas Eve. As the afternoon waned, it was time to go. In the Dudley family, it was hug time, which can take awhile. While the nearby foyer bustled with the business of coats and scarves and packages and bags, Bill stood in his den alone with his two daughters. The daughters wanted a sentimental moment. He was having nothing of it. He parried their sweet thoughts with silly ones. His daughters gave in and engaged in a long familiar game of nonsensical patter.

The moment stopped and silence took the room. He stood there, leaning slightly forward, with a cockeyed grin and a lifted brow, taking in his daughters. They stood, with hands clasped before them like little girls, adoring him. The silence lingered in wordless expression.

Bill Dudley wouldn't have traded that moment, and the countless moments that made it possible, for a ring on every finger.

Bill died on February 4, 2010. He was the last of the high-spirited family that filled the house in Bluefield with music. Brothers Jim and Tom and sister Margaret were gone.

Before he died, Bill was surrounded by his extended family in a three-day vigil in an increasingly crowded hospital room. There were tears and laughter. Becca Stinson recalls the night the vigil ended:

On the night that Daddy died, all but Mama and Jarrett left the hospital to sleep elsewhere. Up until then, we had been staying at the hospital overnight. Jarrett having worked as a hospice worker some, became aware in the early morning hours that Daddy's time was near and informed Mama. She said Mama, who had been resting on a sofa in the room, didn't say anything, but got up, undressed and got into the bed with Daddy. She lay with him whispering and rubbing him until he passed.

Jarrett had called Jim and me, but by the time we arrived at the hospital, Daddy was gone and Mama dressed. The distortions to Daddy's face from the stroke were gone. Jim went to Daddy's bedside, cried, but then declared, "There's no pain in his face, no anguish, only peace."

Mama told us children to come lie with her on the bed next to Daddy, which we did. She said, "Your daddy's still warm." It was quite something, all of us in that hospital bed. And so, we said our physical goodbye to our Daddy much the way we often said our weekend good-mornings or before bedtime goodnights as children—all of us crowded into the same bed.

Jim Dudley delivered the eulogy at the service and marked the touchpoints in his father's life.

God, family, country, community, and service to each were his priorities all his life. He kept things just that simple. Service was, to him, the Golden Opportunity, in and of itself. Very few people look at life this way. The truly great ones always do. Bill Dudley was such a man. In an age when fame and humility seldom dwell in the same house, with Bill Dudley, they were in the same room.

With Libba on the dance floor at their first grandchild's wedding.

LITTLE BILL
By Shelby Dudley, 1955

On the Twenty Second day of December, Nineteen Forty-nine,
From Libba and Bill came a blessing Divine,
The occasion was the birth of a blessed little boy,
Whose arrival filled our hearts with tremendous joy.
Each time I would see him he was jolly and glad,
And he was the spit image of his All-American Dad.
We fell for each other in truly a big way,
And at every opportunity together we would play.
We would use a little bat—and a little ball,
I taught him the strikes—he would laugh at the call.
Strike three! I would say, he would gleefully repeat,
Then in each other's arms we would joyfully meet.
A devotion developed which is difficult to explain,
As I think of it now it gives me inward pain.
Alas! He was stricken with a deadly disease,
God was calling him home that Heaven might be pleased.
He was with me two days before taking his flight,
And thanks be to God for that period of delight.
Three days later while his Dad read him a story,
He slipped from this life into Eternal Glory.
There will be an absence winding through the years
One that will wander back through memory and tears.
Only God knows the hurt of my wounded heart,
So, He will not too long keep us apart.
It should not be thus with this Dad and dear Mother,
For in due time, they may have another.
I thank them so much for giving us Little Bill,
Whom they surrendered to Heaven, according to God's will.

Acknowledgments

I WOULD LIKE TO THANK THE MANY PEOPLE WHO HELPED ME PUT BILL Dudley's story together.

Many thanks go to the Dudley family—Jim Dudley, Jarrett Millard, and Shelby King—for their insights and cherished family memories and dedication to accuracy. To my wife Becca for her willingness to log attic time and lug boxes of documents into my office and for keeping me pointed in the right direction.

To Art Rooney Jr., for his perspective and sense of history.

To Peggy Moody, Bill Calohan, and Sara Rakestraw for painting a picture of life in an insurance agency and painting a portrait of Bill Dudley as a professional there.

To Tom Nowatski for helping me navigate the NFL Alumni staff and to Randy Minniear for his living memory of the NFLAA and his willingness to spend time with me.

To Joe Horrigan of the Pro Football Hall of Fame for his panoramic frame of reference and the players who filled the frame in their lifetimes. And to the many Hall of Fame players who graciously accepted my wife and me as we traveled with Bill.

To Tom Nygaard for his cogent narrative of Bill's medical history.

To the staff of the Lynchburg Museum for giving me access to their documents and for their willingness to supply me with photos.

To Brent Epperson for supplying me with hours of taped conversations with Bill, which were so helpful in filling the gaps in my own interviews.

To Vic Maitland, for one of the most animated and illuminating telephone conversations I'll ever have. And to his son, Jim, for getting me an introduction.

ACKNOWLEDGMENTS

To Mark Lewis of Gridiron Greats for telling me which doors to knock on first.

To Jeff DeBell for his perceptive read-through and to Brian O'Neill for being the first guy I called.

And to Rick Rinehart for asking me if I had any sports books in mind.

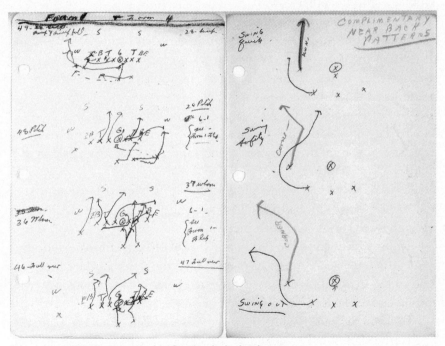

Two pages of Bill's notes in his Steelers' playbook.

Index

Abbey of Gethsemani, 172
Adams, Hunk, 144
All American, 45, 49, 53, 57–60, 86
Alma College, 141
Alma, MI, 140
Alworth, Lance, 217
Ameche, Don, 94–95, 108, 138,149
Ameche, Honey, 95, 138
Amelia Island, GA, 227–28
American Football League (AFL), 182, 213
Anderson, Edwin, 147, 150
Arcaro, Eddie, 138
Army Air Corps, 78, 88
Army Air Force All-Stars, 103
Army Air Force, 313th wing, 99
Army Air Force, 58th wing, 99
Army Air Force, 73rd wing, 99
Army Air Force, 95, 55,103, 106
Arnold, Hap, 95–96
Associated Press, 96
Atomic bomb / A bomb, 102
Aviation Cadet School, 88

B-29, 89, 98, 101
Baltimore Colts, 67, 155,160, 174, 175, 203
Baptist Church, 5, 12, 15, 234
Baugh, Sam, 16, 23, 46, 61, 76, 85, 108, 122, 131, 146, 151–53, 155, 157, 159, 161
Bell, Bert, 62, 70–73, 79, 81, 107, 136–37, 148, 153, 163, 174–75, 214–15, 225, 229, 235

Bell, Herman, 155, 157
Blue Buckle Overall Company, 66
Bluefield, WV, 19, 22
Bluefield Daily Telegraph, 5–6, 9, 11, 20, 24
Bluefield, VA, 6, 11, 14, 28, 33–34, 56, 78, 153
Bond Bowl, 91, 95
Bonelli, Ernie, 130
Boonsboro Country Club, 135. 170
Boston Braves, 144
Boston Yanks, 119–20
Bradshaw, Ahmad, 236
Brooklyn Dodgers, 79, 81, 84, 91, 99, 113, 126
Brown, Paul, 156
Bryant, Eddie "Flash," 49, 54–55
Byrd Organization/Machine, 190, 196, 198
Byrd, Harry F., Jr., 190, 192, 196–98
Byrd, Harry F., Sr., 190, 192, 196–98

Camp Lee Solders, 87
Canton Bulldogs, 49, 51, 178
Canton, OH, 161, 178–79, 204, 211, 216–18
Card-Pitts, 108
Castiglia, James, 202
Cates, Johnny, 185
Catholic Church, 67, 83,135, 172, 183, 233–35
Chapel Hill, NC, 54
Chappuis, Bob, 137
Charlotte News, 57

Charlottesville, VA, 28–30, 33–34, 39, 46, 61, 109, 110, 133–36, 146, 231
Cherundolo, Chuck, 74, 76, 81, 85, 113, 118, 125, 127, 131, 180, 234
Chicago Bears, 46, 60, 62, 72, 75, 85, 91, 144
Chicago Cardinals, 84, 88, 108–9, 116, 118, 144
Christman, Paul, 146
Cifers, Bobby, 91, 137
Clement, Johnny, 113, 116–17, 124, 130, 132
Cleveland Browns, 175
Cleveland Rams, 75, 157, 218
coal mines, 13, 34, 42
Coleman, Art "Tonto," 92
College All Star Game, 58, 60, 71–74, 85–86, 88
College Topics (early version of *Cavalier Daily*), 40, 45, 52
Collier's Magazine, 54
Columbia Pictures, 146
Compagno, Tony, 114, 116
Condit, Merl, 113, 120
Conn, Billy, 69
Considine, Bob, 96
Corcoran, Art, 49
Corum, Bill, 59
Country Club of Detroit, 143
Craig, Ross, 54
Crane, Richard, 146
Crosby, Bing, 149
Crumm, Bill, 89–90, 99
Currence, Stubby, 18

Daley, Art, 96
Dancewicz, Boley, 146
Davis, Burke, 57
Dean, Chubby, 99
Defensive Player of the Year, 145
Dempsey, Jack, 8, 40
Derr, John, 55
Detroit Lions, 84, 123, 135–38, 140–45, 147, 150, 202

DiMaggio, Joe, 149
Dire Need Fund, 202, 204, 209, 212, 218
Dobbs, Glenn, 95
Dorais, Gus, 135–36, 138, 141–42, 144
Dorsey, Tommy, 149
Doyle, Chilly, 75, 80
Dudley Award, 223–24
Dudley Phelps Insurance Agency, 220–21
Dudley Scholarship, 223
Dudley, Becca, 149, 168, 170–71, 185, 238
Dudley, Jarrett, 148, 168, 170–71, 238
Dudley, Jewell, 5–6, 8–9, 60–61, 104, 143, 184, 197
Dudley, Jim (brother), 5–7, 9–10, 13, 14, 28, 31, 42, 163, 166, 191, 219, 238
Dudley, Jim (son), 135, 153, 174, 184, 186–87, 212
Dudley, Libba Leininger, 89, 109–11, 125–27, 133–35, 138, 140–44, 146, 148–53, 156, 168–73, 179, 183–84, 186–87, 189, 191, 195–96, 198–201, 212, 225, 232, 234, 240
Dudley, Little Bill, 152–53, 168–72, 240
Dudley, Margaret, 5, 7, 13–14, 42, 238
Dudley, Sheb, 4–11, 13–15, 25, 31–32, 38, 42, 57, 60, 69–70, 170
Dudley, Tom, 5, 42, 232, 238
Dugger, Jack, 137
Duke University, 53–54
Durden, Chauncey, 30, 57, 82, 140

East-West Shrine Game, 60, 62
Eisenhower, Dwight, 78, 169
Ellington Field, 89
Equitable Insurance, 165–66, 188, 219–22
Eubank, Weeb, 161, 217
Evans, Dippy, 91
Evans, Ray, 95
exhibition game, 31, 38, 72, 75, 79, 141, 175, 212

Farkas, Andy, 85–86
Ferebee, Smith, 165–66, 187
Fernandez, Nanny, 99

Fife, Lyle, 147, 150
Fix, Ted, 12, 15
Flaherty, Red, 82
flying wedge, 206
football fatalities, 206–7
football injuries, 206–8, 214, 218
Forbes Field, 69, 80, 82, 84, 108, 116, 119–20, 125, 143, 155, 230
Ford Motor Company, 148
Ford, Gerald, 212
Fort Pitt Hotel, 69–70, 74
Fort Smith, AK, 65, 70

Garvey, Ed, 213–14
Gehrke, Fred, 148
Geri, Joe, 155
Gifford, Frank, 174–75
Gillespie, Mark, 15, 20
Gillette, Jimmy, 31–32, 34, 36–37, 39–40
Gleason, Jackie, 149
Godwin, Mills, 190, 192–93, 198–99
Goletz, Stan, 99
Goode, Rob, 155
Goodell, Roger, 225
Goodwin, Howard, 54
Goodyear, Johnny, 91, 94, 96
Gordon, Joe, 99–100, 110
Graham G-Men, 4, 6, 8, 11, 14–15, 18–20, 22, 24
Graham High School, 14–15, 18–24, 207, 236
Grange, Red, 209–11, 230
"Greatest Game Ever Played", 135, 137–39, 143, 155, 172, 174, 176, 176, 179, 201
Green Bay Packers, 84, 95, 119, 150, 181
Greensboro Daily News, 55
Grosse Point, MI, 143, 184, 196
Guam, 90, 98, 100–101
Guepe, Art, 33, 35, 49, 133–34, 138
Guyon, Joe, 179

Haggar, 216–18
Halas, George, 62–63, 71, 118–19, 125

Hall of Fame (College Football), 2, 95, 132, 142, 147, 155
Hall of Fame (Equitable Life Assurance), 166
Hall of Fame (Professional Football), 2, 14, 57, 99, 104, 108, 122, 132, 150, 161, 167, 174, 178–81, 202, 204, 216–18, 227–29, 241
Hall of Fame gold jacket, 216–17
Hampden Sydney, 35, 41, 50
Handler, Phil, 108
Harmon, Tom, 146
Hart, Leon, 150, 202–3
Harvard, 43, 157–58
Hayden, Sterling, 46
Hazzard, Wilton, 44
Heikkinen, Ralph, 49
Henry, Gloria, 146
Herber, Arnie, 179
Hershey, PA, 72, 114, 128
Hewitt, Bill, 108
Hickam Field, 102
Hickman, Herman, 157
Higgins, Bob, 76
Hitchcock, Billy, 99
Hoague, Joe, 79–80
Holy Cross Catholic Church, 67, 183
Home Life Insurance, 163–64, 166, 188, 191
Horrigan, Joe, 181, 217, 241
Houston, TX, 89–90
Huff, Sam, 175
Hughson, Tex, 99
Hussey, Ruth, 62
Hutson, Don, 84–85, 122
Hyman, Sig, 176

Illustrated Football Annual, 44, 60
injury clause, 136, 175

Jacksonville, FL, 227
Jacobs, "Indian Jack," 103, 146
Jansante, Val, 114, 116
Japan, 61–62, 90, 98, 101, 102

Jones, Deacon, 181
Junior League, 133, 143, 183
Justice, Charlie (Choo-Choo), 103,155, 159

Kehn, Chet, 99
Kenan Stadium, 1, 56
Kennedy, John F., 191
Kiesling, Walt, 73–74, 77, 79–83, 85, 107–8, 132, 179
Knoxville News Sentinel, 44–45, 59

Lach, Steve, 53–54, 113, 119, 122, 125, 132
Lambeau, Curly, 158
Larson, Swede, 36
Lavelli, Dante, 175, 213
Lawrence, David, 112
Layden, Pete, 91–92, 96
Layne, Bobby, 137, 150
leather helmets, 18, 148, 208–9
LeBaron, Eddie, 159
Leemans, Tuffy, 217
Lehigh University, 43, 50, 52
Leininger, Dot, 67
Leininger, Mary Elizabeth "Inde" Hendricks, 65–67, 134–35
Leininger, Mary, 66, 172
Leininger, Ray "Dutch," 65–67, 110, 134, 143, 171–72
life insurance business, 151, 162–67, 168, 219–22
Litel, John, 146
Lodigiani, Dario, 99
Longworth, Wally, 20
Looney, Don, 75, 91
Los Angeles, CA, 92, 94,136,138,141,148
Louis, Joe, 40, 69
Luckman, Sid, 84, 118, 146
Lynchburg News & Advance, 153, 194
Lynchburg, VA, 33, 62, 64–68, 89, 109, 111, 127, 133–35, 143, 152–53, 156, 168, 170–71, 183–84, 187–89, 191–92, 197, 219, 231–34, 237

Madarik, Tippy, 91, 141
Maitland, Jack, 203
Maitland, Vic, 203–5, 209–12, 216–18
Major League Baseball, WWII, 100, 146
Mandel, Fred, 135, 138, 143,145
March Field Flyers, 94
March Field, 92, 94–95
Mariana Island, 98
Marquette University, 30–31, 49, 95, 133
Marshall, George Preston, 71,151, 155, 157–59, 160, 188
Massive Resistance, 190, 198
Maxwell Football Club, 60
Maxwell Memorial Award, 59–60, 62, 71
Mayhew, Tex, 86
McAfee, George, 122, 179
McCormick, Mike, 99
McDonald, Ned, 169–70
McMann, Dick, 178–79
McMillin, Bo, 15, 147, 150
Mellon, King, 112
Memorial Sloan Kettering Hospital, 171, 173
Merrill, Walt, 91
Military Draft and draft classifications, 77–78, 91, 107
Miller, Creighton, 176
Million Dollar Roundtable, 165
Mills, Buster, 99
Minniear, Randy, 218
Mirman, Bill, 54
Mitchell Stadium, 19
Molloy, Ed, 158
Moody, Peggy, 166,195, 200, 222
Morton, Hugh, 56
Mosconi, Willie, 46
Most Valuable Player (MVP), 2, 84–85, 96, 114, 129–31, 136–37, 149
Motley, Marion, 122, 214
Muha, Joe, 51–52
Munhall, Herb, 56
Murray, DeMarco, 137

Murray, Frank, 25–26, 30–37, 39, 41–44, 46, 48–52, 54, 56, 59–60, 62, 73, 80, 133, 137, 142, 145
mythical championship, 21–22, 24, 58, 96

Nagurski, Bronko, 125, 154, 210–11, 230
Namath, Joe, 189
National Football League (NFL), 2, 31, 46, 51, 62, 70–71, 73–74, 81, 84–85, 91, 95, 104, 108, 113, 131–32, 136–37, 139, 145–48, 152, 154, 156–58, 161, 174–80, 189, 202–18, 220, 225, 227–29, 236–37
Naval Air Corps, 61
Navy (Middies), 35–40
Neale, Greasy, 107
Neff, Johnny, 54–55
New York City, 62, 126, 133, 166, 171, 189
New York Giants, 79, 80, 83, 91, 95, 117, 121, 125–26, 145, 155, 174, 236
New York Jets, 188–89
New York Times, 52, 95–96
New York Titans, 188
Newsweek, 59
Neyland, Bob, 44
NFL Alumni Player of the Year, 228–29
NFL Alumni Village and Center for Athletic Medicine, 205, 209–10
NFL Alumni Association (NFLAA), 202–7, 209–13, 215–18
NFL Draft, 31, 62, 70–71, 91, 137, 236
NFL pension plan, 146, 174–76, 202–4, 213
NFL Players Association, 160, 174–76, 203, 212–13
Niccolai, Armand, 73, 80
Nitschke, Ray, 181, 217, 228
Nixon, Richard, 198–99
Norfolk & Western, 13
Norfolk Shamrocks, 87
Norfolk, VA, 13, 34, 44, 52, 87
North Carolina University (Tarheels), 1, 25, 30, 40, 44–46, 50, 53–56

Notre Dame Box, 73, 135
Nygaard, Tom, 231–32

Oakwood Country Club, 110–11, 133, 168
Olivar, Jordan, 157–58
Oney McManus's Bar, 83
Onion Bowl, 11, 12, 54
Owens, Steve, 121

P-38 Lightning, 90, 94
Palmer, George, 54
Pancake, Flapper, 20, 55
Pearl Harbor, 61, 78, 103, 107
Penn State, 76
Phelps, Steve, 219–22
Philadelphia Eagles, 70, 75, 79, 81–82, 107, 122–27, 136–37, 176
Pittsburgh Athletic Club, 118
Pittsburgh Post Gazette, 137
Pittsburgh Press, 75, 77
PIttsburgh Steelers, 37, 62–63, 69–71, 73–75, 77, 79, 80–86, 95, 104, 107–8, 113–14, 119, 122, 125–32, 135–37, 140
Pittsburgh Sun-Telegrah, 79, 80
Pittsburgh, PA, 69–71, 74, 79, 84, 107–8, 112, 127–28, 138, 172, 192
P.J. Clarke's (Manhattan bar), 149
plastic helmets, 148, 207
Pollet, Howie, 99
Polo Grounds, 83
Ponzi Scheme, 221
Pre-59ers, 177, 202–5, 212–14
Presbyterian Church, 168, 234
Preston, Bill, 54–56
Princeton, WV, 22–24, 26
Pritchard, Bosh, 51–52
Pritchett, Norton, 58

Quadruple Crown, 2, 131, 182

Randolph Field, 88, 90–92, 94–95, 108
Randolph Field Ramblers, 91–92, 94–96, 103, 108, 110, 141

Randolph Macon Woman's College, 68, 109
Ray, Hugh "Shorty," 179
Reagan, Ronald, 199
Rice, Grantland, 54, 59
Richmond Downtown Club, 223
Richmond Times-Dispatch, 31, 35, 38, 57, 59, 88
Riffle, Dick, 79, 81, 84
Riggs, Lew, 99
Roanoke Times, 39, 59
Roberts, Red, 17–18
Robinson, Bradbury, 48
Rockne, Knute, 142
Rojek, Stan, 99
Rookie of the Year, 85
Rooney, Art, 62, 70–71, 73–77, 79, 81–84, 86, 107–9, 113, 115–19, 128–30
Rooney, Art, Jr., 104, 234, 241
Rooney, Dan, 221
Rooney, Tim, 130
Roosevelt, Theodore, 206
Rosenbloom, Carroll, 67, 160, 174, 176
Rozelle, Pete, 176, 210, 225
Ruby, Martin, 91
Russell, Jack, 91, 96, 103
Russell, Jane, 146, 149, 179
Rustburg, 220

Saipan, 90, 98–102
San Antonio TX, 88, 92
Sandig, Curt, 79–81, 83–84
Sauerback, Jack, 54
score in a football game, eleven ways to, 182
Scott Stadium, 29, 186
Seabright, Charlie, 113, 116, 123
Second Air Force, 92, 95
Shearer, Marshall, 15–20, 23–26, 33, 37, 56, 80, 87, 147
Shor, Toots, 149, 173, 192
Shu, Paul, 39
Shula, Don, 175

Shultz, Elbie, 74
single-wing formation, 18, 23, 47–49, 68, 73–74, 114–15, 119, 125, 127, 131–32, 165
Sinkwich, Frank, 53–54
Skil-O-Matic, 226
Skorich, Nick, 124
Slaughter, Enos, 96, 100, 110
Smith, Chester, 75, 85
Smith, Riley, 50
Spring Alumni vs. Varsity game, 177
Stamford TX, 88–89
Steagles, 107–108
Stewart, Jimmy, 62, 89
Stryzkalski, Johnny, 95
Stuart, Mary, 146
Sturm, Johnny, 99
Suhling, Ed, 49–50, 64
Super Bowl, 176, 178, 187, 202–203, 211, 227–29, 236
Superbombers, 95–96
Sutherland, Jock, 63, 69, 113–26, 129–32, 134, 136–37, 141, 143, 159
switching political parties, 198–99
Szymanski, Frank, 202

T-formation, 47–50, 119, 135
Tagliabue, Paul, 208, 225
Taylor, Hugh, 159
Tazewell VA, 19–20, 25–26
Tebbetts, Birdie, 99, 110
Tebell, Gus, 29–30
Third Air Force, 92
Thorpe, Jim, 49, 178, 211, 230
Tinian, 98–101
Todd, Dick, 157
Tomasic, Andy, 73, 79, 113
Touchdown Club, 59, 96
Tower Ground, 9–11, 15–16, 18–19, 23–24
training camp, 74–75, 111, 114, 118, 138, 140–42, 157, 175
Triple Crown, 131
Triple Threat (movie), 146, 188

Trippi, Charlie, 92, 146
Tritico, Frank, 91–92, 94
Turner, Clyde "Bulldog," 179–80
20th Air Force, 98

Unitas, Johnny, 170
University of Maryland, 26, 39, 43
University of Pittsburgh, 63, 69–70, 119
University of Richmond, 32, 51, 88
University of Tennessee (Volunteers), 25,
    41–42, 44
University of Virginia (Cavaliers), 1, 22,
    25–28, 36–40, 44–45, 50–52, 55,
    58, 62, 104, 133, 138, 143, 169, 177,
    183, 223–24, 231
University of Virginia Board of Visitors,
    183, 231
USA Today, 214, 228

Van Brockllin, Norm, 175
Van Burn, Steve, 146
Vanishing Virginian, 62
Virginia Baptist Hospital, 200
Virginia Big Six, 32, 51–52, 58
Virginia Community College system, 192,
    195
Virginia driving age, 192, 194–95
Virginia General Assembly, 185, 194
Virginia liquor by the drink, 192–93
Virginia News-Leader, 39, 59
Virginia Tech, 25, 32, 40, 44, 50, 52
Virginian Pilot, 88
VMI, 25, 32, 29, 40, 44, 50–52, 219

Walker, Doak, 150
Walter Camp Trophy, 59

Washington & Lee (W&L), 9, 13–14, 25,
    27–28, 32, 44, 50, 52
Washington Post, 35, 85–86, 96
Washington Redskins, 12, 17, 23, 46, 61,
    63, 71, 76–77, 80–82, 84–86, 91, 94,
    103, 116, 120, 122, 145, 150–51,
    155–59, 175, 178–79
Waterfield, Bob, 146, 149, 179
Watts, Bobby, 33, 64, 171, 199
Watts, Nida, 171–172
ways to score in a football game, eleven,
    182
Werblin, Sonny, 189
West, Max, 99
Westfall, Bob, 141
White, Jim, 54
White, Paul, 137
White, Whizzer, 71–72, 77
Whitehead, Amy, 143
Whitehead, James, 143
Whitten, Jack "Doc," 25–26
Whittlesey, Merrill, 85
Williamson, Dick, 88
Wilson, Larry, 217
Wismer, Harry, 188
Wojciechowicz, Alex, 202
Wolfe, Hank, 88
Woudenberg, John, 74, 85
Wright, Taft, 99

Yale Daily News, 158
Yale, 43, 50–51, 58, 157–61
Yancey, Robert, 62
Yeager, Charlie, 134, 158

Zirinsky, Walt, 50

About the Author

Steve Stinson is an artist and writer living in Virginia. His first book for adults—*What Would Mary Ann Do? A Guide to Life*—published in 2014, was co-written with Dawn Wells. Bill Dudley was his father-in-law.

BRUCE MUNCY PHOTOGRAPHY